Religion in the Ancient Mediterranean World
Parts I–IV
Glenn S. Holland, Ph.D.

PUBLISHED BY:

THE TEACHING COMPANY
4151 Lafayette Center Drive, Suite 100
Chantilly, Virginia 20151-1232
1-800-TEACH-12
Fax—703-378-3819
www.teach12.com

Glenn S. Holland, Ph.D.

Professor of Religious Studies, Allegheny College

Glenn S. Holland is the Bishop James Mills Thoburn Professor of Religious Studies at Allegheny College in Meadville, Pennsylvania. Born in 1952 and raised in Los Angeles, California, Professor Holland received his A.B. in Drama from Stanford University in 1974. After several years as a writer, Professor Holland entered Mansfield College at the University of Oxford and received a master's degree from Oxford in Theology in 1981. The same year, he entered the Divinity School of the University of Chicago; he received his Ph.D. in Biblical Studies, with a concentration in the works of St. Paul, in 1986. His dissertation was later published as *The Tradition That You Received from Us: 2 Thessalonians in the Pauline Tradition* (Tübingen: J.C.B. Mohr [Paul Siebeck]: 1988).

Professor Holland has written on many topics, including the use of classical rhetoric as a means of analyzing the letters of St. Paul and frank speech as a philosophical, political, and literary virtue in ancient Hellenistic culture. He was a co-editor, with John T. Fitzgerald and Dirk Obbink, of a collection of essays on Philodemus, an Epicurean philosopher of the 1st century B.C.E., *Philodemus and the New Testament World* (Supplements to Novum Testamentum 111, Leiden: Brill, 2004). Professor Holland is also the author of *Divine Irony* (Selinsgrove, PA: Susquehanna University Press, 2000), a study of irony as a person's adoption of the divine perspective on events in the human world, with special attention to Socrates and the letters of the apostle Paul. The professor is a contributor and assistant editor for the award-winning multidisciplinary journal *Common Knowledge*, published three times a year by Duke University Press.

Professor Holland has taught in the Department of Philosophy and Religious Studies at Allegheny College, a traditional four-year liberal arts college, since 1985. It was there that he developed, over many years, the course of lectures that is now *Religion in the Ancient Mediterranean World*. The course has proven to be one of Professor Holland's most popular classes and has introduced many of his students to the academic study of religion. The professor was awarded the Thoburn Chair in Religious Studies in 1992 and the Divisional Professorship in Humanities at Allegheny College in 2003. He is also active with the Allegheny

College Chapter of Phi Beta Kappa and has served as both its secretary and president.

Professor Holland and his wife, Sandra, an elementary mathematics teacher, have two grown sons, Nathaniel and Gregory.

Table of Contents
Religion in the Ancient Mediterranean World

Table of Contents
Religion in the Ancient Mediterranean World

Table of Contents
Religion in the Ancient Mediterranean World

Religion in the Ancient Mediterranean World

Scope:

This course of 48 lectures is an introduction to the religious cultures of the ancient Mediterranean world, from the earliest indications of human religious practices during the prehistoric era to the conversion of the Roman Empire to Christianity in the 4th century of the Common Era. The course examines what we can recover of the religious activities of prehistoric human beings before considering in depth the religious cultures of the great ancient civilizations of Egypt, Mesopotamia, Syria-Palestine, Greece, and the Roman Empire. The emphasis throughout the course is not only on the rituals and mythology of a civilization's official religious culture but also on the beliefs, practices, and yearnings of the common person. The course content is derived in part from primary literary sources that speak about these different religious cultures in the voice of the believer. Comparisons among the different religious cultures will reveal what is unique about each and what ideas, practices, and aspirations appear to be typical of all human religious communities. The course is presented in 4 parts of 12 lectures each.

The first part of the course introduces the subject and addresses the fundamental question "What is religion?" With an understanding of religion as beliefs and practices that express a community's relationship to the sacred, it becomes possible to investigate prehistoric religious cultures on the basis of their physical remains. The course will trace the development of religious practices in the transition from the Paleolithic and Mesolithic eras to the Neolithic era and the beginnings of the first great Near Eastern civilizations. The first of these civilizations to be considered is Egypt, the most straightforward example of an ancient polytheistic religious culture developed in relative isolation from the rest of the world. Because of the richness of the sources and the clear points of focus of Egyptian religious culture—the sun, the Nile, and the king—it is possible not only to reconstruct official Egyptian religious practices and mythology but also to gain some sense of the concerns and sentiments of the common people.

The second part of the course shifts the focus to the other great center of ancient Near Eastern civilization, Mesopotamia. Here, a series of city-states, kingdoms, and empires held sway in succession over the centuries, and the people felt some unease at the power and willfulness of the gods. But Mesopotamia has also left religious literature that brings those gods to life. The course pays particular attention to the creation stories, stories about Ishtar, the impetuous goddess of love, and the first epic poem, the story of the hero Gilgamesh. Points of contact between Mesopotamian religious literature and more familiar biblical literature lead to a consideration of the different concepts of divinity in the ancient Mediterranean world and introduce the religious cultures of Syria-Palestine, especially that of ancient Israel. Here again, despite Israel's distinctive history as a people and a nation and its concern with one God, certain recurring religious ideas and practices, such as prophecy, are seen to reflect more widely spread phenomena common to ancient Near Eastern civilizations.

The third part of the course begins with prophecy as a response to the political and religious crises that arose in the kingdoms of Israel and Judah with the threat posed by the Mesopotamian empires of Assyria and Babylon. Faith in the one God proved particularly resilient, as the experience of exile in Babylon led the prophets of Judah to assert all the more emphatically the uniqueness of the God of Israel. By comparison, the religious cultures of the Aegean Sea made a virtue of diversity. The physical remains of the Minoan civilization of Crete offer some intriguing clues to Minoan religious culture, and the ruins of Mycenaean cities on the Greek mainland provide only glimpses of a world much better known through Homer's *Iliad* and *Odyssey*, themselves products of the succeeding Greek Dark Age. With the rise of Greek civilization and the autonomous city-state during the Archaic era, the pantheon of Greek gods and goddesses begins to assume its familiar appearance. The classical age of the 5th and 4th centuries B.C.E. saw the height of Greek civilization, as well as philosophical and literary reflection on Greek religious culture. After the conquests of Alexander the Great and the spread of Hellenistic culture, mystery religions brought the traditional Greek gods Demeter and Dionysus new prominence as divine patrons who could rescue their devotees from the afflictions of the human situation and fear of the blind power of fate.

The fourth part of the course begins by considering how mystery religions introduced eastern gods, such as Isis and Mithras, into the Hellenistic world. Rome is a prominent example of how a distinctive religious culture is gradually transformed by the incorporation of elements of foreign religious cultures, including those of the Etruscans and the Greeks, as well as by evolving social and political history. Rome came to dominate the Mediterranean world around the turn of the age and continued to accommodate the cosmopolitan expressions of the traditional religious cultures of Greece and the east. The proliferation of religious claims and communities inspired skepticism among the intellectuals of the Roman world, leading to philosophical explanations of religious beliefs and literary attacks against religious charlatans. In this pluralistic context, Jesus of Nazareth appears as a Jewish religious reformer proclaiming a new relationship between the divine and the human worlds. His followers spread a faith based on both his teachings and his person throughout the Mediterranean world, despite official persecution and disagreements among themselves over the proper understanding of who Jesus was and what he taught. The Christian movement's resilience under persecution and its appeal to the religious needs and concerns of the Roman world eventually led to its triumph over traditional Roman religious culture under the emperor Constantine, although the traditional religious culture survived and manifested itself in new ways. The concluding session considers the ways in which the religious cultures of the ancient Mediterranean world are most foreign to our own and the ways in which they appear to have expressed the enduring religious yearnings of all humanity.

Lecture One
Talking About Ancient Religious Cultures

Scope: The lands surrounding the Mediterranean Sea provide the basis for most religious belief and practice in the modern Western world. The religious history of the ancient Mediterranean world begins with its earliest human inhabitants and comes into full flower with the first Near Eastern civilizations to develop written language, in Egypt and Mesopotamia. The religions of ancient Syria-Palestine, Greece, and Rome have left a rich cultural heritage, including the beginnings of the Christian movement. We will discuss ancient religious cultures with the help of archaeological evidence, non-literary records of religious practices, references to religious practices in other non-religious literary works, and religious narratives, such as epics and poems. All religious language is necessarily metaphorical because it describes what lies above, beyond, or behind daily experience in language taken from the natural world.

Outline

I. This course looks at religious cultures in the areas surrounding the Mediterranean Sea in the formative years of human civilization.

   A. The Mediterranean world is often called the "cradle of civilization" in the West.
   1. But this title is appropriate only if we overlook the ancient civilizations in the rest of the world.
   2. The ancient Mediterranean world stretched from the Persian Gulf to the Nile Valley, across the Aegean to the Italian peninsula, and to the straits of Gibraltar.
   3. This vast area includes the ancient civilizations of Mesopotamia, Syria-Palestine, and Egypt.
   4. The Mediterranean basin was also home to the civilizations surrounding the Aegean Sea.
   5. Farther to the west is the Italian peninsula and Rome, destined to become the capital of a world empire.

   B. We will begin with religious activity in the prehistoric era and continue chronologically and topically to early Christianity.

1. We will consider physical remains of prehistoric human beings that seem to point to religious activity and belief.
2. The first religious culture we will discuss that has left literary remains is that of ancient Egypt.
3. We will then move on to religion in Mesopotamian civilizations, notably Sumerian and Babylonian religious culture.
4. The religions of Syria-Palestine include the religious culture of ancient Israel and its rivals.
5. Greek religion is familiar through its mythology, but we will consider Greek religious culture over centuries.
6. We will also discuss the reevaluation of Greek religious culture in the aftermath of the conquests of Alexander the Great.
7. Roman religious culture, and its appropriation of Greek mythology, has strongly influenced our ideas about ancient religious culture.
8. We will consider those elements that make Roman religious culture distinctive and its historical development.
9. Finally, we will talk about the origins of the early Jesus movement and the gradual development of Christianity.

C. We will be able to touch on only the highlights of our very broad and varied subject.
1. Each ancient culture we will consider is an academic discipline in its own right.
2. This course is introductory, an opportunity to learn something about ancient religious belief and practice.
3. The course is intended to provide a sense of the "feel" of these different religious cultures and their distinctive points of view.

II. We will draw on a variety of sources to talk about ancient religious cultures.

A. We have essentially four sources of information about ancient religious cultures available to us.
1. Archaeological evidence provides information about worship practices and household religion.
2. Non-literary writings that may tell us about religious matters include records of rituals performed or festivals celebrated.

3. Literary reconstructions of the religious past are historical accounts written by elite members of a religious culture, usually in contrast to the practices of their own time.
   4. Presentations of religious beliefs, practices, and devotees can be found in ancient literary works.
   5. All these sources of data must be interpreted in terms of what we know about religious cultures in general.

B. This course will concentrate on the *stories* told by and for members of a given religious culture.
   1. Stories best illustrate what a religious culture thought about the relationship between the gods and humanity.
   2. In stories, religious beliefs are expressed both directly and indirectly, as part of a cultural complex that provides the stories' context.
   3. All stories are about relationships, and relationships are central to all religious narrative.
   4. Stories create and shape community, because stories are told and retold within the context of community.
   5. Each story written down is only a snapshot of the development of the story and its religious culture and often represents a single point of view.
   6. But those "snapshots" can give us a sense of what it was like to be part of a particular religious community.

C. We will consider other aspects of religious cultures as they relate to the central relationships revealed in stories.
   1. We will pay particular attention to religious actions and designations of religious space.
   2. Our study will be *developmental* when we examine religious cultures as they grow and change over time.
   3. Our discussion will be *comparative*, because fundamental human needs and interests tend to be expressed in similar ways across cultures.
   4. We will also consider what was unique about each of the ancient religious cultures we discuss.

III. The essential components of religious narratives are *myth* and *metaphor*.

A. When we think of stories about the gods and humanity, we think first of mythology, the familiar stories about gods and heroes.

1. These are stories about human lives lived in the presence of the gods or about the gods themselves.
2. Although some stories explain "how things came to be," more often, they depict "how things are," the ways of nature and of human life.
3. Like all stories, mythological stories are meant both to entertain and to instruct the audience about the world.

B. Any talk about the gods and the divine realm constitutes what scholars call *myth*.
   1. Whenever one talks about the gods and their actions, one engages in *mythic discourse* and speaks from the narrative realm of *myth*.
   2. *Myth* is distinct from *mythology*, which is only one variety of mythic discourse.
   3. *Myth* in this sense also stands in contrast to *history* as the way we talk about notable events in the past.
   4. The use of the word *myth* or *mythic* implies no judgment about the factual nature of what is described.

C. The language of myth is symbolic, because language expresses everyday reality and not what lies beyond it.
   1. Symbolic language refers to the mythic in terms taken from the realm of the everyday.
   2. Symbolic language refers to the supernatural reality it depicts by analogy to everyday phenomena.
   3. We can't know whether the people who told these stories were aware of the symbolic nature of their language.
   4. This means we don't know whether they regarded these stories as reliable accounts of the actions of gods and human beings in the past.
   5. Stories in ancient Mediterranean religious cultures conveyed truths perceived by those who told them: truths about *how* things are and *why* they are that way.
   6. This is one of the central concerns of all religious discourse and all religious cultures.

Supplementary Reading:

Sarah Iles Johnston, ed. *Religions of the Ancient World: A Guide*, pp. 3–16.

Questions to Consider:

1. If all religious language is metaphorical, what determines whether a particular metaphor is more adequate or less adequate to express a particular religious concept or idea?

2. If *myth* and *history* are two different ways of talking about reality, why in our culture is *history* considered to be the more legitimate and "objective" of the two?

Lecture Two
What is Religion?

Scope: The process of defining *religion* begins with the attempt to isolate those features that all religious activities and beliefs have in common that distinguish them from other sorts of activities and beliefs. Much of what is distinctive about religious activities and beliefs is their concern with what we may call the *sacred*. The 19th-century German theologian Rudolf Otto defined the *sacred* as "the overwhelming and awe-inspiring mystery." But how is concern with the sacred expressed within a culture? French sociologist Émile Durkheim devised a definition of religion in the early 20th century that stressed both beliefs and actions, as well as the moral community that is inevitably created by religious observance. There are also traditional ways in which different peoples have understood the divine world and its relationship with the human world, usually based on different models of human relationships in a community.

Outline

I.   Our study must begin with a fundamental question: What is religion?

   A.   This sounds like the sort of annoying question asked by a philosophy major.

      1.   It's an annoying question because we all think we know what religion is until we try to define it.

      2.   "What is religion?" is a question dealt with by historians of religion, who study religious phenomena across cultures.

      3.   The question "What is religion?" is a major problem in systematic treatments of religious communities.

      4.   We will consider what elements seem essential to a definition of religion, then consult two classic definitions.

   B.   One may construct a definition of a complex phenomenon by listing essential elements in all examples of that phenomenon.

      1.   Religion seems to be about worship of a god or gods and obedience to what the god or gods command.

      2.   But there are religious cultures concerned with spirits and some, such as Buddhism, with no gods of any sort.

3. There are also the questions of whether worship is essential and what sort of actions indicate worship.
4. We might identify religion in terms of what it concerns and how people's lives reflect that concern.
5. We might say that religion is the human concern with and response to the supernatural, the mysterious, or the unknown.

C. But this identification leaves questions unanswered and characteristic aspects of religion unaddressed.
1. The *mysterious* or *supernatural* are not clearly identified and may change over time.
2. The distinction between the *natural* and the *supernatural* is primarily a modern one.
3. What responses constitute religious actions, by whom are they performed, in what context, and with what intentions?
4. How do we best describe the object of ultimate concern, and what are the consequences of one's ultimate concern with this object?

D. The German theologian Rudolf Otto (1869–1937) devoted *The Idea of the Holy* to the essential nature of religious concern.
1. Otto approached the subject from the perspective of comparative religious studies and the tradition of German mysticism.
2. Otto defined the *holy* as "the overwhelming and awe-inspiring mystery."
3. For Otto, religion is primary the experience of the holy, the encounter with the overwhelming mystery.
4. Otto's idea of religion shifts the focus from spiritual beings to a general idea of the holy as both awesome and compelling.
5. But Otto conceives of religion as something interior, concerned with feeling and belief.
6. Otto's definition says little about the expression of religious belief in words and actions.

E. The French sociologist Émile Durkheim (1858–1917) developed a definition of religion in *The Elementary Forms of the Religious Life*, in 1912.
1. Durkheim was one of the great pioneers of sociology as an academic discipline.

2. Durkheim wanted a definition of religion based on its simplest forms that would also apply to its most sophisticated forms.

3. Durkheim extensively critiqued several definitions of religion before offering his own attempt.

F. Durkheim's definition is: "A religion is a unified system of beliefs and practices relative to sacred things, that is to say, things set apart and forbidden—beliefs and practices which unite into one single moral community called a church, all those who adhere to them."

1. This definition includes the idea of belief, defines the word *sacred*, and focuses on community.

2. Durkheim's definition has failings, notably defining a religious community as a "church" and sacredness in terms of taboo and emphasizing sacred "things."

G. Durkheim's definition of religion should be modified in light of its shortcomings.

1. A modified definition of a religion is: "A religion is a unified system of beliefs and practices relative to the sacred that unite into a single moral community all those who adhere to them."

2. A definition of the sacred is "that which permeates, influences, and relates to material reality, yet is recognized as part of another reality not subject to the limitations of the material."

3. The basic concepts are an idea of the sacred, the interdependence of beliefs and practices, and the existence of a community.

II. Recurring features in religious cultures are basic to human comprehension of the sacred.

A. These recurring features result from attempts to understand the sacred in terms of the language of everyday life.

1. Each culture's idea of the divine realm is based on the model of its own cultural customs and institutions.

2. Religious symbolism also arises from individual consciousness or is determined by the nature of the religious experience itself.

3. But even in cases where the symbolism is "given," there is an undeniable cultural component.

B. The divine realm is repeatedly believed to be organized on the model of human political organization.
   1. Ancient Mediterranean peoples thought of the gods arranged in a political hierarchy.
   2. The chief god is limited in his or her ability to act by the competing interests of other gods.
   3. The political organization of the divine realm takes on many forms in ancient Mediterranean religious cultures.
C. Different models for how human beings live in relationship to the gods are based on different relationships among human beings.
   1. The idea of the gods as a governing council leads to theories concerning how the gods feel about the human beings under their control.
   2. How a religious culture defines the human predicament depends on the relationship it sees between humanity and the divine world.
   3. The divine realities believed to govern human existence are conceived of in human terms.

Supplementary Reading:

James C. Livingston, *Anatomy of the Sacred*, pp. 3–57.

Questions to Consider:

1. What might be some of the differences between religions with a god or gods and those that have some other conception of the sacred?

2. If human ideas about the sacred are based on human models, how will this affect the way people think about the sacred? Is it a help or a hindrance?

Lecture Three
Early Prehistoric Religion

Scope: Our evidence for prehistoric religious culture is based on material remains of prehistoric human beings, interpreted in the light of the religious cultures of isolated, unsophisticated communities in more recent history. Our earliest evidence consists of burials and artifacts in cave dwellings from the Old Stone Age (before 8300 B.C.E.), indicating some belief in life after death and ritual actions connected to hunting. Bodies were buried with the implements of everyday life and covered with a stone slab, showing awe of the dead. Cave paintings and clay artifacts seem intended to influence the outcome of the hunt. There appears to be a concern with maintaining harmony between humanity and the forces of nature. Artifacts from the Middle Stone Age (8300–4000 B.C.E.) include figures with exaggerated female characteristics, indicating veneration of the earth as mother and source of fertility. Burials become more elaborate and include manmade objects with apparent religious significance.

Outline

I. The earliest indications of prehistoric religion appear during the Old Stone Age.

    A. The primary problem in investigating prehistoric religion is what constitutes evidence.

        1. *Material culture* is the surviving physical remains of prehistoric peoples.

        2. Material culture is our major form of evidence for prehistoric religion, but theories are largely guesswork.

        3. Theories are built in large part on what we know about characteristic forms of religious expression.

        4. We also have data from small groups that were physically and culturally isolated from the world.

        5. Anthropological research provides data that sheds light on the primary religious concerns.

        6. Scholars assume that contemporary isolated, non-agricultural tribal societies resemble similar prehistoric societies.

B. Religion implies that a human being is a part of the world and subject to forces at work in it.

    1. The religious point of view asserts that humanity must live in harmony with its environment.

    2. Religion also asserts that human beings may choose how to relate to their environment.

    3. Human beings are *in* nature but distinct *from* nature and, thus, have to decide how to relate to nature.

    4. The reasoning behind religious activity seems to require a fairly advanced intellectual capacity.

    5. We can know only what material culture reveals about religious ideas and practices among early humans.

C. The prehistoric era begins with the first appearance of pre-human species during the Stone Age.

    1. The earliest Stone Age period is also the longest, the Old Stone Age.

    2. The Old Stone Age lasted to about 17,000 B.C.E. and is further divided into Lower, Middle, and Upper.

    3. The Middle Stone Age (c. 17,000–8300 B.C.E.) saw a gradual shift to a settled life based primarily on agriculture.

    4. The New Stone Age (c. 8300–4000 B.C.E.) saw early city life, improved hunting and agriculture, and early written language.

D. The earliest evidence for religious behavior is based on burial customs and artifacts from the Old Stone Age (the Paleolithic era).

    1. The earliest indications of religious behavior are found among Neanderthals during the Middle Paleolithic era.

    2. Neanderthals buried their dead carefully with food and implements and removed the brains from human skulls.

    3. This practice suggests cannibalism, probably to gain the skills and virtues of the deceased.

    4. Neanderthals also preserved skulls and bones of cave bears on platforms or shelves in their caves.

    5. Discovering a religious or practical explanation for physical remains is the major problem in prehistoric religion.

E. Remains of early human beings from the Upper Paleolithic era show a religious life similar to that of Neanderthals.

    1. *Mousterian* material culture of the Middle Paleolithic appears throughout the Mediterranean basin.

    2. Human beings from this era share with the Neanderthals a concern with proper treatment of the dead.

    3. During this era, the dead were buried carefully, usually with the feet pulled up into a contracted position.

    4. Burials were often in the cave where the group lived or in another cave nearby.

    5. The body was typically buried under a stone slab with ornaments, stone tools, food, and weapons.

F. The Upper Paleolithic era (c. 30,000–17,000 years ago) saw major changes in how human beings lived and expressed themselves.

    1. Early *Homo sapiens* in Europe painted the walls of caves, molded clay figures, and carved antlers.

    2. In the Upper Paleolithic era, exaggerated female clay figurines appear, apparently associated with fertility rites.

    3. Old Stone Age religious practices seem intended to maintain harmony between disparate parties: human and spiritual, living and dead.

    4. The end of the Old Stone Age is marked by substantial climate changes and a revolution in material culture.

    5. Human manufacture extended from tools and hunting implements to address other human needs.

    6. The end of the Paleolithic era leads to changes in religious activities to address changes in how people lived.

II. Religious culture during the Middle Stone Age reflects major changes in human lives.

A. The Mesolithic era (c. 17,000–8300 B.C.E.) began with nomadic hunting and ended in settled agriculture.

    1. Food supplied by nomadic bands was supplemented by wild grains, berries, and nuts gathered by women.

    2. Fishing with hooks or nets and hunting with bow and arrow made the meat supply more dependable.

B. In Syria-Palestine, the Mesolithic era is represented by *Natufian* culture.

    1. Natufians lived in caves or in settlements, most often near marshes, rivers, and lakes.

    2. Natufian settlements are most often in open ground, with huts built on stone foundations.

3. Natufian economy depended on hunting, fishing, and gathering fruit and nuts, with some crops.
4. Natufian culture also shows an interest in art, household items, beads, and decorated shells.
5. Natufian culture is represented at the earlier levels of Jericho, one of the most ancient cities in the world.

C. Religious ideas during the Middle Stone Age include concern for the fertility of the earth and crops.
1. Fertility of the earth is now often represented by figures of the mother-goddess.
2. Aspects of the natural world—sun, moon, trees—were now objects of worship represented in religious art.
3. Objects important to daily life, such as axes and spears, were venerated for their spiritual power as fetishes.
4. Burials became more elaborate, including group burials and secondary burials.

D. In the Middle Stone Age, the same religious impulses are at work to establish harmony and equilibrium.
1. This desire represents recognition of the interrelatedness of life—human, animal, and divine.
2. There was a desire to compensate the sources of food and well-being for the benefits they provided human beings.
3. There is a similar desire for harmony between the living and the dead.
4. The idea of harmony may have been extended to the unseen forces that oversee human life.

Essential Reading:

Robin W. Winks and Susan P. Mattern-Parkes. *The Ancient Mediterranean World: From the Stone Age to A.D. 600*, pp. 1–9.

Supplementary Reading:

The New Larousse Encyclopedia of Mythology, pp. 1–8.

Questions to Consider:

1. What are some of the disadvantages of judging prehistoric religious culture entirely on the basis of material culture? What kinds of misinterpretation might be possible?

2. To what extent does it seem right to say that religious practice is about establishing harmony or equilibrium between the human world and the divine world? To what extent are social rituals aimed at establishing or maintaining harmony among human beings?

Lecture Four
Prehistoric Religion—The Neolithic Era

Scope: The Neolithic era (7000–3000 B.C.E.) saw major changes in the way human beings lived, including cultivation of crops and domestication of animals. Religious concerns included the fertility of crops and animals, with human sexuality often believed to mirror or influence fertility in nature. Funerary practices concentrated on the proper adornment and burial of the body. Although the indications of worship of a mother-goddess are widespread during this era, they do not illuminate the cultural status of women in the Neolithic era. Neolithic religion appears to have focused on the relationship to spiritual beings and forces but also recognized the spiritual power possessed by human beings and by the dead. The power of life and fertility seemed to be tied up with women's power to give birth. Neolithic human beings believed life was meaningful and was lived in relationship both to other human beings and to the divine.

Outline

I. The religious culture of the New Stone Age reflected the changes in human concerns.

    A. The Neolithic era (8300–4000 B.C.E.) saw a rapid pace of change and development in human society.

        1. These changes included cultivation of crops, domestication of herd animals, and population growth.

        2. People tended to live where the conditions were most favorable for agriculture, hunting, and fishing.

        3. The development of pottery, weaving, and sewing led to separation between the activities of men and women.

        4. The Neolithic era saw the invention of the wheel and development of skills not related to procuring food.

    B. One of the major archaeological finds from the New Stone Age is the city of Jericho.

        1. Jericho was founded in the Mesolithic era, about 9300 B.C.E.

        2. Jericho flourished in the Neolithic era, with a population of about 2,000.

3. Jericho was surrounded by a city wall, with a tall round tower in the inside of the wall.
4. Later Neolithic inhabitants of Jericho left two buildings apparently devoted to religious functions, a rectangular room and a temple.
5. Found in the temple were two collections of clay human figures depicting a family group.
6. There were burials under the floor of the temple, but the skulls had been removed and decorated and collected elsewhere in the temple.

C. The Neolithic evidence for religious practices becomes more abundant and more overtly religious.
1. Religious life reflected a growing emphasis on the importance of the fertility of crops and animals.
2. An increasing number of female figurines reflects the growth and spread of the cult of the mother-goddess.
3. In Palestine and elsewhere, large numbers of red-painted representations of genitalia appear.

D. Throughout the Neolithic era, burials became more elaborate in ritual and decoration of bodies.
1. Neolithic funerals might include sacrifice of animals and grain as part of an elaborate ceremony.
2. Graves were covered by boulders, with group burials in stone chambers or cave-like tombs.
3. Bodies were decorated with clothing and accessories worn in life.
4. Ideas about a personal essence that lives on after death may have arisen from funerary rituals.

E. In many ways, Neolithic funerary rituals resemble other rituals of passage.
1. Rituals of passage are associated with birth, puberty, and marriage, as well as death.
2. The progressive yet cyclical nature of these rituals fits into the progression and cycles of time.
3. Death then takes on the aspects of movement from one form of life into another.
4. It appears that Neolithic people regarded death as a cause for sadness but also as part of a natural cycle.

II. The importance of the Neolithic mother-goddess has sparked considerable debate.

   A. Some scholars believe that early matriarchal societies existed that worshiped a mother-goddess.

      1. This theory was originally based on legends that referred to female-led societies (cf. the Amazons).

      2. The theory was later bolstered by archeological evidence provided by female figurines.

      3. The sheer number of these female images suggests that the goddess was central to prehistoric religion.

      4. According to some theories, mother-goddess worship reached its height from roughly 7000–1200 B.C.E.

      5. Some scholars tie patriarchy and worship of a chief male god to the shift from village to urban life.

   B. In these theories, worship is often thought of in terms of a single goddess, "the Goddess" or "the Ancestress."

      1. This goddess was the mother and giver of life for all forms of life and a symbol of fertility.

      2. Some scholars theorize that worship of the goddess was dominated by women.

      3. More extreme theories postulate egalitarian or female-dominated societies devoted to the goddess.

   C. The major tenets of the goddess theory must be recognized as unproven.

      1. It does seem very likely that goddess worship was central to prehistoric and some later religious cultures.

      2. Scholars too often do not consider the contribution of women to religious culture.

      3. There are many cultures, however, that worshiped goddesses but subjected women to very low status.

      4. There is no indication that women necessarily enjoy more equal status in small village cultures.

      5. Conclusions about the breadth in time and space of pre-patriarchal culture are difficult to reach.

      6. Evidence of early goddess-worship should lead historians to take the feminine aspect of religion seriously.

III. We should now recognize some recurring aspects of religious belief in the prehistoric era.

A. Given that our emphasis is on stories, we may ask what "stories" prehistoric religion has to tell us.

  1. First, this is a story about human beings living in relationship to the sacred, spiritual beings and sacred creation.

  2. Second, the story is based on belief in spiritual power, or *mana*, and involves the desire to accumulate mana.

  3. Third, in the story, the dead possess spiritual power and must be eased into death as a new form of existence.

  4. Fourth, the story sees the power of life tied up with women's power to give birth.

B. Finally, the idea of the story is itself part of prehistoric religion, the idea that human life is meaningful.

  1. Life follows cycles comparable to the passage of time, passing through recognizable stages.

  2. Each life is a one-way passage from birth to death, marking each stage of life by rituals of passage.

  3. We will see how these same ideas appear and resonate in the earliest civilizations.

Supplementary Reading:

Henry Jackson Flanders, Jr., Robert Wilson Crapps, and David Anthony Smith. *People of the Covenant: An Introduction to the Hebrew Bible*, pp. 67–78.

Robin W. Winks and Susan P. Mattern-Parkes. *The Ancient Mediterranean World: From the Stone Age to A.D. 600*, pp. 9–13.

Questions to Consider:

1. Is it more likely the case that the Neolithic era produces a richer and more varied religious culture than earlier eras, or that the material culture itself is richer and more varied?

2. Does religious culture become more central to human concerns as human beings gain more control over their lives or when they have less control? What appears to be the connection?

Lecture Five
Egypt—A Unique Religious Culture

Scope: Egyptian civilization began as a series of Neolithic agricultural settlements along the Nile River. These settlements were gradually united into two kingdoms and, finally, into the united kingdom of Upper and Lower Egypt around 3050 B.C.E. Egyptian religion acknowledged the ubiquity of divine power, present on earth in animals, human beings, and especially in the divine pharaoh. The Egyptian gods were very similar to human beings and could even grow old and die. Developments in Egyptian religion arose primarily from political turmoil, but even these changes were moderated by the essential conservatism of Egyptian religion. Egyptian religious culture reflects a dichotomy throughout its history: On the one hand, life in this world under the pharaoh's authority was a mirror of the eternal life of the gods, but on the other, the world was a realm where the suppressed forces of chaos threatened to break out at any time.

Outline

I. Egyptian civilization grew up along the Nile River, its primary focus and source of life.

   A. Egyptian civilization began as a series of Neolithic settlements established along the Nile.
      1. The Nile flows northward from central Africa, forming a broad delta before flowing into the Mediterranean.
      2. The narrow valley flanking the Nile is one of the most fertile agricultural areas in the world.
      3. Upper Egypt was the higher part of the valley to the south, with Lower Egypt near the delta in the north.
      4. The Nile Valley is arid, but the river floods annually in late summer, leaving highly fertile land.

   B. Farming techniques improved in the late Neolithic era, including the use of plows and draft animals.
      1. Farmers learned how to irrigate and drain land, making far better use of available river water.

     2. People lived in homes made of mud bricks, and burials became more elaborate.

  C. By the late fourth millennium, small territories had coalesced under military leaders.

     1. Each *nome*, or small regional unit, had its own god or gods identified with different animals.

     2. The nomes were united by conquest into the Kingdom of Upper Egypt and the Kingdom of Lower Egypt.

     3. Eras of Egyptian history reflect changes in royal dynasties, divided into the Old, Middle, and New Kingdoms.

     4. Most great events in Egyptian history and major developments in religion occurred between 4000 and 1000 B.C.E.

II. Egyptian religious culture arose and developed during the early years of the kingdoms.

  A. According to Egyptian tradition, Upper and Lower Egypt were united by Menes c. 3050 B.C.E.

     1. This would have been near the end of the Chalcolithic era, the "Copper-Stone" Age.

     2. Menes is identified as Narmer or Aha, two kings known from surviving artifacts.

     3. Menes founded the First Dynasty and established his royal capital in Memphis in Lower Egypt.

     4. The Kingdom of Upper and Lower Egypt was united under the power and authority of the pharaoh.

  B. The earliest forms of Egyptian religion represent a belief in the ubiquity of divine power.

     1. Egyptian religious beliefs reflect dependence on the Nile and the power of the divine king.

     2. Egyptians felt a spiritual kinship with animals that also depended on the Nile as a source of life.

     3. The gods were thought of primarily in anthropomorphic terms, carrying out human functions.

     4. Each nome had its own divinities, often represented in animal form but performing human actions.

     5. When the nomes were united, their gods sometimes gained more prominence as regional gods.

     6. Gods were sometimes placed into relationship with gods of other nomes in divine families or in opposition.

      7. Egyptian gods were subject to change in function and appearance to suit their believers' changing needs.

C. This implies variation in the way divine power was conceptualized or expressed in Egyptian religion.
      1. Both the gods and humanity were part of the created order.
      2. Both gods and human beings had a beginning in time and would have an end in time.
      3. The gods were the products of sexual unions and formed their own family units.
      4. The gods acted like human beings, loved, made war, grew old, made plans and carried them out.
      5. The gods could be depicted in a number of forms, using a variety of symbols.
      6. The gods differed from humanity in sacred power, length of life, and their habitation.
      7. Representation of the gods in concrete forms domesticated them but also revealed their divine nature.

III. Egyptian religious culture developed slowly, in response to a number of distinct factors.

A. The stability and conservatism of Egyptian culture ensured that religious culture changed little over centuries.
      1. Developments arose primarily from political turmoil, with each dynasty possibly bringing religious change.
      2. But such changes were moderated by the essential conservatism of Egyptian culture.
      3. Certain ideas and metaphors became traditional and determined Egyptian religion throughout its history.
      4. The full range of ancient Egyptian religion was more or less homogenous throughout its history.

B. The primary trait of ancient Egyptian religion in the modern mind is its sense of the eternal.
      1. This impression is fostered by its major monuments familiar to the modern world.
      2. But this impression of serenity is deliberate, reflecting the pharaoh's imposition of cosmic order over chaos.
      3. Pharaoh's monuments and his self-presentation reflected the life lived under divine order.

4. But the vast majority of Egyptians lived with the constant threat of natural disaster, accident, disease, and death.
5. There were two conflicting stories in Egyptian religious culture, one about life under divine control and one about life constantly threatened by chaos.
6. Such dichotomies reflect the ancient Egyptian way of understanding the created world.
7. Egyptians saw these dichotomies as the expression of the temporal in the eternal and the eternal in the temporal.

Essential Reading:

John Baines, Leonard H. Lesko, and David P. Silverman. *Religion in Ancient Egypt: Gods, Myths, and Personal Practice*, pp. 7–30.

Erik Hornung. *History of Ancient Egypt: An Introduction*, pp. 1–12.

Supplementary Reading:

Jan Assmann. *The Search for God in Ancient Egypt*, pp. 1–14.

Sarah Iles Johnston, ed. *Religions of the Ancient World: A Guide*, pp. 155–164.

Claude Traunecker. *The Gods of Egypt*.

Questions to Consider:

1. What appear to have been some of the most important factors in the development of ancient Egypt's unique religious culture? What did each of these factors contribute?
2. The Egyptians believed animals that depended on the Nile shared a spiritual power and identity comparable to that of human beings. What consequences did this belief have for Egyptian religious culture and the way it was expressed in art?

Lecture Six
Egyptian Creation Stories and Their Meaning

Scope: Creation stories are *cosmogonies*, stories of how things came to be the way they are now. There are four methods of creation: by making, by combat, by sexual generation, and by speaking. The Heliopolis creation story presents Atum standing on a mound in the sea of chaos and releasing the divine life within him, either by spitting or by masturbating. This action creates the first generation of elemental gods, whose descendants include other elemental gods and the gods of the social order. In the Hermopolis creation story, four pairs of couples give birth to a god, either Thoth or Atum, who in turn, creates all the other gods. In Thebes, humanity is the creation of the divine craftsman Khnum. At Memphis, Ptah was credited with creating the cosmos by speaking, "breathing" his will into being. All Egyptian creation stories seem to be variants of a single master story of creation.

Outline

I. Creation stories tend to follow certain forms and patterns in ancient religious cultures.

    A. Creation stories fall under the category of *cosmogony*, accounts of the origins of the cosmos.

        1. Creation stories are mythic accounts of the cosmos as the work of a god or gods in a "beginning" time.

        2. In polytheistic religious systems, creation stories are usually about the origins of the gods as well.

        3. The order of the gods' creation doesn't necessarily reflect the importance of the gods involved.

        4. This is because the initiative for creation usually arises spontaneously out of primordial matter.

    B. There are four means of creation in classical mythic cosmogonies.

        1. There is creation by making, when a god acts upon undifferentiated primordial matter.

        2. There is creation through conflict between the creator god and some principle of chaos.

3. There is creation through sexual generation, when a god and goddess create divine offspring through sexual intercourse.
4. There is creation by word, based on the spoken word as a means of controlling all that exists.

C. These four means of creation appear to be common to all ancient Mediterranean religious cultures.
   1. Creation through sexual generation shows the least intention to create on the gods' part.
   2. Both creation by making and creation by word reveal a clear intention to create.

II. Egyptian creation mythology appears to represent variations on several basic ideas.

A. Egyptian creation mythology is distinctive in seeing creation as the deliberate work of a god.
   1. Egypt has several cosmogonies that credit a "self-generated" god with initiating creation.
   2. In Egypt, the three powers necessary for creation were *Hu*, divine utterance; *Heka*, magic; and *Sia*, divine knowledge.

B. Several methods of creation are involved in the Heliopolis creation story, focusing on Atum.
   1. Heliopolis is the Greek name for Iwnw (biblical On), "Sun City," the primary site for the worship of Atum.
   2. Before creation, the waters of the depths, Nun, already existed as a principle of chaos.
   3. In the midst of Nun, Atum stood on the Benben, a primeval pyramidical hill that arose out of the waters.
   4. Atum is the creative force who contains within himself the life-essence of every other deity.
   5. Atum releases the divine life-essence within himself, either by spitting or by masturbating.
   6. The two elemental gods created in this way are Shu, god of the air, and Tefnut, the goddess of moisture.
   7. Tefnut gives birth to two children, Geb, the god of the earth, and Nut, the goddess of the sky.
   8. Nut gives birth to her four children by Geb, Osiris, Isis, Seth, and Nephthys.
   9. The children of Geb and Nut are the gods of the political order who rule over human beings.

C. Another creation story comes from Hermopolis, city of Thoth, god of the moon and wisdom.

    1. Here the agents of creation are the Ogdoad, a group of four pairs of gods and goddesses.

    2. The Ogdoad existed initially as entities within the primordial sea.

    3. The four couples were essentially male and female aspects of the same principles, as revealed by their names, masculine and feminine forms of the same word.

    4. From these four couples comes an egg containing the god who is responsible for the creation.

    5. In some versions of the story, it is Thoth who stands on the Benben mound and creates the Ogdoad.

D. An interesting variation on Egyptian creation stories comes from Thebes, focusing on the god Khnum.

    1. Khnum is portrayed as a ram-headed man, a craftsman who is a builder of ferryboats and ladders.

    2. In the Theban story, Khnum is responsible specifically for the creation of human beings.

    3. Khnum creates human beings on a potter's wheel, both their outer forms and their internal systems.

    4. As a result, Khnum is intimately involved with human beings and their health.

    5. In some stories, Khnum is also responsible for the individual creation of the pharaoh.

E. Amun became the dominant god of Egypt during the New Kingdom, when he was designated the transcendent creator.

    1. Amun was originally a sun god but gained an unparalleled primacy over the other gods.

    2. Amun was believed to be not only king of the gods but also the divine essence found in all gods.

    3. Amun is understood as "self-generated," active in creation as the impulse of creative energy prompting the Ogdoad into action.

    4. Because of the conservative nature of Egyptian religion, Amun could be incorporated into creation only by finding a place in an existing creation myth.

F. Finally, we have an example of creation by word in the creation story of the god Ptah.

    1. Ptah was worshiped from the early dynastic era, but his distinctive role as the patron of artisans came later.

    2. Ptah was the chief god of Memphis and came to prominence in the Fourth Dynasty.

    3. Ptah was usually depicted as a mummified figure holding a scepter representing life, stability, and omnipotence.

    4. Ptah creates by speaking a word, giving spirit to a divine idea and "breathing" it into being.

    5. Ptah is responsible for the creation of all the gods and their *kas*, their creative intellectual capacity.

    6. Ptah's act of creation was an act of both the heart, the seat of the intellect, and the tongue, the organ of speech.

    7. Again, we see how traditional stories are modified with the addition of new chief creator gods.

G. There appears to be one master creation narrative that lies behind most Egyptian creation myths.

    1. Before creation, there existed a primordial sea, the dark waters of the abyss.

    2. A mound of earth arises from the depths and, from this mound, a god initiates the process of creation.

    3. The process moves from the creation of elemental gods to the generation of the gods of the political realm.

    4. Shu and Tefnut, Geb and Nut, Osiris and Isis, Seth and Nephthys, and a creator god form the Ennead, the nine principal gods.

    5. Creation of the cosmos is separated by three generations from the gods with sovereignty over human beings.

    6. The creation of human beings plays little or no part in this schema.

Essential Reading:

John Baines, Leonard H. Lesko, and David P. Silverman. *Religion in Ancient Egypt: Gods, Myths, and Personal Practice*, pp. 88–122.

Lucia Gahlin. *Egypt: Gods, Myths and Religion*, pp. 50–57.

Donald B. Redford, ed. *The Ancient Gods Speak: A Guide to Egyptian Religion*, pp. 246–251.

Supplementary Reading:

George Hart. *Egyptian Myths*, pp. 9–28.

James C. Livingston. *Anatomy of the Sacred*, pp. 196–222.

Questions to Consider:

1. Read Genesis 1 and 2; which methods of creation are at work in the biblical account? Why are these methods favored over others?

2. In what ways is the creation story of Ptah from Memphis similar to the biblical account of creation in Genesis 1? In what ways is it different? What does the comparison say about the two religious systems represented?

Lecture Seven
The Egyptian Pantheon

Scope: The Egyptian pantheon is not easily categorized, because a god's or goddess's importance does not necessarily arise from association with a part of creation or a realm of human endeavor. The gods may be divided into categories as gods that represent natural phenomena, regional gods, funerary gods, or gods identified with professions. Such categories do not reflect the way the Egyptians thought about their gods, however. There was inevitable overlapping in association and function among the gods in Egyptian religious culture, as in any polytheistic system, especially as some gods waxed and waned in importance over the centuries. This phenomenon is clearest in the case of the many Egyptian solar deities, including Horus, Atum, Rē, Amun, and Aten. Often, these gods are harmonized, with each representing a different aspect of the sun, although Aten was the subject of almost exclusive worship for a brief period during the New Kingdom.

Outline

I. The Egyptian pantheon or hierarchy of gods includes a wide variety of deities.

    A. There is no single obvious way to categorize the gods of ancient Egypt.

        1. The Egyptians thought of the gods as forming a hierarchy similar to their own hierarchical society.

        2. The Ennead, the first nine gods of creation, stands at the head of the divine hierarchy.

        3. We may classify gods by their primary associations, but many gods transcended their primary attributes.

    B. The creation stories deal with many of the gods that represent cosmic elements.

        1. Among this group are the eight gods of the Ogdoad, as well as Shu and Tefnut (air and moisture) and Geb and Nut (earth and sky).

2. To them, we may add two different moon gods, Thoth, who is also the divine scribe, and Khonsu.
3. Other gods of nature include the various sun gods and Hathor, goddess of joy and divine vengeance.
4. The personalization of natural phenomena as gods humanized the forces that controlled nature.

C. National deities appear to have developed from the local gods of the ancient nomes.
1. Distinctly local gods took on additional significance when one nome conquered another.
2. It is possible that some gods were recognized very early as local manifestations of universal gods.
3. A god sacred to all Egypt might still have a special association with a particular locality or city.

D. One group of gods with significance for all Egyptians consisted of the funerary deities.
1. The earliest god of the dead and the underworld seems to have been the jackal-headed god Anubis.
2. Anubis was succeeded as god of the underworld by Osiris, who died and left his earthly realm to his son Horus.
3. Osiris presided over the realm of the dead with his consort Isis and their sister Nephthys.
4. The work of judgment of the souls of the dead also involved the gods of the Egyptian nomes.

E. There were gods who represented and served as patrons to particular professions.
1. Ptah performed an artisan in the divine realm but also served as the patron of artisans and craftsmen.
2. Thoth, the scribe of the gods, was also patron of scribes in the royal bureaucracy.
3. A host of gods served as patrons of doctors, including Imhotep, himself a deified official.
4. Other, more universal gods might be invoked by those in need in particular situations.
5. Some minor gods seem to have been invoked primarily as protectors.

F. This survey of the Egyptian pantheon underscores several significant points.

      1. The multiplicity of gods in Egypt means an inevitable overlap in their functions and concerns.

      2. The fortunes of gods rise with the waxing of the realm of human concern over which they preside.

      3. The multiplicity of gods also exhibits gradual evolution in the human conception of a particular god, his or her claims, and comparative power.

II. Duplication and overlapping of divine functions is particularly clear among Egyptian solar deities.

  A. The primary example of historical change and development is found among the Egyptian solar deities.

      1. The different Egyptian sun gods rose and fell in importance as a result of cultural factors.

      2. Because the sun was a primary reality of Egyptian life, sun gods were often identified as chief gods.

      3. Egyptians apparently had no trouble with these gods simultaneously representing the divine aspects of the sun.

  B. Different divine aspects of the sun were identified with different solar gods.

      1. Atum was identified with the sun at its setting and, thus, was sometimes depicted as an old man.

      2. Kheprer was represented by the scarab or dung beetle, identified with the sun at its rising.

  C. Horus was the earliest of the sun gods and the chief god of Lower Egypt.

      1. The name *Horus* is generally believed to mean "the distant one" and appears in many compound forms.

      2. Horus was represented as a falcon or falcon-headed man, often wearing a crown or sun disk.

      3. Horus inherited the heavenly throne after Osiris was murdered by Seth, providing a model for royal succession.

      4. The association between Horus and pharaoh largely overshadows Horus's identity as sun god.

  D. The dominant solar deity was Rē, especially during the early dynasties of the Old Kingdom.

      1. Rē is identified with the sun at its zenith but also represents the divine essence of the sun.

2. The creative power associated with the sun led to the identification of Rē as creator god.
3. From the Fourth Dynasty, the pharaoh was called "the son of Rē."
4. One of Rē's names, Rē-Horakhty, "Rē, Horus of the Horizon," indicates this relationship.
5. Such combination names indicate the unity of the divine powers associated with the sun.
6. Rē sailed across the sky each day in his royal barge and entered the underworld each night.
7. Sometimes, the sun's course across the sky was thought of as mimicking the human lifespan.

E. Amun gained supremacy as Amun-Rē and enjoyed widespread exclusive worship.
1. Amun was, very early on, a god of Thebes, together with Montu, the god of war.
2. As Thebes became politically prominent, Amun grew more powerful and received the name Amun-Rē before 2000 B.C.E.
3. After the expulsion of the west Semitic Hyksos rulers circa 1540 B.C.E., worship of Amun-Rē represented the reassertion of native Egyptian power.
4. During the New Kingdom, worship of Amun-Rē came close to monotheism in practice if not theory.

F. The power of Amun-Rē's priests led to the attempt to replace him with Aten, the solar disk.
1. Devotion to Aten reached its height during the reign of Amenophis IV, later known as Akhenaten (1353–1336 B.C.E.).
2. Akhenaten's reign signaled a break with tradition in many ways but most notably in the worship of Aten.
3. Aten was not represented in anthropomorphic form, as most gods were, but as the light radiating from the sun disk.
4. Aten was not identified with other sun gods, and the worship of Amun-Rē in particular was suppressed.
5. Whether the royal worship of Aten was truly monotheistic is an open question, but it stands in contrast to Egypt's prevailing polytheism.
6. Soon after Akhenaten's death, the worship of the old gods was restored.

7. Akhenaten's innovations are further evidence for the sun god's inevitable place at the head of the Egyptian pantheon.

Essential Reading:

John Baines, Leonard H. Lesko, and David P. Silverman. *Religion in Ancient Egypt: Gods, Myths, and Personal Practice*, pp. 30–87.

Lucia Gahlin. *Egypt: Gods, Myths and Religion*, pp. 16–47, 126–133.

Erik Hornung. *History of Ancient Egypt: An Introduction*, pp. 76–124.

Donald B. Redford, ed. *The Ancient Gods Speak: A Guide to Egyptian Religion*, pp. 255–261.

Supplementary Reading:

George Hart. *Egyptian Myths*, pp. 50–61.

Jan Assmann. *The Search for God in Ancient Egypt*, pp. 198–221.

Questions to Consider:

1. What are some of the consequences of hierarchical structuring of the pantheon of gods in a polytheistic religious culture?

2. What factors seem to determine whether a particular god takes a high place in the Egyptian pantheon? Do the more important gods share any general characteristics?

Lecture Eight
Egyptian Myths of Kingship

Scope: The pharaoh was at the center of Egyptian religious culture. First regarded as the embodiment of Horus and later as "son of Rē," the pharaoh was enforcer of *ma'at*, cosmic balance. He made both human and divine activity possible. In time, the individual kings were regarded as human beings in whom the sun god dwelt, but each king was regarded as divine in his role as pharaoh. The myth of Egyptian kingship is the story of Osiris's death at the hands of his brother Seth and Isis's quest to recover Osiris's body and bear his son. The second part of the myth recounts the contest between Seth and Horus, Osiris's son, to gain sovereignty over the cosmos. During his reign, each pharaoh was identified with Horus but at death assumed the role of Osiris, the king of the underworld, leaving his earthly realm to the new pharaoh.

Outline

I. The divine pharaoh took a dominant place in the religious culture of ancient Egypt.

   A. The king provided stability not only for his human subjects but for the gods as well.

      1. The pharaoh was traditionally the focus of religious concern, although it took different forms.

      2. Pharaohs of the First and Second Dynasty (3000–2670 B.C.E.) were venerated as incarnations of Horus.

      3. Pharaohs of the Old Kingdom (from about 2670 to 2200 B.C.E.) were called "son of Rē."

      4. Old Kingdom pharaohs established a royal administration filled with officials to help them govern their domain.

      5. The vast majority of Egyptians were subsistence farmers and craftsmen.

   B. The divine honors afforded pharaoh reflect his central importance to the entire cosmic order.

      1. The primary role of the pharaoh was to establish *ma'at*: "truth," "order," "cosmic balance."

2. *Ma'at* was both a principle and a goddess, representing the ideal state of being.

3. Ancient Egyptians were aware of sharp physical and spiritual contrasts that stood in tension in the world.

4. The king was responsible for maintaining order and defeating the forces of chaos that threatened order.

C. The role of the pharaoh is necessary for both the good of humanity and the good of the gods.

1. Pharaoh exists simultaneously in the divine and the human worlds and is necessary to both.

2. The concept of *ma'at* implies reason and decorum as the motivating forces in pharaoh's actions.

3. Each king was understood to be also the one divine and eternal, ever-reigning pharaoh.

D. The pharaoh's role tells us something concerning Egyptian ideas about the divine.

1. The pharaoh was considered to be an incarnate god during the First and Second Dynasties.

2. The office of the pharaoh, his royal identity, was divine and eternal.

3. Each pharaoh was identified with Horus on his accession to the throne.

4. Later in history, the pharaoh became a human being in whom the sun god dwelt.

II. The myth of kingship was the basic explanation for both the divine and the earthly order.

A. The divine model for pharaoh's rule was the contest between Horus and Seth for kingship.

1. This story appears in a variety of sources, including Plutarch's 1st-century C.E. Greek version.

2. The Egyptian sources are fragmentary and reluctant to address the death of Osiris.

B. The story begins with Osiris ruling over the earth until he is murdered by his brother Seth.

1. Osiris ruled with his sister and consort Isis during a golden age of peace and prosperity.

2. Osiris's younger brother Seth grew jealous and killed Osiris, scattering the pieces of his body.

3. Seth assumed rule, but Isis went into deep mourning until Nephthys decided to help her.

C. The sister goddesses searched for the pieces of Osiris's body and reassembled it at Abydos.

  1. Isis was able to revive her husband sufficiently that she was able to conceive the god Horus.

  2. Osiris departed from his earthly domain and entered the underworld, where he ruled as king.

D. This part of the story has some fairly clear symbolic significance.

  1. The story of Osiris is tied to the fertility of crops provided by the annual flooding of the Nile.

  2. The scattering of pieces of Osiris's body may justify the many cultic sites sacred to him.

  3. Seth, although a god of disorder and violence, is part of the cosmic order of creation and not a force of primordial chaos.

E. The second part of the myth shifts attention to the combat between Seth and Horus.

  1. Horus is represented as a falcon, while Seth was represented by a strange composite animal.

  2. Isis hid the child Horus from Seth and served as his protector and advocate.

  3. Once grown, Horus asked for his legitimate right of succession to assume the throne.

  4. The contest between Horus and his uncle Seth takes on different forms in various sources.

  5. The central contest is legal, Horus's plea for the divine council to recognize his legal rights.

  6. During the combat, Horus was blinded in one eye, while Seth lost both testicles.

  7. The blinding and healing of Horus are the origins of a powerful amulet, the Eye of Horus.

  8. The combat resulted in a series of victories for Horus and losses and humiliations for Seth.

  9. Rē gave Seth the job of protecting Rē's barge from the chaos monster Apophis during Rē's daily journey across the sky.

F. This story has a complicated web of connections and meanings relevant to royal rule.

1. At death, a pharaoh assumes the role of Osiris, leaving behind his heir in the role of Horus.
2. In this way, the continuity of the rule of the eternal divine pharaoh is maintained.
3. The contest is sometimes understood as a contest between Horus as representative of Lower Egypt and Seth as representative of Upper Egypt.
4. On a more primary level, the contest is between kingly authority and social chaos.

G. The story of Osiris, Seth, and Horus is, in part, an explanation and justification for "the way things are."
1. In this sense, the story is a creation myth explaining how the world assumed its current shape.
2. The myth is also the basis for beliefs about Isis, the most important Egyptian goddess.
3. It is also a story that explains the continuity between the realm of Horus and the realm of Osiris, the land of the living and the land of the dead.

Essential Reading:

Lucia Gahlin. *Egypt: Gods, Myths and Religion*, pp. 58–69.

Donald B. Redford, ed. *The Ancient Gods Speak: A Guide to Egyptian Religion*, pp. 251–255, 302–307.

Supplementary Reading:

George Hart. *Egyptian Myths*, pp. 29–41.

Questions to Consider:

1. What are some of the reasons the pharaohs became identified with the sun gods? Is this more a reflection of political propaganda or of the common people's regard for a ruler so far elevated above their own station in life?

2. How might we interpret the myth of kingship in the context of inner-family dynamics? In what ways does the Egyptian idea of family represented in the myth resemble or conflict with our own ideas of family and family dynamics?

Lecture Nine
Egyptian Myths of the Underworld

Scope: The Egyptians show more concern with preparation for the afterlife than any other ancient civilization known to us. Their beliefs about the afterlife were particularly vivid and evolved over a period of centuries. A person was believed to consist of the body; the name; the shadow; the *ba*, or alter ego; and the *ka*, or spiritual identity. The long and expensive process of mummification and the elaborate decoration and furnishing of the tomb were intended to provide for the needs and well-being of the departed in the afterlife. The dominant conception of the afterlife was the kingdom of Osiris, where the departed made a negative confession of the sins he or she had not committed before being subjected to a form of trial by ordeal. If the deceased passed the trial, he or she was welcomed into the company of the gods and the souls of the blessed.

Outline

I. Ancient Egyptian burial practices reflected and supported ideas about the afterlife.
- **A.** Egyptian civilization showed more concern with the next life than any other known to us.
  - **1.** The apparent preoccupation with death arises from our primary sources for Egyptian culture: tombs.
  - **2.** The abundance of material argues that concern with the afterlife was, in fact, central to Egyptian religion.
- **B.** The Egyptians' vivid beliefs about the afterlife stand out among ancient cultures.
  - **1.** Prehistoric religious culture included belief in an afterlife.
  - **2.** The earliest Egyptian burials are consistent with other Neolithic burials.
  - **3.** Burials were gradually moved away from village settlements and the homes of the living.
  - **4.** Some scholars argue that belief in an afterlife stems from the preservative qualities of Egypt's arid climate.
- **C.** Beliefs about the afterlife evolved slowly over the centuries.

1. An afterlife was originally restricted to the divine pharaoh, an aspect of his divine status.
2. After the end of the Old Kingdom (c. 2000 B.C.E.), the afterlife was opened to nearly everyone.

D. Beliefs about the afterlife involve the whole person: body, name, shadow, *ba*, and *ka*.
1. The name was an essential expression of the personality, in this life and the afterlife.
2. The shadow was the physical presence of a person distinct from the body in both life and afterlife.
3. The *ba* was an alter ego, the impression others receive of a person's spirit through what he or she does.
4. The *ka* relates to the interaction of the mind and the body that comes into being at birth.
5. Egyptian burial practices were determined by these beliefs about the person and the afterlife.

E. The practice of mummification involved an elaborate process carried out over weeks.
1. The brain was removed and discarded, but the heart was left in place as an abode for the *ba*.
2. Internal organs were removed and either placed in canopic jars or later put back into the body.
3. The body was washed, soaked in natron for two months, then sewn up and wrapped in linen bands.
4. The body was often padded and decorated to make it appear as lifelike as possible.
5. The finished mummy was placed in two or more coffins decorated to resemble the deceased.

F. Tomb furniture and decoration were to serve the needs of the deceased as an eternal habitation.
1. The pyramid evolved from early mud-brick tombs covering a burial, topped by a mound of sand.
2. Given that the *ba* and shadow resided in the tomb, furniture and decorations were needed to accommodate them.
3. Also left in the tomb were models of male and female slaves called *ushebtis*, "answerers."

G. Part of the preparation of the tomb was the "opening of the mouth" ceremony.

1. The rituals for "opening the mouth" were performed on *ushebtis*, other human figures, and the mummy.
2. These rituals included purification with water, animal sacrifice, and recitation of spells.
3. The deceased was nourished by daily offerings of food at the tomb, given by the eldest son.
4. Although the tomb was carefully designed, the afterlife took place in the kingdom of Osiris.

II. The kingdom of Osiris was the dominant idea of the afterlife among several alternatives.

A. Just as with Egyptian creation myths, so too, were there competing conceptions of the afterlife.
1. Egyptian beliefs about the fate of the dead were, for the most part, meant to be evocative.
2. A person's beliefs about the afterlife often depended on the chief god he or she worshiped.
3. Amun-Rē and Osiris represent two different aspects of the afterlife, rejuvenation and eternal life.

B. We have three primary textual sources of information about the situation of the dead.
1. The Pyramid Texts are inscribed on the walls of pyramids from the Old Kingdom.
2. These texts were collected and edited during the Middle Kingdom into the Coffin Texts.
3. During the New Kingdom, the *Books of Going Forth by Day* was a guide to a blessed afterlife.

C. Among the oldest beliefs were those that envisioned the underworld as the kingdom of Osiris.
1. These beliefs depended on the myth of kingship, when Osiris was murdered by Seth.
2. After his death, Osiris left his earthly kingdom to Horus and descended to the underworld.
3. Osiris's realm was variously located in the western desert, the Nile Delta, Syria, or the Milky Way.
4. In Osiris's kingdom, the deceased would live at leisure while slaves provided for his or her needs.

D. Entrance into the kingdom of Osiris was determined by an elaborate process of judgment.

1. Details differ, but we can sketch out a general account of the process.
2. After death, the deceased is guided by Anubis into the kingdom of Osiris and his courtroom.
3. Here, Osiris sits in state, attended by Isis and Nephthys, who mourn and protect the dead.
4. The deceased makes a negative confession affirming that he or she has not committed a list of offenses.
5. The deceased repeats this confession before a series of 42 divine judges.

E. After the confession, the deceased is subjected to what amounts to a trial by ordeal.
1. The heart of the deceased is placed in a balance opposite an ostrich feather.
2. In paintings, this scene takes place before Osiris, Isis and Nephthys, and sometimes, Anubis.
3. If the heart is heavier than the ostrich feather, it has been made heavy by evil deeds and is destroyed.
4. If the heart is lighter than the ostrich feather, it has been made light by virtue.
5. In this happy event, the deceased is welcomed into Osiris's kingdom to enjoy it for eternity.
6. The *Books of Going Forth by Day* records the traditional favorable decree of Osiris.
7. The ideal of the afterlife was to live like a god, partaking of daily memorial offerings.
8. Even so, generally, the greatest good was believed to be a long life enjoyed on earth.

Supplementary Reading:

Lucia Gahlin. *Egypt: Gods, Myths and Religion*, pp. 138–187.

Donald B. Redford, ed. *The Ancient Gods Speak: A Guide to Egyptian Religion*, pp. 34–57, 134–154, 293–298.

Questions to Consider:

1. Which aspects of Egyptian burial practices appear to be most similar to the practices of the Neolithic era? Which represent innovations?

2. Can the rather complicated idea of the components of a human person tell us anything about how the Egyptians thought about human consciousness, moral responsibility, or personality?

Lecture Ten
Egypt—The Power of Goddesses

Scope: Goddesses play an important role in Egyptian creation mythology, both as personifications of the cosmic elements and as mothers to new generations of gods. Other goddesses have a multitude of concerns and functions. Hathor, originally a fertility deity, was the goddess of love and joy, associated with all aspects of erotic pleasure. But Hathor was also goddess of fate and the warrior of divine retribution. In one story, Hathor had to be distracted to prevent her from destroying all of humanity. Isis plays an important role in the Egyptian myth of kingship, both as sister and wife to Osiris and mother to Horus. In this connection, Isis was protector of the pharaoh's throne. Isis gained the power of magic and spells by tricking Rē into revealing his secret name to her. As a group, the Egyptian goddesses display strength, initiative, cleverness, and other virtues traditionally associated with women.

Outline

I. Some Egyptian goddesses represented different elements of the divine order of creation.

    A. Goddesses played major roles in the process of creation and as part of the created order.

        1. The divine world reflected the natural world, including the duality between male and female.

        2. Creation through sexual generation involved male and female deities giving birth to a new generation of gods.

        3. In the Hermopolis creation, the origin of living creatures is an egg produced by the male and female pairs of the Ogdoad.

    B. In the Heliopolis myth, Shu and Tefnut are the first gods created and the first who are sexually differentiated.

        1. Tefnut represented the moist air of the heavens and the atmosphere of the underworld.

        2. Tefnut is depicted as a woman with the head of a lioness, crowned with a solar disk and *uraeus*, the sacred asp that symbolizes supreme power.

       3. Shu and Tefnut are the first divine couple, and Tefnut is the first mother.

  C. Nut, the daughter of Tefnut and Shu, was the sky-goddess, consort to Geb, god of the earth.

       1. After Nut gave birth to the gods of the political order, her father, Shu, lifted her up to separate her from her husband Geb.

       2. Geb wept tears that created the oceans, and Nut is often portrayed as stretching over Geb's reclining body.

       3. In other depictions, Nut has wings that spread over the earth to form the sky.

       4. Nut is sometimes mother of Rē, giving birth to him each dawn and swallowing him at dusk.

       5. Nut and Geb reverse the usual association of gods with the sky and goddesses with the earth.

II. We find a considerably more complex divine figure in Hathor.

  A. Hathor was a popular and important goddess who filled a number of related functions.

       1. Hathor's origins seem to lie in a prehistoric cow goddess representing nature and fertility.

       2. She is represented as a cow, or as a goddess with horns, or with a human face and cow's ears.

       3. Her name means "House of Horus," and she was identified with various abodes of Horus.

  B. Hathor was goddess of love and joy and was associated with all aspects of erotic love.

       1. Hathor was patroness of singers, dancers, and artists and protected women in childbirth.

       2. She is sometimes associated with the god Rē, either as his mother or his daughter.

       3. She plays a small part in the *Contendings of Horus and Seth* when she amuses Rē.

       4. Perhaps because of her associations with fertility, Hathor is goddess of fate and a prophetess.

  C. Hathor as goddess of fate is also the warrior goddess of divine vengeance.

       1. Hathor inflicts punishment against those who offend the gods or overstep human limits.

    2. Hathor is sometimes identified with Sekhmet, the lioness-goddess known as the "Powerful One."

    3. In one story, when human beings plot to overthrow Rē, he orders Hathor to take vengeance.

    4. At the end of the day, Hathor has destroyed half of humanity, threatening to wipe it out.

    5. Rē procures a vast quantity of beer and mixes it with red ocher, pouring it all over the earth.

    6. Hathor mistakes the beer for blood and drinks until she is intoxicated; thus, humanity is saved.

D. Hathor's rituals and festivals reflect her primary characteristics.

    1. Her rituals often included music and dance to the sound of her sacred instrument, the sistrum.

    2. On New Year's Day, Hathor's cult statue was taken out to stand in the sun's ray, reuniting her with her father, Rē.

    3. Later in the same month, she was happily honored by a "festival of drunkenness."

    4. Hathor sometimes appeared as the wife of Horus and was honored in a summer rite of "sacred marriage."

    5. Hathor's many associations are typical of major goddesses worshiped in ancient Mediterranean religions.

III. Isis is the sister and consort of Osiris but gains importance to become Queen of Heaven.

A. Isis plays a major role in the myth of kingship as Osiris's wife and Horus's mother and protector.

    1. Isis is a model of a devoted wife, widow, and mother, reflecting roles relevant to all women.

    2. Isis's tears of mourning for Osiris cause the flooding of the Nile, ensuring Egypt's fertility.

B. Isis intrudes several times into the contest between Horus and Seth.

    1. Isis appears repeatedly in the *Contendings of Horus and Seth* to help Horus gain the kingship.

    2. She argues Horus's case before a tribunal of the gods, but Rē opposes Isis and bans her from the court.

    3. Isis is not only wise but clever, with the ability to develop successful schemes.

4. At one point, Isis uses magic to disguise herself and trick Seth into condemning himself.
5. Once the trial between Horus and Seth turns into a physical contest, Isis intercedes repeatedly.
6. The contest is finally resolved by the intervention of Osiris, and Seth renounces his claim.

C. As these stories make clear, Isis is closely associated with pharaoh as the embodiment of Horus.
1. The goddess protects pharaoh, acting as his divine patroness and symbol of his sovereignty.
2. Isis also protects the dead pharaoh, identified with Osiris, and helps him gain immortality.
3. As protector of the pharaoh, Isis is identified with Hathor; thus, Isis is also depicted crowned with horns.

D. Isis's power of magic and healing made her important to the average Egyptian.
1. Isis was believed to have knowledge of elixirs that could confer health and immortality.
2. Isis was associated with protective spells against hostile animals or harmful insects.
3. Many of these spells are set in the context of Isis's protection of Horus.

E. According to a myth from about 1200 B.C.E., Isis gained power to cast spells by knowing Rē's secret name.
1. In Egypt, the name was the expression of the essence of a person's or god's hidden being.
2. As part of her plan to put Horus on the throne, Isis schemes to make Rē reveal his secret name.
3. She knows nothing created can hurt Rē, so she collects his saliva when he dozes and drools.
4. Using Rē's saliva, Isis creates a venomous snake and places it where Rē will pass.
5. When the snake bites Rē, only Isis has the power to help, and she demands to know his secret name.
6. Rē tries to get around Isis but finally capitulates, telling Isis to put Horus on oath to keep the secret.
7. Isis agrees and learns Rē's secret name, using it to enhance her own magical power.

F. Goddesses of Egypt were envisioned in ways consistent with the feminine role in Egyptian society.

   1. Goddesses act as maternal protectors, but they provide blessings associated with nurturing mothers.

   2. Goddesses such as Tefnut and Isis are faithful to their husbands even after separation or death.

   3. Goddesses also become an expression of the dynamic life of the cosmos.

   4. Hathor, in her role as warrior goddess, is a protective deity, ensuring the inviolability of divine decrees.

   5. Egyptians believed the powers represented by goddesses to be fundamental to divine order, *ma'at*, who was herself also presented as a goddess.

Essential Reading:

Lucia Gahlin. *Egypt: Gods, Myths and Religion*, pp. 58–75.

Donald B. Redford, ed. *The Ancient Gods Speak: A Guide to Egyptian Religion*, pp. 157–161, 169–172, 277–278, 352–353.

Supplementary Reading:

George Hart. *Egyptian Myths*, pp. 29–45.

Questions to Consider:

1. What is the connection with sexuality and joy in a goddess such as Hathor? What is the association between fate and divine vengeance? Is there a common cord tying all these attributes together?

2. What are some of the points of continuity in Isis's different roles and associations? Are these all typically "feminine" attributes, or does the goddess sometimes represent what we might call "masculine" virtues or powers?

Lecture Eleven
Egypt—Religion in Everyday Life

Scope: Official Egyptian religious ritual took place in a sanctuary that included the temple and other sacred spaces. Daily rituals consisted of washing, dressing, and "feeding" the cult statue of the temple. Animals might also serve as representatives of the gods. Religious festivals were dedicated to the honor of the gods or pharaoh. Processions carrying the cult statue allowed common people a rare opportunity to "see" the god. The popular religious culture in ancient Egypt focused on gods who would hear prayer. The primary religious activities of common people were "magical" practices and rituals, including the use of spells and amulets or practices aimed at gaining insight into a problem or gaining foresight into the future. *The Tale of Sinuhe* from Dynasty 12 tells the story of an official far from home and provides a vivid portrait of an ancient Egyptian's longing for his country and the company of his gods.

Outline

I. Official Egyptian religion was centered on temple worship carried out in pharaoh's name.

    A. The concerns of official Egyptian religion are expressed in "cult," that is, ritual, worship.

        1. The focus of cultic worship was not only gods but living kings, sacred animals, the dead, and heroes.

        2. Although the pharaoh was officially chief cultic official, priests conducted worship on his behalf.

        3. The temple estate provided everything necessary to support worship.

        4. There were two orders of priests responsible for different aspects of worship.

        5. There were other cultic functionaries, as well as musicians, singers, and dancers, both men and women.

    B. The main temple ritual took place in the morning, coinciding with the sun's rebirth.

1. The priest would unlock and open the doors of the temple just as the sun rose.
2. The temple would be purified before the doors of the god's shrine were opened and the cultic statue removed.
3. Most of these statues were relatively small and made of stone, word, or metal.
4. The cult statue would be stripped, then decorated and anointed with oil and dressed again in fresh clothing.
5. During this ritual, the cultic statue was also presented the day's offering of food.
6. At the end of the ceremony, the priests replaced the cult statue in its shrine and left the temple.

C. Other rituals were commonly performed as well, in temples and other sacred spaces.
1. Other temple rituals were typically conducted during other times of the day, mostly to purify the god's shrine.
2. Rituals were celebrated in honor of the divine pharaoh both during his life and after his death.
3. There were funerary cults to provide offerings for all the dead who had been prepared to enter the afterlife.

D. The Egyptians also devoted cults to animals as manifestations of the *ba* and *ka* of the gods.
1. Temple animals were carefully chosen and honored as manifestations of the god.
2. They and other animals of the same species were kept in the temple estate and, at death, were mummified.
3. Other animals of species sacred to the gods were kept in homes and honored as the gods' representatives.

E. Official Egyptian religion also included a variety of festivals honoring pharaoh or the gods.
1. The pharaoh played the leading role in several annual festivals.
2. A major feature of festivals was the transportation of the cult statue of the god in a *bark*, a boat-shaped shrine.
3. The transportation of the bark brought the temple gods out where they could be seen by the people.
4. Festivals provided an opportunity for an encounter between official religion and popular religion.

II. It is difficult to reconstruct religious culture among the common people in ancient Egypt.

    A. There are far fewer sources for what we might call popular religion than for official religious culture.

        1. The ruling elite and administrators made up, with their families, only a small percentage of the kingdom.

        2. The life of most Egyptians was very different, based in manual labor.

        3. For the mass of ancient Egyptians, life was a constant process of loss.

        4. The gods of greatest interest to the common Egyptians were those who could help them.

    B. The common people invoked the major gods, but only if the gods were believed to hear their concerns.

        1. Both Amun and Ptah, for example, were said to hear common people's prayers.

        2. An increase in piety during the New Kingdom reflects belief in universal accessibility to the gods.

        3. During the New Kingdom, we find an increase in devotional items in the homes of common people.

    C. The primary religious activities of common people of Egypt focused on "magical" practices and rituals.

        1. In ancient Egypt, magic was part of the divine panoply of power, as in the case of Isis.

        2. Spells were invoked to subdue chaos and maintain the divine equilibrium that imposed *ma'at*, divine order.

        3. Magical practices stood alongside other, more practical ways of interacting with the natural world.

        4. The most common form of magical protection was the amulet, with its power to drive away evil forces.

    D. Other forms of religious activity among common people focused on gaining divine insight or foresight.

        1. One reason to visit a temple or attend a religious festival was to obtain an oracle.

        2. Messages from the gods might also be given through portentous dreams that required interpretation.

        3. A questioner might also consult a "wise woman," a female seer with the gift of foresight.

E. We find essentially two different faces to religious practice in ancient Egypt.

    1. One, the face of the official religious culture, is centered in the temple and the tomb.

    2. The other, the face of popular religion, seeks the intercession of the gods through prayers and votive offerings.

    3. Both faces represent the spirit of Egyptian religion as it was experienced by its devotees.

III. *The Tale of Sinuhe* gives narrative expression to this spirit in everyday Egyptian life

    A. *The Tale of Sinuhe* is about a courtier who leaves Egypt and lives many years in Syria-Palestine before returning home.

        1. The story is set in the Middle Kingdom and begins with the death of Amenemhet I in a political coup.

        2. Sinuhe, a harem official, flees and enters Syria-Palestine, where he is welcomed by a Bedouin chieftain.

        3. Sinuhe serves the ruler of Upper Retenu, who also gives one of his daughters to Sinuhe as a wife.

        4. The Lord of Retenu places Sinuhe over a district of his domain, where Sinuhe lives for many years.

        5. Ultimately, Sinuhe is summoned back to Egypt by Amenemhet's son Senwosret I.

        6. Sinuhe returns to Egypt to be honored by the pharaoh and happily lives there the rest of his days.

    B. *The Tale of Sinuhe* provides a portrait of the attitudes of an Egyptian official of its time.

        1. Pharaoh is presented as a divine figure who is the source of all blessings and the sum of all virtues.

        2. In the story, Sinuhe refers to God in the singular but also mentions many Egyptian gods and goddesses.

        3. What is striking is Sinuhe's longing for his home, for the gods, rulers, customs, and comforts of Egypt.

        4. Although he finds a home among the Bedouins, he expresses some Egyptian disdain for their uncivilized ways.

        5. This is especially clear when he returns to the comforts of Egypt.

        6. For Sinuhe, Egypt is home, and its customs and comforts are the best the world has to offer.

7. Sinuhe's love for his country, his king, and his gods reflects the spirit of Egyptian religion.

Supplementary Reading:

John Baines, Leonard H. Lesko, and David P. Silverman. *Religion in Ancient Egypt: Gods, Myths, and Personal Practice*, pp. 123–200.

John L. Foster, ed. and trans. *Ancient Egyptian Literature: An Anthology*, pp. 124–148.

Erik Hornung. *History of Ancient Egypt: An Introduction*, pp. 124–148.

Lucia Gahlin. *Egypt: Gods, Myths and Religion*, pp. 100–125, 188–235.

Donald B. Redford, ed. *The Ancient Gods Speak: A Guide to Egyptian Religion*, pp. 191–214, 279–293.

Questions to Consider:

1. What seems to be the intention or rationale behind the daily rituals in a god's temple involving the god's shrine and cultic statue?

2. The *ba* and *ka* of a god were believed to reside in a cultic statue or in a sacred animal. How does this idea conform to and differ from our own ideas of "idolatry" as a practice typical of polytheistic religious cultures?

Lecture Twelve
Egypt—The Beginning of Wisdom

Scope: Proverbial wisdom, based on common experience and typically expressed in brief, pithy form, is part of the cultural heritage of all peoples throughout history. The systematic compilation of proverbial wisdom is found throughout the ancient Near East, including Egypt, where its setting was the scribal school. Wisdom literature is essentially pragmatic, intended to provide a student with the practical wisdom to get things done and lead a successful and happy life. In Egypt, wisdom literature took several forms. There are instructions from a king to his son that combine guidance for wise living with ruthless political advice. There are the more typical collections of teachings from a father to a son, but the subject matter varies considerably. Finally, there are instances of wisdom teaching in unexpected forms, such as songs, often expressing the injunction *carpe diem*—"seize the day"—in order to enjoy life while it lasts.

Outline

I. The wisdom tradition grants religious status to the practical experiences of daily life.

   A. Proverbial wisdom is part of the cultural heritage of all peoples throughout history.
      1. *Proverbs* are pithy maxims that expose one facet of the truth and often contradict each other.
      2. The systematic compilation of proverbial wisdom is found throughout the ancient Near East.
      3. The most extensive wisdom collections come from Egypt and have parallels in the Hebrew Bible.

   B. Wisdom literature offers practical advice intended to teach how one might best get along in life.
      1. Wisdom literature forms a counterpart to creation mythology, which explains how things got to be the way they are now.
      2. The student learns wisdom to achieve a happy life that can be enjoyed to the fullest.
      3. Wisdom teaching is *anthropocentric*, based on a predictable pattern in the ways of nature and humanity.

      4. Its basis is common experience, producing a community-based ethic that can be learned.

C. Wisdom literature's home is the scribal school, where boys were taught to read, write, and calculate.

      1. Wisdom sayings are meant to be memorized, and their form is inherently poetic.

      2. We often find wisdom literature presented as the teaching of a father to a son.

      3. A common feature is the contrast between the deeds and fate of the wise man and the fool.

      4. Both wise man and fool are students of wisdom, with no reference to the rest of humanity.

D. The basis of wisdom literature is a social and natural order based on divine control over creation.

      1. Wisdom teaching is generally deterministic but optimistic, granting humanity a measure of free will.

      2. The primary example of this optimistic determinism is the idea of retributive justice, that good works bring good to a person and evil works bring evil.

      3. In some strains of wisdom, determinism overwhelms optimism, leading to resignation.

II. The wisdom tradition in Egypt is expressed and preserved in different forms of literature.

A. Examples of Egyptian wisdom literature fall into several categories.

      1. There are instructions from a king to his son combining advice for living with more ruthless political counsel.

      2. The more usual teachings from a father to a son focus on diverse subject matter.

      3. Instances of wisdom teaching in unexpected forms usually advise the student to enjoy life as it comes.

      4. Wisdom literature in the Egyptian tradition is attributed to specific individuals; it is not anonymous.

B. Instruction from a king to his son appears in "The Testament of Amenemhet."

      1. Amenemhet I ruled from 1938–1909 B.C.E., including a co-regency with his son Senwosret.

      2. Amenemhet appears to his son "risen as a god" before taking his place in the afterlife.

3. Amenemhet was killed during a palace coup and warns Senwosret to be wary of underlings.
4. The king recounts highlights of his reign and encourages his son to emulate him.

C. "The Instruction for Merikare" is presented as advice from his father, Kheti III, of Dynasty 10.
   1. This work combines the pious and the practical with the military and the politically ruthless.
   2. Kheti advises his son on how to conduct himself in both personal and governmental matters.
   3. Kheti reminds his son that his eternal destiny depends on how he conducts himself during his life.
   4. He advises Merikare to focus on Osiris's kingdom and, thus, learn to do justice.
   5. There is specific advice on how to govern Egypt and deal with the threat from Syria-Palestine.
   6. Kheti is particularly ruthless when it comes to dealing with potential traitors.
   7. Merikare, despite this good advice, lost his throne to Inyotef I of Dynasty 11.

D. Wisdom teaching of a father to a son appears in *The Wisdom of Amenemopet* (c. 800–600 B.C.E.)*.
   1. The author describes his work as "meditations on good living, the guide to health and happiness."
   2. The book includes a prologue, 30 chapters of various lengths, and an epilogue.
   3. Most of the teachings invoke the value of wisdom and conducting oneself in an exemplary way.
   4. The primary virtues are honesty, humility, respect, mercy, generosity, careful speech, and good judgment.
   5. The intended audience is the scribe, whose patron god is Thoth.
   6. *The Wisdom of Amenemopet* has close parallels in Proverbs 22:17–24:34.
   7. The book's epilogue extols writers and the value of their work.

E. "The Instruction for Little Pepi" makes it clear that wisdom belongs to the scribe's world.
   1. The bulk of this work is a satire on the trades, written from the perspective of a scribe.

2. Kheti warns his son Pepi to study in order to avoid the woes suffered by artisans and laborers.
3. The litany of woes is followed by instructions on proper conduct and praise for scribal skills.
4. Kheti's disdain for manual labor, his perspective, and his advice all reflect his pride in being a scribe.

F. Wisdom themes and ideas echo in other literature, such as the poems called "Harpers' Songs."
   1. These songs reflect uncertainty about the fate of the dead or, perhaps, prefer the joys of life.
   2. One from the tomb of Pharaoh Intef reviews the fate of humanity and advises enjoying life.
   3. A Harper's Song reviews the austere facts of life, similar to Ecclesiastes, and advises "Seize the day!"
   4. Wisdom literature teaches that integrity and diligence can lead to a happy life, but fate lies in the gods' hands.
   5. This and other aspects of Egyptian religious culture are paralleled in other ancient religious cultures.

Supplementary Reading:

John L. Foster, ed. and trans. *Ancient Egyptian Literature: An Anthology*, pp. 32–42, 85–88, 179–182, 186–228.

Questions to Consider:

1. What are some examples of proverbial wisdom from our own culture? What do these proverbs advise and why? Are they a sound basis for making judgments in life?

2. What are some of the modern equivalents to the wisdom literature produced by scribal schools? What are the sources of "traditional" practical advice in our own time? For what sort of situations is this traditional practical advice most useful? For what sort of situations is it least useful?

Erratum: Professor Holland inadvertently gives these dates as 8000–6000 B.C.E.

Lecture Thirteen
Mesopotamia—The Land Between the Rivers

Scope: Mesopotamia is the land "between the rivers" Tigris and Euphrates, roughly equivalent to modern Iraq. It lies in the eastern end of the Fertile Crescent and was subject to frequent invasion and ethnic migrations. The climate is semi-arid, and the land is generally flat and must be irrigated to be productive. Civilization grew up there beginning in the fourth millennium B.C.E. with the rise of powerful city-states. Some of these city-states went on to dominate the surrounding peoples between the 24th century and the 6th century B.C.E.: Akkad, Sumer, Babylon, and Asshur. Mesopotamian civilization was the first to develop writing, about 3200 B.C.E. in Sumer, and written law, notably the Code of Hammurabi in Babylon in the 18th century B.C.E. Ancient Mesopotamia's history was marked by war, unrest, political upheaval, and the threat of chaos, leaving an unmistakable mark on Mesopotamian religious culture.

Outline

I. The geography of Mesopotamia was a determining factor in its early history.

   A. *Mesopotamia* is Greek for "between the rivers," the land between the Tigris and Euphrates Rivers.
      1. This area is roughly equivalent to the modern nation of Iraq, but its ancient people called it only "the land."
      2. Assyria included the northern Tigris Valley, with Babylonia in Lower Mesopotamia to the south.
      3. This is diverse country with a fertile area around the rivers but foothills, steppes, and desert as well.
      4. Agriculture has always been dependent on carefully managed irrigation of the rivers' waters.

   B. The fourth millennium saw the incursion of a number of different peoples into Mesopotamia.
      1. Neolithic settlers called Ubaidians were the region's earliest identifiable ethnic group.

    2. The Ubaidians settled in the south, in villages that expanded into small cities of several thousand.

    3. Ubaidian loan words appear in Sumerian, referring to the work of farmers, craftsmen, priests, and merchants.

    4. The Sumerians entered Mesopotamia about 3100 B.C.E., followed about two centuries later by Amorites.

C. Mesopotamian civilization began in the fourth millennium B.C.E. with a series of powerful city-states.

    1. The city-state included a walled city and adjacent irrigated agricultural settlements.

    2. The city-state was a center for crafts and trade, as well as the political and religious center of the area.

    3. Writing was first developed about 3200 B.C.E. among the Sumerians and used primarily for accounting.

    4. Initially, the priests were the city leaders, but recurring warfare demanded military kingship.

    5. Each city had its king, and cities might enter into confederations, with one city dominant over others.

II. Mesopotamia was ruled by the sovereigns of a succession of kingdoms over its long history.

A. The first kings to rule over larger territories were Akkadian, the descendants of the Semitic Amorites.

    1. The Akkadian Sargon the Great (2334–2279 B.C.E.) was the first to unite the city-states under his rule.

    2. Sargon destroyed the walls of conquered cities and demanded their kings' loyalty or replaced them.

    3. Sargon was the first king to have a standing army and placed military outposts throughout his kingdom.

    4. Sargon's kingdom lasted a little more than a century; his capital, Akkad, quickly sank into obscurity.

B. Sumerian supremacy was reestablished by Ur-Nammu around 2111 B.C.E., shifting power to the south.

    1. Ur-Nammu appointed governors, centralized his administration, and enforced history's first law code.

    2. Ur-Nammu's dynasty lasted about a century, ending in Ur's devastation by the Elamites in 2004 B.C.E.

    3. In the next century, Akkadian displaced Sumerian as the language of Mesopotamia.

C. Babylon came to prominence in the 18th century B.C.E. under Hammurabi.

   1. Hammurabi (1792–1750 B.C.E.) established Babylon as the seat of kingship, but his kingdom barely survived him.

   2. During the next two centuries, Mesopotamia was invaded by non-Semitic peoples from the west.

   3. One such people, the Kassites, founded a dynasty that ruled Mesopotamia for more than 400 years.

D. In the mid-14th century B.C.E., the Assyrians under Tukulti-Ninurta I came to rule over Mesopotamia.

   1. Tukulti-Ninurta (1244–1208 B.C.E.) sacked Babylon in 1235 B.C.E., asserting sovereignty over the south.

   2. The 12th century B.C.E. was a period of renewed ethnic migrations at the end of the Bronze Age.

   3. Aramaic, an alphabetic Semitic language, began to replace Akkadian.

E. Tiglath-Pileser I (r. 1115–1077 B.C.E.) increased the size of Assyria to an unprecedented extent.

   1. In the 9th century, Assyrian power extended to the Mediterranean under Assur-nasirpal II (r. 883–859 B.C.E.).

   2. His son Shalmaneser III (r. 858–824 B.C.E.) made a vassal of Israel under Jehu (r. 842–815 B.C.E.).

   3. The Assyrian empire achieved its greatest size under Tiglath-Pileser III (r. 744–727 B.C.E.).

   4. Assurbanipal (r. 669–627 B.C.E.) gained control over Babylon and defeated the Elamites.

F. During the period of Assyrian hegemony, Babylon came under the control of the Chaldeans.

   1. After Assurbanipal's death, the Assyrian empire was dismantled by the Medians and Neo-Babylonians.

   2. Nebuchadnezzar II (r. 604–562 B.C.E.) led the Babylonians against Egypt and conquered Judah.

   3. Nebuchadnezzar's successor was Nabonidus (r. 556–539 B.C.E.), who abandoned Babylon to live in an oasis.

   4. In Babylon, his son Belshazzar presided over a worsening economic and military situation.

   5. The Persians under Cyrus invaded Babylon and took control of the city in 539 B.C.E.

6. Mesopotamia came under the control of a series of world empires until the 20th century.

III. This history of instability and upheaval forms the context for Mesopotamian religion.

    A. This historical review illuminates differences between Egyptian culture and Mesopotamian culture.

        1. Despite mutual histories of upheaval, Egyptian culture was more homogenous than Mesopotamian culture.

        2. The different groups that came to dominance identified themselves with the heritage of earlier Mesopotamian cultures.

        3. They also introduced changes that extended into the religious culture of the successive civilizations.

    B. Religious culture reflects its historical situation, and Mesopotamia's history was full of the threat of chaos.

        1. This may have been the inevitable result of Mesopotamia's geographical situation.

        2. Mesopotamia was the natural pathway for successive waves of migrating peoples.

        3. Lower Mesopotamia is a flat, marshy land at the mercy of natural catastrophes.

    C. In this relatively flat land, the monumental religious structure was the ziggurat.

        1. Ziggurats were massive pyramidical brick buildings intended to represent the sacred mountain.

        2. At the pinnacle and on terraces were temples dedicated to various gods and, perhaps, a site for the ritual of sacred marriage.

        3. Ziggurats were square or rectangular at the base; one dedicated to Nanna at Ur measured 64×46 meters by 12 meters high.

        4. The ziggurat was a physical manifestation of the intersection of heaven and earth.

    D. Life between the rivers seemed to be overshadowed by the unpredictability of both nature and human events.

        1. Anxiety seems to lie beneath a sense that the gods might do as they please without regard for humanity.

2. Mesopotamia was the crossroads of the ancient civilizations of the East and West.
3. Mesopotamian civilizations exerted influence through the Assyrian and Neo-Babylonian empires.
4. Mesopotamian religious culture had points of overlap with official Egyptian religious culture but also clear distinctions.
5. Mesopotamian mythology and religious literature conveys dominant religious ideas familiar in the West.

Essential Reading:

Jean Bottéro. *Religion in Ancient Mesopotamia*, pp. 7–20.

George Roux. *Ancient Iraq*, pp. 1–84 (or entire text).

Supplementary Reading:

Sarah Iles Johnston, ed. *Religions of the Ancient World: A Guide*, pp. 165–172.

Joan Oates. *Babylon*, pp. 9–135.

Questions to Consider:

1. Considering the differences between the geographical and historical situations of Egypt and Mesopotamia, what differences might we expect to find in their respective religious cultures?

2. Temple priests were originally the city leaders in Mesopotamian city-states. How might we expect this fact and their later loss of power to military kings to have influenced the development of Mesopotamian religion?

Lecture Fourteen
Mesopotamia—Stories of Creation

Scope The gods of the Mesopotamian pantheon are like human overlords, except they are endowed with supernatural power and authority. The Babylonian saga of creation, *Enuma Elish*, begins with the birth of the earliest gods through the sexual congress of Apsu, the depths, and Tiamat, the waters. The uproar made by the young gods leads Apsu to decide to kill them, but he is killed instead. Tiamat marries another god, Qingu, and with him, makes war on the younger gods. The younger gods call for a champion, Marduk, to defend them. In return, he asks to be acknowledged king of the gods. He defeats Tiamat and splits her in half to create heaven and earth and makes humanity from Qingu's clotted blood. Another story tells how the sage Adapa lost the opportunity for human beings to become immortal. Both stories explain how things came to be the way they are now.

Outline

I. The Mesopotamian pantheon is difficult to define or to arrange in any sort of systematic way.

    A. It is not clear what the Sumerian and Akkadian terms that refer to gods are supposed to mean.

        1. The terms are *dingar* in Sumerian and *ilu* in Akkadian, with ideograms associating them with the heavens.

        2. The primary attribute of the gods is superiority, but that may mean any superiority over the human.

        3. The gods have a power called the *m e* that seems to combine authority and supernatural power.

        4. Mesopotamian gods are like overlords in a political hierarchy but with divine authority and power.

        5. The hierarchical model suits the multitude of gods who fill offices resembling a royal administration.

    B. The earliest list of the gods (c. 2600 B.C.E.) lists 560 gods by their Sumerian names.

        1. An (Akk. Anu), "Sky," was god of the sky and chief god in the early Mesopotamian pantheon.

    2. Enlil (Akk. Bel), "Wind," was moist wind and chief god of Sumer; he carried the Tablets of Destiny.

    3. Inanna (Akk. Ishtar) was a fertility goddess who gathered a wide range of associations and powers.

    4. Enki (Akk. Ea), "Manager of the Soil," god of sweet water, was the source of knowledge and magic.

    5. Nanna (Akk. Sin) was god of the moon, associated with the passing of time and guardian of night.

    6. Utu (Akk. Shamash), "Sun," drove his chariot across the sky daily and was dispenser of justice.

C. Other gods, such as Asshur and Marduk, later became prominent in the Mesopotamian pantheon.

    1. The goddess Ninhursaga, associated with foothills and desert, was a woman's protectress during childbirth.

    2. Nergal and his consort Ereshkigal, "Lady of the Great Earth," were deities of the underworld.

    3. Asshur, the Assyrian war god, became chief god and creator, identified with a primordial god, Anshar.

    4. Marduk, patron god of Babylon, became head of the pantheon under Babylonian dominion.

    5. The relationships among the gods and between the gods and creation form the content of cosmogonies.

II. The Babylonian story of creation reflects Marduk's dominance as the patron god of Babylon.

A. Cosmogony considers creation in mythic terms, in terms of the *why* and the *who* of creation.

    1. These stories assume some sort of being before creation, most often, undifferentiated matter.

    2. Most creation stories are more broadly about how things got to be the way they are now.

    3. "How things are now" notably involves the problem of humanity's status before the gods.

B. *Enuma Elish*, the Babylonian creation story, was probably composed around the 12th century B.C.E.

    1. Marduk is the divine hero, and the climax of the poem is the creation of the city of Babylon.

    2. If the original hero was an Amorite god, the poem was created by Semitic ancestors of the Akkadians.

3. In its current form, the poem was probably performed during the New Year's festival in late April.

C. *Enuma Elish* begins with three uncreated elements, the god Apsu, his consort Tiamat, and Mummu.
   1. Apsu represents the abyss of the seas of chaos, divine energy dissipated in unfocused activity.
   2. Tiamat is a body of water, the bitter sea waters that support the earth.
   3. Like the waters of the abyss, Tiamat is formless and exerts power without purpose.
   4. Mummu seems to represent the forces that oppose the gods' creative energy.

D. As Apsu and Tiamat slumber, various elements mingle to create new elements and gods.
   1. The water of the abyss mingles with the seas, creating the gods Lahmu and Lahamu, "silt."
   2. Anshar and Kishar, the two horizons, are separated by the birth of Anu, "Sky."
   3. Anu, in turn, engenders Ea-Nudimmud, god of the waters of earth and of wisdom.
   4. The gods' divine energy cannot be contained; they disagree and make an uproar in Tiamat's belly.
   5. Because the gods' noise keeps Apsu from sleeping, Apsu is determined to kill his children.
   6. Ea casts a spell on Apsu, putting him to sleep; Ea kills him and binds and imprisons Mummu.

E. At this point, the poem describes the birth of Marduk, the son of Ea and his consort Damkina.
   1. The poem describes Marduk's divinity in multiples to indicate how far he surpasses other gods.
   2. His birth awakens Tiamat and leads the lesser gods to prod her into action against Anu and Ea.
   3. Tiamat takes a new husband, Qingu, making him general over an army of monstrous creatures.
   4. Neither Ea nor Anu can stand against Tiamat; thus, Anshar calls a council and summons Marduk as champion.
   5. Marduk accepts on the condition that all the gods will acknowledge him as their king.

F. Marduk then arms himself and sets out to find Tiamat to fight and destroy her.

    1. Marduk arms himself with bow and arrow, a mace, and a net, as well as natural forces.

    2. When Tiamat tries to devour Marduk, the tempest winds inflate her, while Marduk pierces her with an arrow.

    3. Marduk quickly subdues the lesser gods, puts the monsters in chains, and binds Qingu.

    4. Finally, Marduk smashes Tiamat's head and splits her body in two to form the heavens and earth.

    5. The forces of chaos, Apsu, Tiamat, and Mummu, become part of the created order.

G. To finish off the work of creation, Marduk brings order to the divine world.

    1. Marduk builds temples on earth and assigns the gods places in the firmament, creating the calendar.

    2. All the gods pay homage to Marduk, who puts on his kingly robes and fastens the Tablets of Destiny to his chest.

    3. Marduk kills his captive Qingu and uses his blood to create humanity to serve the gods.

    4. Marduk builds Babylon as his dwelling-place and the crown of his work of bringing order to creation.

    5. The second half of the poem is a recitation and explanation of the 50 names of Marduk.

    6. Marduk represents the power of civilization and the achievements of human activity and reason.

III. The story of Adapa the sage provides a different explanation of the human situation.

    A. Another explanation for "the way things are now" appears in the Akkadian story of Adapa.

        1. Ea sent the seven sages to humanity with the skills necessary for civilized life.

        2. The story of one of these sages, Adapa, is preserved in two fragmentary versions.

    B. The poem begins with a description of Adapa and sets up the situation of his quest.

        1. Adapa was a priest of Ea in Eridu, traditionally the oldest Mesopotamian city.

2. Adapa is clever and scrupulous in carrying out the rituals of Ea's temple, including fishing.
3. One day while fishing, Adapa was thwarted by the South Wind and, in revenge, prevented her from blowing.
4. Ea summons Adapa and advises him to appear before Anu but tells him not to take bread offered him.
5. Adapa goes to Anu's court and refuses the bread offered to him as the Bread of Life (that is, of immortality).
6. As a result, humanity loses its chance at immortality and is sentenced to death.
7. The key appears to be a play on words, but whether Ea intended to deceive Adapa is open to question.
8. The story also presents rules for hospitality, with notes on garb and behavior for mourning the dead.

C. In both of these stories, we find the same unease about the human situation in relation to the gods.
   1. In *Enuma Elish*, humanity is made from a god's blood to relieve the gods of the burden of physical labor.
   2. In the story of Adapa, the sage is led astray by the directions of the gods, and all humanity must suffer death as a result.
   3. Both stories place humanity at the bottom of the cosmic hierarchy, at the mercy of the gods.

Essential Reading:

Jean Bottéro. *Religion in Ancient Mesopotamia*, pp. 44–113.

Stephanie Dalley, ed. and trans. *Myths from Mesopotamia: Creation, the Flood, Gilgamesh, and Others*, pp. 182–188, 228–277.

Supplementary Reading:

History of Mesopotamian Religion, pp. 93–135, 165–191.

Thorkild Jacobsen. *The Treasures of Darkness: A H*Samuel Noah Kramer. *Sumerian Mythology: A Study of Spiritual and Literary Achievement in the Third Millennium B.C.*, pp. 30–75.

Questions to Consider:

1. *Enuma Elish* distinguishes between the "slumber" of chaos and the activity of creation. What basic ideas about the nature of the world and the gods seem to lie behind this distinction?

2. To what extent does the poem *Enuma Elish* parallel some of our own more scientific ideas about the beginnings and development of life on earth? Where does it most differ?

Lecture Fifteen
Mesopotamia—Inanna the Goddess

Scope: The Mesopotamian fertility goddess was worshiped in Sumer as Inanna and later in Babylon as Ishtar. Inanna was consort to Dumuzi, a pastoral god. Her rituals included a *sacred marriage*, that is, sexual intercourse between the king and a priestess of Inanna to ensure the kingdom's fertility. Inanna is associated with all aspects of fertility and sexuality but also with the impetuous fury of natural disasters and the frenzy of battle. She became Queen of Heaven and Earth by tricking Enki, god of wisdom, into offering her all his powers while he was drunk. Inanna traveled into the underworld, the realm of her sister Ereshkigal, to conquer it but became trapped there instead. She was rescued through the efforts of her chamberlain, but someone needed to take her place in the underworld. Dumuzi is chosen, and his annual six-month stay in the underworld established the cycle of the seasons.

Outline

I. The Mesopotamian fertility goddess Inanna soon also became a goddess of sexuality.

    A. Inanna was worshiped in Sumer c. 4000–1000 B.C.E. and later in Babylon as Ishtar.

        1. Inanna was originally paired with Dumuzi-Ama-ushumgal-anna, who represented ripe clusters of dates.

        2. Inanna was identified with the storehouse for the date harvest and, thus, also with plentiful yields of produce.

        3. Inanna was also the fertile earth and its powers of generation; her presence brought life and abundance.

    B. The power of fertility inspired by Inanna and Dumuzi was celebrated in a yearly rite of sacred marriage.

        1. The ritual apparently involved sexual intercourse between Inanna's priestess and the city king in the goddess's temple.

        2. The purpose was to ensure fertility through the symbolic action of the representatives of Inanna and Dumuzi.

    C. Inanna's association with fertility was expressed primarily in active sexuality and sexual activity.

1. In her mythology, Inanna is eager for sex, especially with Dumuzi, and descriptions of their sexual activity carry echoes of fertility.
2. Her sexuality has overtones of danger, and she is often sexually voracious.
3. Religious poetry about Inanna and Dumuzi is often heavily and frankly erotic.

D. Inanna is connected with many different aspects of human sexuality.
1. The goddess is noted for her own beauty and the beauty of her robes and adornments.
2. Inanna is patroness of prostitutes and the evening star and is herself sometimes depicted as a prostitute.
3. Inanna *is* sexual desire in all its forms, and without her, there cannot be human or animal life.
4. Desire sometimes becomes a threat to civilized life, a force of deep, churning emotion and chaos beyond human control.

E. Inanna's power is dangerous and unpredictable in association with natural disasters and the heat of battle.
1. Inanna's wrath is expressed through such natural phenomena as lightning, flood, storm, and wind.
2. These extreme phenomena were taken as signs of Inanna's strong emotions, which have their roots in her sexuality.
3. Mesopotamians were wary of divine power that might lash out at them in unexpected and violent ways.
4. Inanna loved war and battles for the deep passions—anger, hate, fear, revenge—they provoked.
5. Sumerians called battle "the dance of Inanna" and believed she was present in the thick of the fighting.

II. Inanna's power grew until she was regarded as supreme, as Queen of Heaven and Earth.

A. As Queen of Heaven and Earth, Inanna is at the top of the Mesopotamian pantheon.
1. In this role, Inanna is depicted as the ruler of the gods in heaven and the director of human affairs on earth.
2. Inanna's ties to the fertility cycle and heavenly bodies give her power to regulate their movements.

3. Thus, Inanna is also guardian of the social order, as well as the overseer of judgment in legal matters.

B. According to one story, Inanna gained sovereign power from Enki/Ea, the god of wisdom, by trickery.
   1. Inanna put on her adornments and robes of power to visit Enki, who welcomed her into his house.
   2. They soon engaged in a drinking bout, matching each other drink for drink—but only Enki got drunk.
   3. Enki offered Inanna his powers one by one, and once he'd offered them all, she took them and left him.
   4. When Enki sobered up, he tried to regain his powers from Inanna, but she refused to return them.
   5. This story resembles the Egyptian story of how Isis gained magical power from Rē by trickery.

C. We can see that Inanna presents us with a series of apparent contradictions.
   1. She represents fertility and the joys of sexuality, but she's also dangerous, predatory, and uncontrollable.
   2. As Queen of Heaven and Earth, she oversees the social order, yet she's fond of grabbing and wielding power.
   3. All these conflicting attributes are on display in the story of Inanna's journey into the underworld.

III. The major story about Inanna recounts her journey into the underworld to conquer it.

A. Inanna's journey is an attempt to extend her sovereignty over the kingdom of her elder sister, Ereshkigal.
   1. The beginning of the poem already hints at Inanna's insatiable ambition and her predicament once she enters the underworld.
   2. Inanna prepared to go down into the pit by adorning herself with the physical signs of her sovereignty.
   3. At the gates of the underworld, Inanna threatened to smash the gates and free the dead to eat the living.
   4. As Inanna descended, her sister Ereshkigal saw her and vented her anger at Inanna's ambitions and presumption.
   5. Ereshkigal's gatekeeper made Inanna lay aside one of her adornments at each of the gates leading to the underworld.

6. Inanna laid aside her adornments of power one by one; without them, she entered the underworld stripped of both clothing and power.

7. Ereshkigal had her vizier send 60 diseases against Inanna, who sickened and died.

B. Papsukkal, the gods' vizier, interceded with Ea to bring Inanna back to life and return her to earth.

    1. Ea created a person, "Good-looks the playboy," to go down into the underworld and rescue Inanna.

    2. Good-looks was to go down into Ereshkigal's realm and ask for a water-skin.

    3. The playboy's appearance would please Ereshkigal, but he was, in some sense, not human and, thus, impervious to Ereshkigal's power.

    4. Ereshkigal became angry and cursed Good-looks, but she also ordered Namtar, her vizier, to revive Inanna.

    5. Namtar sprinkled Inanna with the water of life and restored her to life; as Inanna departed, she regained one of her adornments at each gate.

C. But Inanna was also required to pay a ransom and to find someone to take her place in the underworld.

    1. This is common motif: Once a place has been filled among the dead, it cannot be left vacant.

    2. Inanna's replacement in the underworld was Dumuzi, who was prepared for burial and mourned in the story as if dead.

    3. Dumuzi's sister Belili pleaded that he might be allowed to return to the land of the living periodically.

    4. When Dumuzi goes down into the underworld, the earth is infertile; when Dumuzi returns to earth, fertility is restored.

    5. Details of the story suggest religious rituals to mark the end and the beginning of the agricultural year.

D. The intention of the myth was, in part, to clarify the balance between the roles of the two goddesses Inanna and Ereshkigal.

    1. Although Inanna is Queen of Heaven and Earth, there is a third realm that lies beyond her control, the realm of her sister and symbolic opposite, Ereshkigal.

    2. The story may be an answer to the question: "Why is there suffering and death?"

3. The story also recognizes a connection between the power of fertility and the role of death in allowing new life to appear.

E. Inanna is "lady of myriad offices," but the different aspects of her divinity are based on a few of her fundamental traits.
  1. One of these traits is the impetuosity expressed in the unrestricted outlet of energy.
  2. Her sexual nature is both uninhibited and dangerous in her insatiability and carelessness toward lovers.
  3. One might associate Inanna with the force and energy of life in all its aspects, both benign and threatening.
  4. Inanna is Queen of Heaven and Earth in part because she embodies in herself the full range of human activity.

Essential Reading:

Stephanie Dalley, ed. and trans. *Myths from Mesopotamia: Creation, the Flood, Gilgamesh, and Others*, pp.154–164.

Diane Wolkstein and Samuel Noah Kramer. *Inanna, Queen of Heaven and Earth: Her Stories and Hymns from Sumer*, pp. 3–110.

Supplementary Reading:

Thorkild Jacobsen. *The Treasures of Darkness: A History of Mesopotamian Religion*, pp.135–143.

Questions to Consider:

1. How can one divine figure represent both the force of divine order and the chaotic powers that threaten order? How are these apparent opposites reconciled in the case of Inanna?

2. Which of Inanna's primary characteristics seems to be more important, her association with fertility or her association with sexuality? What secondary characteristics seem to arise from each association?

Lecture Sixteen
Mesopotamia—Gilgamesh the King

Scope: *The Epic of Gilgamesh* is the oldest surviving example of an epic poem, the story of a hero who has a series of adventures lived out in conscious relationship to the divine world. The first part of the epic concerns Gilgamesh as king of Uruk, where his people feel oppressed because he takes their sons for his armies and deflowers virgin brides. The people complain to the gods, who make Gilgamesh's equal, a man of the wilderness named Enkidu. He is civilized through intercourse with a prostitute, who teaches him refined ways. Enkidu soon enters Uruk to confront Gilgamesh. The two warriors grapple with each other, but Gilgamesh overcomes Enkidu. Enkidu becomes Gilgamesh's comrade, reflecting ancient ideas about friendship. The two heroes set out on a long journey to find Humbaba, a monster of the wilderness. They defeat and kill him, thereby eliminating the threat he poses to humanity.

Outline

I. *The Epic of Gilgamesh* is the earliest surviving example of an epic poem.

    A. An epic poem generally presents a hero who has a series of adventures lived out in conscious relationship to the divine world.

        1. The most familiar examples are Homer's *Iliad* and *Odyssey*, products of Greece, and Virgil's *Aeneid*, from Rome.

        2. The adventures usually incorporate feats of derring-do beyond the capacity of ordinary human beings.

        3. Although the epic hero interacts with the gods directly, his adventures reflect human capability and free will.

        4. The epic hero strains at the limitations of humanity, pushing at the barriers between human and divine.

    B. *The Epic of Gilgamesh* was written in Akkadian, but individual incidents circulated in oral form for generations.

        1. Gilgamesh was a historical figure, a king of the city of Uruk between 2800 and 2500 B.C.E.

2. There are many stories about Gilgamesh that appear in many different written versions.
3. Transcribing a story did not affect its continued telling, and versions of the stories reappear in other oral traditions from other cultures.

II. The first part of *The Epic of Gilgamesh* is concerned with Gilgamesh as king and the events leading to his friendship with Enkidu.

A. The epic begins with a prologue that extols Gilgamesh's heroic deeds and accomplishments as king.
1. Gilgamesh is presented as a paragon of strength and beauty, created by the gods for heroism and kingship.
2. Two-thirds of Gilgamesh was divine and one-third mortal, foreshadowing his rejection of death.
3. Gilgamesh is both a warrior who makes civilized life possible and a king who presides over civilized life.

B. It soon becomes clear that Gilgamesh has faults as a king, most of them arising from his unbridled appetites.
1. His appetite for battle meant constant warfare, leaving families bereft of their male children.
2. His sexual appetite led him to exercise the king's right to deflower virgin brides before they marry.
3. His subjects complain to the gods, who decide to find a solution to the problem.
4. The description of Gilgamesh as king and his subjects' complaints provide insight into Mesopotamian ideas about kingship.

C. The gods' solution to the problem posed by Gilgamesh is to create his equal, Enkidu.
1. A goddess creates Enkidu and places him in the wilderness, away from human habitations and civilization.
2. Enkidu is a primitive man covered with shaggy hair, who eats grass and drinks from forest pools.
3. When a hunter discovers that Enkidu is freeing animals from his traps, he goes to Uruk to complain to Gilgamesh.
4. Gilgamesh tells the hunter to take a prostitute to Enkidu to seduce him.

D. The prostitute seduces Enkidu; after he has sexual intercourse with her, he becomes "civilized."

1. Enkidu is cut off from nature and the animals that now flee from him in fear.
2. His separation from nature is described both in terms of weakness and in terms of wisdom.
3. The prostitute instructs Enkidu in the arts of civilization, how to eat bread and drink wine.

E. Soon Enkidu comes to Uruk and challenges Gilgamesh to determine which of them is stronger.
   1. Enkidu confronts Gilgamesh at his father-in-law's house, where the two men grapple and wrestle in the street.
   2. The two are evenly matched, and their struggle sends tremors through the city.
   3. The description of the outcome of the contest is lost, but when the text resumes, Enkidu is listening to Gilgamesh and crying.
   4. The Old Babylonian text suggests that Gilgamesh used a wrestling trick to subdue Enkidu.
   5. The two men become friends, embrace one another, and from this point on, will be comrades in adventures.

F. The friendship between Gilgamesh and Enkidu exemplifies an ancient ideal of friendship.
   1. The ancient ideal is the friend who is the "other self," one who mirrors the background, intelligence, and skills of his friend.
   2. This ideal finds fulfillment in the case of Gilgamesh and Enkidu, because the goddess creates Enkidu as "another Gilgamesh."
   3. Emphasis throughout this part of the poem is on the resemblance between the two men.
   4. Gilgamesh and Enkidu each find an ideal companion and perfect comrade in the mirror image provided by his twin.

III. Gilgamesh and Enkidu join in seeking out and fighting the elemental monster Humbaba.

A. Enkidu tells Gilgamesh about Humbaba, the monster guardian of the forest who terrorizes those who enter it.
   1. The great god Enlil has made Humbaba guardian of the forest and its animals.
   2. Humbaba represents all the dangers of that unknown territory that threaten civilized people.

3. Gilgamesh is determined to destroy Humbaba, with no clear reason why, except that Humbaba is a threat.

B. Once Gilgamesh has decided on his course, he gains assistance from both human beings and gods.
1. Gilgamesh must rely on Enkidu, who will counsel him, protect him, and bring him home.
2. Gilgamesh goes to his mother, Ninsun, who offers him advice and makes offerings to Shamash, the sun god.
3. Finally, Gilgamesh and Enkidu themselves make offerings and vows to the gods.
4. The long journey to the great Pine Forest is marked by repeated actions, words, and motifs.

C. Once Gilgamesh and Enkidu enter the Pine Forest, they soon encounter Humbaba.
1. Humbaba mocks the heroes' small size, as if they were hardly worth his notice or the bother of killing them.
2. Gilgamesh is unnerved at the sight of the monster, and it falls to Enkidu to rally his spirits.
3. The account of the battle is fragmentary, but it is won by the heroes' efforts and 13 winds sent by Shamash.

D. Overcome, Humbaba begs Gilgamesh to let him live, offering promises and bribes.
1. Humbaba's promises to Gilgamesh reveal his original identity as a god of the forest.
2. Enkidu tells Gilgamesh to destroy Humbaba, both to eliminate the threat he poses and to gain everlasting fame.
3. Gilgamesh finally kills Humbaba, and the heroes cut down trees to make a door for Enlil's temple as an offering.

E. This fairly traditional story includes touches of irony and foreshadowing of events to come.
1. Most intriguing are the parallels between Humbaba and Enkidu, the "primitive" man who has embraced civilization.
2. The story is filled with forebodings of death for Enkidu, who will soon be cut down in his prime.
3. Gilgamesh's recklessness in this story shows he is straining at the limits of human destiny and wishes to become "immortal."
4. These motifs intertwine in the second half of the epic, a melancholy counterpoint to the adventures of the first half.

Essential Reading:

Jeremy Black and Anthony Green. *Gods, Demons and Symbols of Ancient Mesopotamia: An Illustrated Dictionary*, appropriate entries.

Stephanie Dalley, ed. and trans. *Myths from Mesopotamia: Creation, the Flood, Gilgamesh, and Others*, pp. 39–77.

Supplementary Reading:

Stephen Mitchell. *Gilgamesh: A New English Version*, pp. 1–35, 69–129.

Karen Rhea Nemet-Nejat. *Daily Life in Ancient Mesopotamia*, pp. 163–174.

Questions to Consider:

1. Gilgamesh the hero had obvious failings as king of Uruk. What are the tensions between the characteristics of the "hero" and those of the "ruler"?

2. The ancient ideal of friendship was based on the idea that friends mirrored each other's character and status. Is this an appropriate or adequate way of understanding friendship?

Lecture Seventeen
Mesopotamia—The Search for Eternal Life

Scope: After the victory over Humbaba, Ishtar asks Gilgamesh to be her lover. He refuses, reminding her of the sad fate of the others she has loved. She sends the Bull of Heaven to kill Gilgamesh and Enkidu, but they defeat it. When Enkidu threatens Ishtar, she sends him a fatal illness. Enkidu's death frightens Gilgamesh, leading him to a quest for everlasting life. In the garden of the sun god, the alewife Siduri offers advice and directs Gilgamesh to the home of Ut-napishtim, survivor of an ancient flood. Ut-napishtim tells Gilgamesh the story of the flood but cannot help him gain eternal life. However, Ut-napishtim does tell Gilgamesh about a rejuvenating plant. Gilgamesh finds the plant, but it is stolen by a snake. Gilgamesh returns to Uruk and follows the advice he received repeatedly during his quest: to enjoy the pleasures life has to offer as long as it lasts.

Outline

I. After defeating the beast Humbaba, Gilgamesh faces danger from the beauty Ishtar.

    A. After his victory over Humbaba, Gilgamesh attracts the attention of Ishtar, the goddess of erotic love.

        1. Here, Ishtar appears in her role as an insatiable sexual predator as she attempts to seduce Gilgamesh.

        2. But Gilgamesh resists Ishtar's advances and lists the lovers she has betrayed, including Dumuzi.

        3. Ishtar is infuriated and asks Anu to send the Bull of Heaven to destroy Gilgamesh.

        4. The Bull of Heaven wreaks havoc in Uruk but is quickly overcome by Gilgamesh.

        5. Ishtar rages against Enkidu and Gilgamesh, while Enkidu threatens the goddess.

    B. But Ishtar takes revenge; Enkidu has a prophetic dream that makes it clear he must die.

        1. In despair, Enkidu prays to Shamash to curse the hunter and Shamhat, the prostitute who civilized him.

    2. Shamash rebukes Enkidu, because Shamhat, by civilizing Enkidu, has brought him Gilgamesh's friendship.

    3. Enkidu relents and blesses Shamhat but soon becomes ill and dies.

    4. Enkidu's death confronts Gilgamesh with the inevitability of his own death.

C. Mesopotamian beliefs about the afterlife were very different from the optimistic view in Egyptian religion.

    1. The underworld was located beneath the earth's surface and was associated with darkness, dryness, and thirst.

    2. Here, all the dead, both good and evil, continued to exist in a shadowy, semiconscious state.

    3. The realm of the dead was under the control of a god but separated from the gods of heaven and earth.

    4. Distinction between the fates of the good and the wicked was a late development outside of Egypt.

D. Death's permanence and inevitability lead Gilgamesh to search for the secret of everlasting life.

    1. Gilgamesh regards the pleasures and glories of his life as nothing, because they must end in death.

    2. There is a connection between Gilgamesh's fear of death and his role as a hero who deprives others of life.

    3. Gilgamesh's quest is a search for wisdom and the meaning of life, for what makes life worth living.

II. Gilgamesh's search for everlasting life takes him far from civilization into the wilderness.

A. In his search, Gilgamesh forsakes the trappings of civilization, turning to life in the wild.

    1. Gilgamesh lives by hunting and wears animal skins, becoming like Enkidu before he was civilized.

    2. Gilgamesh wishes to find Ut-napishtim, the only human being to gain everlasting life from the gods.

    3. His quest takes him through the mountain Mashu, where his way is blocked by Scorpion monsters.

    4. The monsters warn Gilgamesh that the way under the mountain is too dark for anyone except Shamash.

    5. Regardless, Gilgamesh plunges into the darkness and, after 10 leagues, emerges into the garden of the sun god.

B. In the garden of the sun god, Gilgamesh has a conversation with Siduri the alewife.
1. The alewife was a woman who sold beer to travelers and was free to interact with men.
2. When Siduri first spots Gilgamesh, she asks why his face is wasted with grief.
3. Gilgamesh replies at length, giving both the cause for his grief and the deeper anguish it has engendered.
4. Gilgamesh asks Siduri for directions to the home of Ut-napishtim, which she supplies, and he departs.

C. In the Old Babylonian version, Gilgamesh's reasons for his quest are explained to both Shamash and Siduri.
1. These conversations appear in the Old Babylonian version but not the version preserved at Nineveh.
2. Gilgamesh is first met by Shamash, who is concerned about him, but who also says that his quest is futile.
3. Gilgamesh's reply makes his anguish clear; he wants to see the sun and live, rather than sleep in darkness.
4. Siduri appears in an Akkadian list as "Ishtar of wisdom," perhaps explaining her role in the Old Babylonian version.
5. Siduri repeats the words of Shamash, asking Gilgamesh the point of his quest.
6. But Siduri offers Gilgamesh advice: The best thing is to enjoy what life has to offer while it lasts.
7. This advice recalls the Egyptian Harpers' Songs and similar ideas elsewhere in ancient wisdom literature.

III. Gilgamesh seeks out Ut-napishtim the Faraway to learn the secret of everlasting life.

A. Gilgamesh continues his journey to find Ut-napishtim, finally coming to the "waters of death."
1. Gilgamesh intimidates Ur-shanabi the ferryman into carrying him across the waters to Ut-napishtim.
2. At Ur-shanabi's direction, Gilgamesh pulls the ferry to the place where Ut-napishtim lives.

B. Gilgamesh's search for Ut-napishtim is a search for an ancient ancestor to learn the meaning life in the face of death.
1. Ut-napishtim survived a worldwide flood, and in the epic, he is presented as a depository of ancient wisdom.

     2.   Ut-napishtim greets Gilgamesh with the same words he has heard from Siduri and others.

     3.   Gilgamesh repeats his explanation: Because he fears death, he has come to learn how to attain everlasting life.

     4.   Ut-napishtim has no wisdom to offer Gilgamesh, except to accept human life as the gods have created it.

     5.   Gilgamesh is surprised that Ut-napishtim is not a hero, even though the gods have exempted him from death.

     6.   Ut-napishtim tells the story of the primeval flood, a story that parallels the Mesopotamian story of Atrahasis and the biblical story of Noah.

C. Gilgamesh falls asleep and awakes a week later in despair; he asks Ut-napishtim what he should do.

     1.   Gilgamesh is still dogged by the fear of death, which seems to haunt him or threaten his every step.

     2.   Ut-napishtim orders Ur-shanabi to allow Gilgamesh to wash and put on fresh clothing to return to Uruk.

     3.   Ut-napishtim also tells Gilgamesh a secret: A certain plant in the abyss will restore a person's youth.

     4.   Gilgamesh ties stones to his feet and plunges into the water of the abyss to find the plant.

     5.   He finds it, but on his way home, Gilgamesh bathes in a pool, where a snake steals the plant from him.

     6.   Gilgamesh weeps at his loss, but he and Ur-shanabi continue their journey to Uruk.

     7.   The last section of the poem is an addition, a Sumerian version of the death of Enkidu.

D. By the end of the epic, Gilgamesh has come to understand how things are and why they are that way.

     1.   He appears to come to terms with his ultimate fate and he returns to his role in the civilized world.

     2.   Gilgamesh resumes his kingship and devotes himself to those works celebrated at the epic's beginning.

     3.   Gilgamesh makes peace with his human destiny and enjoys what pleasures life has to offer while it lasts.

Essential Reading:

Jeremy Black and Anthony Green. *Gods, Demons and Symbols of Ancient Mesopotamia: An Illustrated Dictionary*, appropriate entries.

Stephanie Dalley, ed. and trans. *Myths from Mesopotamia: Creation, the Flood, Gilgamesh, and Others*, pp. 77–109, 116–153.

Supplementary Reading:

Jean Bottéro. *Everyday Life in Ancient Mesopotamia*, pp. 230–245.

Thorkild Jacobsen. *The Treasures of Darkness: A History of Mesopotamian Religion*, pp. 193–219.

Stephen Mitchell. *Gilgamesh: A New English Version*, pp. 35–64, 130–180, 193–200.

Questions to Consider:

1. How is Gilgamesh's search for everlasting life comparable to his adventures in the rest of the epic? How is his quest consistent with his role as a hero who makes civilized life possible?

2. Gilgamesh hears the same advice about how to live from different people throughout this part of the epic. What does this repetition contribute to the plot and the literary impact of the poem, as well as to its religious message?

Lecture Eighteen
Mesopotamia—The Great Flood

Scope: The story of Ut-napishtim and the primeval flood in *The Epic of Gilgamesh* has clear parallels with the story of another Mesopotamian hero, Atrahasis, and the biblical story of Noah. The gods decide to send a flood because humanity makes too much noise. Ea, the god of wisdom, reveals the gods' plan to Ut-napishtim. Ut-napishtim builds a boat and loads it with his family, craftsmen, animals, and his worldly goods. The flood is so fierce it scares the gods, who regret agreeing to destroy humanity. When the flood ends, the gods gather around Ut-napishtim's sacrifice. In the very similar story of Atrahasis, the flood is the gods' last attempt to control the human population. The story of Noah stands apart, because a single god both destroys life on earth and ensures its survival. Instead of divine wrath and repentance, it is a story about divine justice and mercy.

Outline

I. Ut-napishtim's appearance in the *Epic of Gilgamesh* includes his account of the great flood.

  A. His account is distinct from the rest of the epic by virtue of its parallels to similar stories.
  1. Ut-napishtim speaks in the first person but narrates all the events of the story, divine as well as human.
  2. Ut-napishtim speaks more as a traditional storyteller than as a participant in the events he describes.

  B. The story begins "in those days" when the great gods, the Igigi, send a flood to destroy humanity.
  1. No reason is given for the flood, nor is its extent originally indicated.
  2. There is no debate among the great gods, including Anu, Enlil, Ninurta, Ennugi, and Ea, god of wisdom.
  3. Ea reveals the plan to Ut-napishtim by telling the secret to his house, allowing Ut-napishtim to "overhear."

  C. Ea tells Ut-napishtim to build a boat and gives him all the instructions he needs to carry out the plan.

      1. Ea gives Ut-napishtim the dimensions of the boat and tells him to bring all living things on board.

      2. Ut-napishtim asks Ea what he is to tell his neighbors, and Ea gives him a highly ironic answer.

      3. The story describes in detail the building of the boat and the efforts of the many workmen.

      4. Ut-napishtim loads the boat with all his gold and silver, his family, the animals, and the craftsmen.

D. The mechanics of the storm and the flood are described with a wealth of detail.

      1. All the gods are implicated in the flood; all of them—except Ea—bear guilt for the decision to destroy humanity.

      2. The flood is created by a storm and the unleashing of the waters of the abyss.

      3. The gods themselves are frightened by the flood and ascend to the highest heaven to escape it.

      4. Even Ishtar regrets the decision to destroy humanity, whom she calls "my own people."

E. The flood lasts six days and nights; afterward, the waters slowly recede.

      1. Ut-napishtim's boat runs aground on Mount Nimush and remains there for a week.

      2. Ut-napishtim sends out a series of birds to see if the waters have receded and offers a sacrifice.

      3. The gods smell the sweet savor and gather like flies around the sacrifice, but Ishtar bars Enlil.

      4. Enlil arrives, outraged that anyone has survived the flood, and Ea is accused of revealing the plan.

      5. Ea argues that the flood was too devastating and indiscriminate, introducing the idea of justice and proportion.

      6. Enlil relents and blesses Ut-napishtim and his wife, granting them everlasting life at the mouths of the two rivers.

II. Another Mesopotamian flood story, the story of Atrahasis, is a much fuller account.

    A. In "Atrahasis," the flood story is the climax of a longer story about the creation of human beings.

      1. There are some overlaps and parallels to the creation story in *Enuma Elish.*

2. There is an account of the divine hierarchy and the creation of human beings to work for the gods.

3. Also as in *Enuma Elish*, human beings are made in part from a sacrificed god.

B. In "Atrahasis," the flood is only one of the gods' attempts to decrease the size of the human population.

   1. At first, human beings are immortal, and as they reproduce, they add to the population.

   2. When they become too many and too noisy, the gods send some catastrophe to decimate the population.

   3. The gods send wasting illness, two drought-induced famines, another plague, and another famine.

   4. Each time the gods send a calamity, Atrahasis asks Enki/Ea to tell him how to save humanity.

   5. Each time, Enki replies with a strategy to bring an end to the calamity.

   6. Finally, the gods agree to send a great flood to wipe humanity from the earth.

C. Atrahasis's preparation for the flood and the flood itself are very close to the Ut-napishtim story.

   1. Here, the command to save the animals is muted, and there is an emphasis on Atrahasis's anxiety.

   2. Nintu/Mami, who created humanity, mourns them, and the gods suffer from the lack of sacrifices.

   3. Once the flood is over, Nintu blames Anu and Enlil for the disaster and, like Ishtar, promises to remember.

   4. At the end of the story, Atrahasis and his wife do not gain immortality but, instead, *retain* immortality.

   5. All other human beings, however, are now subject to a limited lifespan and the other means the gods devise to limit the human population.

III. The biblical story of Noah stands apart not least in involving only one god, not a multitude.

A. The story of Noah has some obvious parallels to the stories of Ut-napishtim and Atrahasis.

   1. Each includes a divine decision to send a flood, with one person selected to save his family and all animals.

2. The building of the boat, the gathering of animals, the flood, the release of birds, and the sacrifice appear in all three stories.
3. The parallels suggest reliance on a tradition common to the entire eastern Mediterranean.

B. There are also notable differences between the Mesopotamian and Israelite versions of the story.
1. In Genesis, there is no deceptive story for Noah's neighbors and no gold and silver as cargo, and the members of Noah's family are the only human beings on the ark.
2. In the Mesopotamian stories, the storm is brief but extremely violent.
3. In Genesis, the rain falls 40 days and nights, while the flood itself lasts for 150 days.
4. Unlike Ut-napishtim, Noah and his family have the responsibility to replenish the human world.

C. More important are the differences that change the tone and message of the entire story.
1. In the Mesopotamian stories, the flood is divine vengeance against a teeming humanity.
2. In Genesis, the flood is a reaction to human wickedness, but God also provides for humanity's future.
3. In the Mesopotamian stories, the gods squabble, change their minds, and show fear and shortsightedness.
4. The gods are very much like human beings, with competing desires that can lead to disaster.
5. In Genesis, God's moral character leads him both to destroy the unrighteous and to save the righteous.
6. In the Mesopotamian story, there is no guarantee that chaos will not break out again to threaten humanity.
7. Uncertainty about human security in the hands of unreliable gods is a hallmark of Mesopotamian religious culture.
8. The Genesis account concludes with God making a covenant with Noah, promising never again to destroy the earth with a flood.
9. These differences reflect a fundamental difference between Mesopotamian and Israelite conceptions of the divine and the nature of the relationship between the divine world and creation.

Essential Reading:

Jeremy Black and Anthony Green. *Gods, Demons and Symbols of Ancient Mesopotamia: An Illustrated Dictionary*, appropriate entries.

Stephanie Dalley, ed. and trans. *Myths from Mesopotamia: Creation, the Flood, Gilgamesh, and Others*, pp. 1–38, 109–116.

Genesis 6–9.

Supplementary Reading:

Jean Bottéro. *Everyday Life in Ancient Mesopotamia*, pp. 213–229.

Samuel Noah Kramer. *History Begins at Sumer: Thirty-Nine Firsts in Recorded History*, pp. 148–153.

Stephen Mitchell. *Gilgamesh: A New English Version*, pp. 181–192.

Questions to Consider:

1. In these stories of the near-destruction of humanity, the means of destruction is a flood. What factors make a flood a particularly effective means of destruction and salvation in these stories?

2. What differences and similarities between the depictions of the gods in the Mesopotamian stories and the Lord in the biblical story seem particularly significant? What do they tell us about their respective religious cultures?

Lecture Nineteen
Ancient Concepts of the Divine

Scope: Western concepts of divinity have evolved from a series of choices: thinking of the sacred in terms of deity separate from and transcendent over creation, yet intimately involved with creation by choice. In polytheistic religious cultures, such as those of Egypt and Mesopotamia, there are innumerable gods organized into a divine hierarchy, with each god identified with a particular realm of concern. These gods interact much as human beings do and are under the power of an impersonal force, such as fate. A henotheistic system worships only one god, usually a national god committed to its people's protection, although other gods are believed to exist. A monotheistic system posits a single god in complete control of the cosmos created by the god, who is the absolute moral arbiter over creation and morally perfect. Henotheism tends toward monotheism, although monotheism runs counter in many ways to our experience of the world and human society.

Outline

I. Certain beliefs about the nature of the sacred seem to be typical of Western cultures.

   A. How people in the Western world think about the sacred is the result of choices made in the course of early Western history.

      1. First, there is the choice to think about the sacred in terms of deities as self-conscious controllers of numinous power, instead of in terms of an impersonal, immanent force.

      2. Second, there is the choice to think about the divine as something separate from creation and creatures, instead of something identical with creation, itself a manifestation of the divine.

      3. Third, there is the choice to think of deity as transcendent over the human world, yet involved in it by choice, instead of something that exists only in and through creation.

      4. Thinking about the sacred in particular ways unites the religious cultures of the ancient Mediterranean world.

B. The religious cultures of Egypt and Mesopotamia are polytheistic, believing in a number of gods.
  1. In a polytheistic system, the multitude of gods is divided into categories, ranks, and hierarchies.
  2. Polytheistic systems have chief gods in control of lower gods and other supernatural beings.
  3. The gods can be categorized by their attributes, their places in the divine hierarchy, or their importance in daily life.
  4. The gods' essential nature and concerns are usually connected to their places in the divine hierarchy.
  5. In a polytheistic system, the gods have no specific moral character and interact as human beings do.
  6. They can be capricious in their treatment of human beings and are easily offended by them.
  7. Usually an impersonal factor, such as fate, regulates disputes among the gods and curbs divine power.
  8. The problem of unjust treatment of human beings does not really arise in polytheistic religious cultures.

C. Sometimes in a polytheistic system, the chief god will assume dominance over the other gods.
  1. We can see this process at work with Marduk in the Mesopotamian creation narrative, *Enuma Elish*.
  2. In the poem, Marduk serves as the gods' champion and gains dominance over them as a result.
  3. Marduk proves himself mightier than the other gods and is declared sovereign by the divine assembly.
  4. Marduk becomes the dominant god by combat, by acclamation, and by bringing order to creation.

II. Standing apart from polytheism are henotheism and monotheism, each of which focuses on a single god.

A. In henotheistic religious cultures, one god is worshiped out of the many gods that exist.
  1. Like polytheism, henotheism assumes a multitude of gods but asserts that only one god is worthy of worship.
  2. Usually the one god worshiped is believed to be supreme over other gods in power, influence, and moral character.
  3. This god might be a national god that interacts with and protects a people the god has set apart.

4. For the most part, the favor of this god is what determines how a person or nation fares in the world.
5. In henotheistic religious cultures, the one god receives exclusive worship.
6. Usually, "other gods" means the gods of other, hostile peoples and, thus, gods hostile to one's own god.
7. Lesser gods associated with the god in a henotheistic system are demoted to lower forms of deity or other spiritual beings.
8. In a henotheistic system, the god's actions must be justified as consistent with the god's power and moral character.

B. A monotheistic religious culture maintains that there is one and only one god, and no others exist.
1. Monotheism appears to grow out of henotheism, as the claims for the single god become more exclusive and more absolute.
2. In a monotheistic system, the one god is all-powerful, a creator distinct from the creation, from everything else that exists.
3. The one god is the moral arbiter of right and wrong and is believed to be absolutely morally good.
4. Omnipotence and absolute moral rectitude raise the problem of theodicy, proving that the god is in the right despite appearances to the contrary.
5. Monotheism, in many ways, runs counter to the experience of both nature and human society.
6. The idea that a single deity controls the cosmos results more from theological reflection than from direct observation.

C. Henotheism tends toward monotheism, but the difference is sometimes difficult to identify.
1. Absolutist claims made for a god in a polytheistic religious culture are henotheistic rather than exclusive.
2. The absolutist claims made by Akhenaten for the god Aten were primarily a rejection of similar claims made by worshipers of Amun, and neither was truly monotheistic.
3. There is a much clearer shift from henotheistic worship to true monotheism in the development of Israelite religious culture.

Supplementary Reading:

Sarah Iles Johnston, ed. *Religions of the Ancient World: A Guide*, pp. 17–31.

James C. Livingston. *Anatomy of the Sacred*, pp. 165–195.

Questions to Consider:

1. What are some of the consequences of thinking about the sacred in terms of gods, as opposed to impersonal forces or an all-pervading spiritual power?

2. To what extent does a polytheistic religious system appear to be consistent with the world as we experience it? In what ways might it be inconsistent with our experience of the world?

Lecture Twenty
The Gods of Syria-Palestine

Scope: Syria-Palestine features very different landscapes and ways of life in close proximity. As the land bridge between Mesopotamia and Egypt, Syria-Palestine was subject to repeated waves of ethnic migration and military conquest. The chief god of the Syro-Palestinian pantheon was 'El, creator of all things and father of the gods. His son Ba'al, god of storms and fertility, became the dominant god of Syro-Palestinian polytheism. His mythology recalls several Mesopotamian myths. The worship of the Lord in Israel was both different from and consistent with other Syro-Palestinian religious cultures. The Lord's divine name YHWH appears to mean "He is." The Lord was originally associated with the wilderness and became the god of Israel's nomadic ancestors. This relationship was understood in terms of a covenant, a legal contract between the Lord and Israel. The substance of the covenant was: "You shall be my people, and I shall be your god."

Outline

I.   The geographical situation of ancient Syria-Palestine opened it to a range of influences.

   A.   We have seen how geographical setting can influence the development of a nation's religious culture.
      1.   Egypt's relatively secure and isolated situation produced a serene official religion with hopes of a blessed afterlife.
      2.   Mesopotamia's place as a crossroads between Asia and the Near East produced a sense of life's precariousness.
      3.   In spite of their geographical differences, there were similarities between these two religious cultures.
      4.   These similarities seem to reflect universal concerns that will also resonate in religions of Syria-Palestine.

   B.   The area of Syria-Palestine comprises the western arm of the Fertile Crescent.
      1.   Syria-Palestine lies to the east of the Mediterranean and to the west of the Arabian desert.

2. Syria-Palestine is also the passage between Egypt and Mesopotamia, two centers of Near Eastern empire.
3. This relatively small area is divided into four climatic zones, from fertile plains to rocky highlands to scrubland.

C. People in Syria-Palestine have lived different sorts of lives dependent on different economies in close proximity.
   1. There were three sorts of traditional culture: nomadic pastoral culture, settled farming culture, and urban culture.
   2. The proximity of these distinct cultures has led to conflicts between cultural and religious groups.

D. Syria-Palestine was also subject to historical developments that shaped the culture of its inhabitants.
   1. Syria-Palestine was subject to successive waves of migration that changed the ethnic face of the region.
   2. There was a general development from pastoral herding to settled agriculture and the growth of cities.
   3. Syria-Palestine saw a certain uniformity in religious cultures based on fertility and urban political cults.

II. Religious cultures in Syria-Palestine all shared some general influences and characteristics.

A. Religious communities in Syria-Palestine were coterminous with secular communities.
   1. In this respect, they were like the religious communities in Mesopotamia or Egypt.
   2. Equivalence of the political and religious community meant that the political leader was also the chief cultic official.
   3. Priests and other religious officials were also officials of the political order as members of the royal administration.
   4. The common religion of Syria-Palestine was polytheistic, with the gods arranged in a royal hierarchy.
   5. The religious culture featured *syncretism*, the combination of elements of one system of gods, myths, and rituals with elements of another.

B. The chief god of the Syro-Palestinian pantheon was 'El, the creator of all things and father of the gods.
   1. 'El was the oldest of the gods, head of the divine council, and well respected for his wisdom in judgment.

2. 'El's home was in the mountains to the far north, the source of the waters of the cosmos.
3. 'El's most significant epithet is "the Bull 'El," an indication of his virile power and strength.
4. 'El also appears enjoying the recreations and prerogatives of a patriarch: hunting, feasting, and engaging in sexual intercourse.
5. 'El appears as a divine warrior in his work of creation, but later, the work of the divine warrior falls to his son Ba'al.

C. Ba'al became the dominant god of Syria-Palestine, apart from the Lord of Israel.
1. The name *Ba'al* means "Lord" or "Master," and, like 'El, became a generic identification.
2. Ba'al was initially a god of the storm, who made the earth fertile through rain.
3. In one story, 'El forces Ba'al to serve Prince Sea, but Ba'al overcomes Prince Sea and destroys him.
4. In another story, Ba'al becomes a slave to Mot, ruler of the underworld, but later returns to earth.
5. In yet another story, Ba'al and 'Anat fight a primordial sea monster, Lotan, related to the biblical Leviathan.
6. Biblical scholars have noted substantial echoes and overtones between the stories and attributes of Ba'al and those of the Lord of Israel.

D. Other gods of Syria-Palestine were chief gods of ethnic groups or local manifestations of major gods.
1. The Jebusites had a chief god called Salim, and the Philistines had the half-man, half-fish god Dagon.
2. Gods identified by attributes included 'El Shaddai, "'El of the Mountains," and Ba'al-zebub, "Ba'al of the Vermin."
3. Ba'al was sometimes identified with local gods through syncretism; one example is Ba'al Melqart, a god of the Phoenician city of Tyre.
4. The god people worshiped could often be identified by the names given to the worshipers' children.
5. We find examples of such names in the Hebrew Bible, including names sacred to Salim, 'El, Ba'al, and the Lord.

E. Israel's worship of the Lord stood apart in some respects from the common religious culture of Syria-Palestine.

   1. The name of the Lord appears in the Hebrew Bible as four consonants, YHWH.

   2. The Lord may have originally been a god of the storm or of the mountain.

   3. The Lord was clearly associated with the wilderness, the "no-man's-land" away from villages and cities.

   4. The basis for the Lord's association with Israel appears to have been the god's connection with Abraham.

   5. The relationship between the Lord and Israel is understood in terms of a covenant, a binding legal contract between two parties.

   6. After the sojourn in Egypt, the covenant is renewed but also expanded to suit the people's new situation.

   7. The covenant between the Lord and Israel made at Sinai imposes stipulations on both parties.

   8. Observance of the covenant is the means by which Israel maintains harmony and equilibrium between the human and the divine world.

Essential Reading:

Henry Jackson Flanders, Jr., Robert Wilson Crapps, and David Anthony Smith. *People of the Covenant: An Introduction to the Hebrew Bible*, pp. 48–67.

Siegfried Hermann. *A History of Israel in Old Testament Times*, pp. 3–38.

Supplementary Reading:

Sarah Iles Johnston, ed. *Religions of the Ancient World: A Guide*, pp. 173–180.

Frank Moore Cross. *Canaanite Myth and Hebrew Epic: Essays in the History of the Religion of Israel*, pp. 3–75.

The New Larousse Encyclopedia of Mythology, pp. 73–84.

Questions to Consider:

1. What are some points of similarity between 'El and Ba'al and some of the gods of Egypt and Mesopotamia? What characteristics make them distinctive from these other gods?

2. In the ancient Mediterranean world, the names given children often indicated the gods worshiped by their parents. What ideas or information are the names given children intended to express in our own culture?

Lecture Twenty-One
Israel's Ancestral History

Scope: The stories about Israel's ancestors in Genesis reflect the life of nomadic herders in the Middle and Late Bronze Ages (c. 2200–1200 B.C.E.). The patriarch had absolute authority over every member of the household and would have several wives to ensure the survival of the bloodline. Israel's story begins with the Lord's choice of Abraham to receive his blessing. Abraham proves himself when he is willing to sacrifice his son Isaac. The story of Jacob and Esau emphasizes the Lord's freedom to bless whom he chooses, and the theme of fraternal rivalry continues into the story of Joseph. The Exodus story begins when the Lord appears to Moses and reveals his divine name. The Exodus story combines several traditional storytelling motifs. The covenant at Sinai establishes a legal relationship between the Lord and Israel and represents Israel's decision to worship the Lord alone out of all the gods that exist.

Outline

I. The "historical" situation depicted in the stories about Israel's ancestors does not reflect the ancient reality.

   A. The Genesis account of Israel's ancestors reflects a deliberate attempt to place its stories in the context of "things as they used to be."

      1. In the stories, Abraham comes into contact with peoples that historically only entered Syria-Palestine around the 12th century B.C.E.

      2. Likewise, Israel's ancestors are associated with cities that did not exist before the kingdom of Israel was founded.

      3. Abraham is said to come from "Ur of the Chaldeans," but the Chaldeans did not occupy Ur until about 1000 B.C.E.

      4. In the stories, the ancestors have domesticated camels, but camels were not domesticated much before about 1000 B.C.E.

      5. Such details suggest that the traditions about Israel's ancestors were written down during the early monarchy in Israel and the details added to reflect older times.

B. The basic narrative of the ancestral history, however, appears accurately to reflect life in Syria-Palestine during the Middle and Late Bronze Ages (c. 2200–1200 B.C.E.).

    1. Tablets from the Mesopotamian city of Mari provide a general idea of the lives of nomadic herdsmen during this era.

    2. The structure of the family was patriarchal, giving the father absolute authority over members of the family.

    3. The eldest son inherited, but he could forfeit his rights or the patriarch could designate another son as "eldest."

    4. Adoption was practiced within the family and in a direct line to ensure purity of the bloodline.

    5. Marriage among blood relatives, such as cousins, was preferred for the same reason.

    6. Polygamy ensured a host of children for the patriarchal line, with status based on seniority among wives who had borne children.

    7. The patriarchal "house" included the father, his wives, the unmarried daughters, grown sons and their wives, the children, and servants.

    8. These nomadic patriarchal families appear to have lived independently and autonomously.

II. Israel's ancestral history provides an origin story for Israel as a people.

  A. Every people maintains an oral tradition about its origins as members of a particular group.

    1. The ancestral history accurately reflects how nomadic herdsmen lived when Israel's forebears entered Syria-Palestine.

    2. At the same time, stories about the ancestors in Genesis have literary intentions unrelated to historical reminiscences.

    3. The stories are part of the "beginnings" narrative, because they explain "how things got to be the way they are now."

    4. Many scholars assume that the ancestral history was derived from stories told by different groups only later united as "Israel."

    5. They cite the two names of Isaac's younger son—Jacob and Israel—as evidence that two traditions have been combined into a single narrative.

B. The ancestral history begins when the Lord picks Abraham among all humanity to make a covenantal promise with him.

   1. There is no justification for the Lord's choice of Abraham, and Abraham is initially told only to go into Canaan.

   2. However, Abraham's subsequent behavior in response to the Lord's promise demonstrates Abraham's trust in the Lord and the promises he has made.

   3. Abraham also intercedes when the Lord decides to destroy Sodom, arguing that the Lord must show himself righteous.

C. The story of Jacob and Esau emphasizes the Lord's freedom to decide whom he will choose as "covenant-bearer."

   1. Previously, the Lord had chosen Isaac over Ishmael, Abraham's son by Sarah's maid Hagar.

   2. Jacob and Esau are twins, but Esau forfeits his inheritance, while Jacob gains the blessing Isaac intended for Esau by trickery.

   3. This pattern of fraternal rivalry is echoed in the later story of Joseph and his brothers.

   4. The ancestral history explains the origins of Israel and of many of the nations surrounding Israel through stories about Abraham's family.

   5. Israel's ancestors live in relationship with the Lord, who uses both their good and bad behavior to fulfill his intentions.

III. The God of Abraham is explicitly identified with the Lord who later reveals himself to Moses.

A. The God of Abraham, Isaac, and Jacob is definitively identified as "the Lord" in the Exodus narrative.

   1. When the Lord appears to Moses in the burning bush, Moses asks the name of the god of his ancestors.

   2. Moses's request is, to some extent, a request for permission to "call upon the name" of the god he encounters.

   3. The Lord gives Moses what amounts to three replies, each originating in a different level of the tradition (3:14–15).

   4. The explanation "I am who I am" indicates that the Lord is "the Living God" who at all times Is.

B. The appearance to Moses establishes both continuity and change in the Lord's way of dealing with Israel.

     1. God is now to be known exclusively as the Lord and is not to be identified with the gods worshiped by other peoples.

     2. The Lord will be known through his actions in history, because his relationship with Israel will be based on a covenant.

     3. But Israel's escape from Egypt and entry into Canaan is tied to the Lord's earlier promises to Abraham.

     4. Israel's religion as understood and practiced throughout its history begins with the revelation to Moses.

C. The account of the Exodus itself reflects elements of at least two different traditions in several respects.

     1. The story of the plagues has folkloric elements, including the cycle of plague–capitulation–relief–renewed oppression.

     2. This cycle indicates that the plagues are really nine "warnings," followed by the final plague.

     3. There are two versions of the circumstances in which the people leave, either as expulsion or escape.

     4. There are also two versions of the miracle at the Reed Sea, one more overtly supernatural than the other.

D. The Exodus becomes the basis for the covenant at Sinai, with binding stipulations on both parties.

     1. The covenantal agreement as it appears in Exodus 19:3b–8 recalls an ancient Near Eastern suzerainty treaty.

     2. The Lord's covenant with Israel is based on the Exodus, because it demonstrated what sort of god the Lord is for Israel.

     3. The covenantal stipulations in Exodus 19:3b–8 are expressed in terms of a conditional blessing based on obedience.

     4. Like the stipulations in a suzerainty treaty, Israel's responsibilities are laid out in second-person imperatives.

     5. The covenantal stipulations are assumed to be known in this summary, and the people give their solemn assent.

E. The covenant confirms the Lord's status as Israel's national god out of all the gods that exist.

     1. The first commandment in Exodus 20:2 reflects this idea: "You shall have no other gods besides me."

     2. The Lord's "jealousy" is the jealousy of a henotheistic deity, who alone of all the gods is to be worshiped.

3. Observance of the covenant is the means by which Israel certifies its allegiance to the Lord.
4. Although it is true that the Lord chooses Israel, Israel chooses the Lord as well, and this is the basis for their mutual history.

Essential Reading:

Exodus 1–20.

Henry Jackson Flanders, Jr., Robert Wilson Crapps, and David Anthony Smith. *People of the Covenant: An Introduction to the Hebrew Bible*, pp. 133–221.

Genesis 12–50.

Siegfried Hermann. *A History of Israel in Old Testament Times*, pp. 41–127.

Supplementary Reading:

Sarah Iles Johnston, ed. *Religions of the Ancient World: A Guide*, pp. 181–188.

Questions to Consider:

1. What are some of the points of similarity between a story about the origins of the gods in Egypt or Mesopotamian myth and the story of the origins of the people of Israel in Genesis? In what important points do they differ?
2. The emphasis in the story of Abraham's family is on the Lord's freedom to choose whom he will bless and who will serve as the bearer of his covenantal promises. What are some of the implications of the Lord's freedom to make such choices for Israel's self-understanding?

Lecture Twenty-Two
Israel's National History

Scope: When the Israelites settled in Palestine, their way of life changed, a change reflected in their religious culture, as Ba'al became a rival to the Lord. During the 1st century or so in Palestine, Israel was led by "judges," charismatic war leaders and city princes. When the Sea Peoples entered Syria-Palestine, Israelites needed a military king to protect them and chose Saul. The later conflict between Saul and David was a conflict between an unsuccessful military king and a younger, successful general. David managed to gain the support of the people and finally took the throne of Israel from Saul's son, uniting Israel with Judah. David's rule was legitimized by the Lord's covenant promising him an eternal dynasty. David's choice of the Jebusite city of Jerusalem as his capital reflects his own background as a Jebusite. The books of Samuel and Kings view history from Judah's perspective, exalting David and Jerusalem.

Outline

I. Israel's national history begins when the people enter and settle in the land of Canaan.

    A. Israel's history in the Hebrew Bible is composed of traditions collected and presented by different authors at different times.

        1. As a result, we find conflicting points of view on events and issues arising in Israel's history.

        2. This polemical re-presentation of traditional material has parallels in such re-workings of mythology as *Enuma Elish*.

        3. The Hebrew Bible presents an interplay of theological perspectives more revealing than an imposed "orthodoxy."

    B. After the death of Moses, Joshua led the people into Canaan, where they established themselves as farmers and village dwellers.

        1. The nature of Israel's settlement in Canaan is open to question, but Israelite religious culture inevitably changed as a result.

        2. The Lord was associated with the wilderness, far away from settled life in Canaan.

3. The needs of farmers and village dwellers are different from those of nomadic herders of sheep and goats.

4. Israelites almost inevitably participated in rituals associated with foreign gods who ensured fertility.

5. Israel's religious history reflects a continual struggle between the Lord's henotheistic claims and the people's polytheistic practices.

6. Most often, the Israelites would combine worship of the Lord with ritual recognition of other gods.

C. During the 1st century in Palestine, the people were ruled by charismatic war leaders and city princes.

1. The word *judge* derives from a verb meaning "to rule"; these were leaders who ruled over some part of Israel.

2. Israel at this time was a small territory located in the central hill country of Palestine, with few cities.

3. Stories about the judges resemble tall tales and reflect a more or less wide-open religious culture.

4. The author of Judges notes several times, "In those days . . . all people did what was right in their own eyes" (cf. 21:25).

5. The last judge was Samuel, who oversaw the transition from territorial rule to a centralized military monarchy.

D. The change in rule from Samuel to Saul is also a change in the sort of leadership Israel needed.

1. In religious terms, Samuel and Saul were similar, given that both were believed to have been chosen by the Lord to rule over Israel.

2. Both Samuel and Saul attempted to establish dynasties, and both men served cultic functions in Israel's ritual worship.

3. The primary difference between them was that Saul was a successful military leader over a standing army.

II. Israel's transition to a monarchy also brought about changes in the nation's religious culture.

A. It is difficult to reconstruct the religious culture of Israel at the birth of the monarchy.

1. Before Samuel, worship of the Lord appears to have been overshadowed by devotion to other gods.

2. The Lord remained the God of Israel, although the names of Israel's princes indicate that kings might also worship other gods.

3. David's loyalty to the Lord may have arisen in part from his need to legitimate himself as a successor to Saul.

B. During the monarchy, the king was not only ruler but also the representative of his people before the Lord.

1. As the people's leader, each king was believed to be the Lord's chosen representative before him.

2. The historian who wrote Samuel and Kings holds each king responsible for the nation's faithfulness to the Lord.

3. Israel's kings determined the religious policies of the nation, but these reflected both political and religious intentions.

C. The conflict between Saul and David was a conflict between an unsuccessful king and a successful general.

1. David was not born an Israelite; his mother came from Moab, and his father from Bethlehem, a Jebusite city.

2. David formed his connection to Israel by loyalty to its king and to the Lord as the God of Israel.

3. Saul's defeat and the rout of his army by the Philistines left David without opposition in both Israel and Judah.

4. It may have been during David's reign that the idea that all Israel descended from Abraham was devised.

D. The Jebusite character of Jerusalem influenced the conduct of the worship of the Lord in the royal capital.

1. The Jebusites worshiped the gods 'El-Elyon ("'El the Highest") and Salim, among others.

2. The "true" Israelite religion at the time was the religion of the north, unassociated with temples or the monarchy.

3. David and the Jerusalem priests modified Israelite religion in the light of Jebusite practice.

E. David's reign was further legitimated by the *Davidic covenant*, a covenant of grant from the Lord.

1. The fate of Israel was to be tied to a royal "house," and its governance was defined in terms of David's dynasty.

2. After Solomon's reign, the kingdom divided into its component parts, Israel to the north and Judah to the south.

F. The accommodation of Israelite worship to the new national situation found its fullest expression in the Jerusalem Temple.

    1. Previously, the Lord had been worshiped in a tent that reflected the nomadic life of Israel.

    2. Several sites in the north, including Bethel and Shiloh, had long been cultic sites for worship of the Lord.

    3. Once Jerusalem became the political and cultic center of Israel, Solomon built the Temple as part of his palace complex.

    4. The so-called "high places" (*bamoth*) were national shrines devoted to the worship of the Lord.

    5. The primacy of the Jerusalem Temple remained a point of contention between Judah and Israel.

G. The historical narrative in the books of Samuel and Kings generally represents the Judahite perspective.

    1. The historian presents David's dynasty as designated rulers of all Israel, and the Temple as the one legitimate cultic site.

    2. Generally speaking, the historian reflects the strict moral standards typical of the book of Deuteronomy.

    3. The historian's position may be summarized as one God, one people, one cult, and one temple for all Israel.

    4. The historian attributes the fall of Israel to the Lord's wrath, because Israel had rebelled against the Lord's chosen king and temple.

    5. The historian subsequently blames the fall of Judah on its failure to worship the Lord only in the Jerusalem Temple.

    6. The religious policy of Israel and Judah should be understood in its own terms, not judged by the historian's ideals.

    7. Those ideals reflect the work of the prophets, whose support for exclusive worship of the Lord in time led to the development of a genuine monotheistic faith.

Essential Reading:

1 Kings 1–13.

1–2 Samuel.

Henry Jackson Flanders, Jr., Robert Wilson Crapps, and David Anthony Smith. *People of the Covenant: An Introduction to the Hebrew Bible*, pp. 257–303.

Siegfried Hermann. *A History of Israel in Old Testament Times*, pp. 131–173.

Supplementary Reading:

Michael D. Coogan, ed. *The Oxford History of the Biblical World*, pp. 165–205.

John H. Hayes and J. Maxwell Miller, eds. *Israelite and Judaean History*, pp. 332–380.

Questions to Consider:

1. What specific changes would be likely to appear in Israel's religious culture as a result of the change from a nomadic herding culture to a settled agricultural and village culture in Canaan?

2. In 1 Samuel 8, Samuel argues that the people's desire to have a king rule over them is, in effect, a rejection of the Lord's rule over them. What does this argument tell us about both the nature of the Lord's relationship with Israel and the nature of kingship in ancient Near Eastern kingdoms?

Lecture Twenty-Three
Prophecy in the Ancient Near East

Scope: A basic motivation for religious action is the desire to establish harmony between the human and divine worlds. Some methods of discerning the divine will are controlled by religious authorities, while others arise from an individual's sensitivity to divine communication. A prophet has an inaugural experience indicating that he or she has been set aside to speak on the god's behalf. The god's message is received in an ecstatic state as something seen, something heard, or both. The message is delivered in the name of the god and addresses its audience's situation from the divine perspective. The prophet may communicate the message by word or symbolic actions. The prophet may also have oracles written down as verification that the god has spoken. The voice of prophecy represents an independent voice of divine authority over against that of the religious establishment and sometimes finds itself in conflict with it.

Outline

I. In the ancient world, there were several means of gaining insight into the divine will.

  A. The basic motivation for religious action is the desire to maintain harmony between the human and the divine world.

    1. Religious activity arises when people feel separated from, but in relationship with, supernatural forces at work in the world.

    2. Part of maintaining equilibrium is gaining insight into the will of the gods in order to respond appropriately.

    3. Insight into the will of the gods is part of creation mythology that lays out the basic conditions of human life.

    4. But crises in community life give rise to the need to determine the gods' will much more specifically.

    5. This is when religious officials are called upon to discern the will of the gods on the community's behalf.

  B. Practices to discern the will of the gods through divinatory methods tend to be controlled by established religious authority.

      1. One such method uses a simple apparatus to gain a divine response to a yes-or-no query.

      2. Another is to seek a revelatory dream by incubation, sleeping within the precincts of the god's temple.

      3. Spontaneous dreams and other sorts of oracles required interpretation, and interpreters were typically part of the official religious authority.

  C. There were also divinatory practices based on a particular person's sensitivity to divine communication.

      1. In these cases, the method used is secondary to the gifts of the person using them.

      2. Seers, diviners, and mediums used different methods to gain knowledge of the divine world.

      3. These gifted individuals were generally free of the stricture of official religious authority and provided a counterbalance to it.

      4. The response to seers and diviners from the official religious authority might be positive or negative.

      5. As in the story of Joseph, spiritual gifts associated with interpreting dreams are often considered a form of practical wisdom.

  D. Both spiritual insight and wisdom allow a person to make decisions about how best to live in the world.

      1. Part of wisdom was knowing how to interact with the divine world; thus, the spiritual adept was also considered a wise person.

      2. There is also a continuing association in the ancient world between wisdom and magic, as with Inanna and Isis.

      3. *Execration texts*, names written on clay vessels, then smashed, were a means of breaking an enemy's power.

      4. The spiritual adept had the power of effective cursing, calling down divine wrath on enemies.

      5. A humorous example of effective cursing appears in Numbers 22–24, in the story of Balak and Balaam.

II. Prophecy was a powerful form of divine insight and communication in the ancient Near East.

  A. Although prophecy belongs to this realm of religious phenomena, it also stands apart in some respects.

1. The prophet is set apart by the gods and submits to them, speaking out on the basis of religious experience.
2. The prophet usually feels under constraint to speak the message given by the gods, even against his or her will.
3. The Greek term *prophetes* means "*forth*-teller," because the prophet proclaims the message given by the god.

B. The prophet's ministry usually begins with an inaugural experience when the call to prophesy is received.
1. The prophet experiences *ecstasy*, "standing outside" the self, when the perception of reality is temporarily interrupted.
2. A vision may involve seeing what isn't there or insight into the true nature or significance of something that is there.
3. An *audition* is hearing something in ecstatic experience, the aural equivalent of a vision.
4. In all forms of prophetic experience, the prophet is convinced that the god has conveyed a message and the prophet must proclaim it.

C. The prophet's proclamation of the message is not restricted to a public forum or to speaking alone.
1. The prophetic message may be addressed to an individual, a group, or the people in general.
2. A prophet may perform a *prophetic action* as part of the message, an action that may take many forms.
3. Part of the prophet's mission may be to record the prophecies in writing as verification that the god has spoken.
4. The Hebrew Bible includes collections of prophecies, some including the divine order to record them.
5. The divine word is sometimes depicted as a scroll swallowed by the prophet and later to be spoken aloud.

D. An Egyptian text from the 20th century B.C.E. is a literary presentation dependent on the tradition of written prophecies.
1. "The Prophecy of Neferty," was supposedly given during the reign of Snofru (2600–2571 B.C.E.), but it is, in fact, much later.
2. The text may reflect prophecy as it was practiced in Egypt, but it is not itself a prophetic text.
3. Neferty gives a poetic description of a future catastrophe when the Asiatics will overrun Egypt.

4. But the nation will be saved by a king from the south, Ameny, who will drive the Asiatics out of Egypt.
5. The narrative is really a review of history presented as prophecy to extol the pharaoh as the gods' champion for Egypt.
6. Apocalyptic works also present themselves as prophecy but, in fact, serve another purpose, cf. Daniel.

E. The proclamation of a divine message makes the prophet potentially dangerous to authorized religious officials.
1. The prophet may display eccentric behavior as a part of the prophetic ministry.
2. Prophecy might be practiced in the context of the temple or the court, to provide divine guidance.
3. But prophecy can also be practiced without official authorization, making the prophet an independent voice for the god.
4. In this capacity, a prophet may have great influence as a protesting voice against the religious or secular power structure.
5. In Israel, the dissenting voice of the prophet may challenge the official practices of both king and cult.

Supplementary Reading:

Joseph Blenkinsopp. *A History of Prophecy in Israel: From the Settlement in the Land to the Hellenistic Period*, pp. 19–52.

John L. Foster, ed. and trans. *Ancient Egyptian Literature: An Anthology*, pp. 76–84.

Numbers 22–24.

Questions to Consider:

1. What are some traditional or contemporary ways that people attempt to gain insight into the future in our own time and culture?

2. Sensitivity to the spiritual realm places the seer or prophet at the margins of normal human experience. How might this "marginal" status have affected the seer's or the prophet's ability to have his or her message heard and taken seriously by society at large?

Lecture Twenty-Four
Early Prophecy in Israel

Scope: Various methods for gaining insight into the divine will were practiced in Israel, but in time, these were overshadowed and de-legitimized by prophecy. Biblical scholars have identified three general types of prophecy in ancient Israel: *guild prophecy*, carried out by groups of ecstatic prophets under the leadership of a head prophet; *official prophecy*, carried out in connection with the royal court or the cult; and *independent prophecy*, carried out by prophets whose only claim to authority came from the prophetic word they proclaimed. An example of the independent prophet is Elijah, who championed the exclusive worship of the Lord in the face of opposition from Ahab and Jezebel, who imported the worship of Ba'al-Melqart into Israel. Elijah represents something of a turning point in the history of Israelite prophecy.

Outline

I. Several of the methods for gaining insight into the divine world we have discussed were present in ancient Israel, but over time, prophecy became the dominant method.

    A. Various kinds of seers are mentioned in the Hebrew Bible, but gradually, they and their practices were more and more likely to be rejected as illegitimate and pagan.

        1. Joseph is a wise man whose talents include the ability to interpret dreams and to read omens from the dregs of the wine in a cup (Gen. 40–41; 44:5, 15).

        2. Oracles were derived from the sound and movement of trees, but *necromancy*, the consultation of dead spirits, was forbidden in Israel.

        3. Later prophets reject the oracles of diviners, dreamers, soothsayers, and sorcerers in favor of the Lord's word revealed to the prophet.

    B. Samuel presents an interesting case at the very beginning of the Israelite monarchy: He is priest, magistrate, and prophet but also appears as a seer.

1. Samuel appears in the role of a seer in 1 Samuel 9, when Saul consults him for help in finding his father's she-donkeys.
2. Samuel is both a seer and "a man of God" in this story, and the historian conflates the role of "seer" with what he regards as the more respectable role of "prophet."
3. Samuel represents the emerging dominance of inspired prophecy over other forms of gaining insight into the divine will.

II. Biblical scholars have identified three primary forms of Israelite prophecy, although there is overlap among the categories.

A. *Guild prophets* were prophets who lived and prophesied in groups under a leader and were apparently known as "the sons of the prophets."
   1. Guild prophets experienced such extreme forms of ecstasy as dancing, whirling, going into catatonic trances, and stripping off their clothing.
   2. The form of ecstasy they experienced was contagious.
   3. Guild prophets appear to have set themselves apart by distinctive clothing and some sort of head mark or tonsure that indicated they were prophets.
   4. Over time, the guild prophets appear to have fallen into disrepute.

B. *Official prophets* were professional prophets who worked within the context of the royal court or the shrine to determine God's intentions.
   1. Court prophets served as advisors to kings in formulating national and foreign policy or, in time of war, strategy and tactics.
   2. Cultic prophets were associated with the shrines dedicated to the Lord to discern the Lord's will for individual petitioners or for the proper maintenance of cultic worship.
   3. Because official prophets formed part of the royal or religious establishment, they are sometimes regarded with suspicion by the biblical authors.

C. *Independent prophets* are what we usually associate with prophecy in Israel, prophets who speak on the Lord's behalf without royal authority and often in opposition to it.

1. Independent prophets seemed to be called from a variety of professions to speak the word of the Lord at the Lord's instigation.
2. The classical examples are Elijah, who spoke out repeatedly against the political and religious policies of Ahab, and Jeremiah, who faced opposition to his prophetic message in Judah.
3. Most of the prophets in the Hebrew Bible were official prophets who also had the status of independent prophets.

III. An example of an independent prophet without official standing is Elijah the Tishbite.

A. Elijah is the first of the major prophets of Israel and Judah.
1. Elijah's prophetic career includes the reign of Ahab of Israel (871–851 B.C.E.) and the reign of his son Ahaziah (851–850 B.C.E.).
2. Elijah found himself in almost continual opposition to Ahab, although Ahab appears to have reluctantly recognized Elijah's authority as a prophet of the Lord.

B. Ahab was the son of Omri, the greatest of the kings of the northern kingdom of Israel.
1. Omri had consolidated his territory, founded Samaria, and made peace with Judah on very favorable terms.
2. He made alliances with nations surrounding Israel and consolidated these alliances with royal marriages, as when his son Ahab married Jezebel, the daughter of the king of Tyre.

C. Jezebel was a worshiper of Ba'al-Melqart, the Phoenician representation of Ba'al.
1. Jezebel brought 400 Ba'alite priests to Israel to establish cultic sites for Ba'al-Melqart.
2. Jezebel's support for Ba'alite worship aroused Elijah's opposition as champion of "the Lord alone" for Israel.
3. The stories about Elijah all have the same point: The Lord is the giver of all gifts and the only God for Israel to worship.

D. The story about the contest on Mt. Carmel in 1 Kings 18:20–40 is primarily about a jurisdictional dispute between the Lord and Ba'al.
1. In the ancient Near East, gods were assumed to manifest their divine power in the places where they were worshiped.

2. The more shrines a god had, the greater his power and his ability to act in response to the prayers and offerings of his devotees and the larger his realm of operation.
3. Mt. Carmel was roughly equidistant from Tyre, the home of Ba'al-Melqart, and the city of Samaria, the cultic home of the Lord.
4. The question was: Which of the two gods was able to act in response to his worshipers on Mt. Carmel?

E. The contest involves the preparation of two identical sacrifices and invocation of each god to send fire to ignite the sacrifice.
1. The Ba'alite priests prepare their sacrifice and call upon Ba'al but receive no answer.
2. Elijah ridicules the priests by insisting that Ba'al must have a reason for not hearing them.
3. When Elijah prepares the sacrifice and calls upon the name of the Lord, fire immediately consumes the sacrifice.
4. The contest settles the question: The Lord alone is the god to be worshiped in Israel.

F. Elijah does not represent a monotheistic point of view but henotheistic worship of the Lord.
1. Elijah does not deny the existence of Ba'al, only his capacity to act on Mt. Carmel.
2. Elijah fights only against Ba'alism, not against other religious offenses that the historian who wrote the book of Kings condemns.

G. Elijah's encounter with the Lord at Mt. Horeb in 1 Kings 19 illustrates the changing nature of Israelite prophecy.
1. Jezebel reacts to Elijah's victory at Mt. Carmel by persecuting worshipers of the Lord.
2. Elijah flees into the wilderness, where his experiences parallel the experience of Israel's ancestors in the wilderness.
3. The Lord's appearance to Elijah at Horeb stands in continuity and contrast with the Lord's appearance to Moses at Sinai.
4. Elijah is told not to expect a miraculous overthrow of the Lord's enemies but their elimination by the mechanics of human history.

Essential Reading:

1 Kings 16–22.

Joseph Blenkinsopp. *A History of Prophecy in Israel: From the Settlement in the Land to the Hellenistic Period*, pp. 53–79.

Henry Jackson Flanders, Jr., Robert Wilson Crapps, and David Anthony Smith. *People of the Covenant: An Introduction to the Hebrew Bible*, pp. 322–338.

Supplementary Reading:

Klaus Koch. *The Prophets*: Vol. 1: *The Assyrian Period*, pp. 1–35.

Questions to Consider:

1. There seems to be a conscious rejection in ancient Israel of other ways of determining the Lord's will in favor of inspired prophecy. What is gained and what is lost in the process?

2. There is an obvious tension between the king as the Lord's anointed ruler and the prophet as a proclaimer of the Lord's word. How do we strike a balance between political realities and theological ideals?

Lecture Twenty-Five
Classical Israelite Prophecy

Scope: After the reign of Solomon, the nation of Israel split into two parts, Israel with its capital, Samaria, to the north and Judah with its capital, Jerusalem, to the south. Both nations flourished in the absence of a regional military power, but the rise of Assyria threatened all the nations of Syria-Palestine. The religious policies of both Israel and Judah were determined by the king and the priesthood, reflecting not only the traditional worship of the Lord but foreign religious influences, as well. The prophets represented an independent voice of religious authority that often came into conflict with official religious practice and political policies. Amos presented a prophetic voice that challenged social injustice in Israel, while Isaiah of Jerusalem urged trust in the Lord, rather than military alliances in political matters. Both prophets emphasized the Lord's love for his people and his faithfulness to his covenantal promises.

Outline

I. The political situation in Israel and Judah after the reign of Solomon led to a variety of religious practices in both nations, only some of them consistent with later orthodoxies.

    A. The united monarchy of Judah and Israel broke into its component parts during the reign of Solomon's son Rehoboam (r. 928–911 B.C.E.).

        1. The people of the northern territory of Israel felt oppressed by Solomon's practice of requiring forced labor from them but not from the people of Judah.

        2. In the eyes of the northerners, Solomon was a foreign monarch ruling them from a foreign capital and demanding worship in a foreign temple under foreign priests.

        3. The north rebelled against David and Solomon and finally broke away during Rehoboam's reign, under the leadership of Jeroboam (r. 928–907 B.C.E.).

4. The northern kingdom had a series of short-lived dynasties until Omri (r. 882–871 B.C.E.), who made Israel militarily and politically secure.

5. Judah continued to be ruled by David's dynasty and engaged in frequent warfare with Israel.

B. Both Israel and Judah flourished in a period marked by the absence of a major world power in the Near East between about 1250 and 850 B.C.E.

1. After the fall of the Hittite empire, while Egypt was preoccupied with internal problems, Syria-Palestine was free of external domination.

2. A number of native kingdoms arose and developed, including Edom, Moab, Ammon, Sidon, Aram-Damascus, and the Philistine kingdoms.

3. These kingdoms fought among themselves or formed alliances; they survived until the Assyrian encroachment on Syria-Palestine in the 9th century B.C.E.

4. From that time on, the political fortunes of both Israel and Judah depended on the actions of the Assyrian kings as allies, opponents, or conquerors.

C. After the kingdom divided in 928 B.C.E., the people continued to worship the Lord in their own territories according to their ancestral traditions.

1. Judah continued to worship at the Jerusalem Temple but also at other altars dedicated to worship of the Lord located elsewhere.

2. Israel worshiped at the traditional cultic sites of Dan and Bethel, as well as other altars dedicated to worship of the Lord.

D. Both Israel and Judah incorporated the worship of foreign gods in various ways.

1. The worship of a foreign god might be practiced by resident aliens.

2. Women of the king's harem would bring their own gods and religious customs with them.

3. Official worship of a foreign god might be introduced as a sign of allegiance to a foreign nation as ally or as conqueror.

4. Religious orthodoxy was determined by the political and religious authorities as custodians of the religious culture of Israel and Judah.

E. The most common source of conflict between the authorities and the prophets was their different ideas of what the Lord demanded of his people.
   1. Political leaders were concerned with how best to respond to external threats and how to ensure the nation's security.
   2. Like most of their contemporaries, the religious authorities believed that the primary religious duty of the people was to obey the king and support the national cult.
   3. The prophets proclaimed that the primary duty of both king and people was obedience to the Lord in moral action, as well as proper worship.
   4. The prophets represented an independent, self-authenticating voice of religious authority.

F. The conflict: Was the will of the Lord expressed by the actions of the king and the priests or by the words and actions of the prophets?
   1. The prophets tended to represent either a rejection of royal authority in favor of divine authority or an evolving monotheism.
   2. The idea that the Lord alone should rule over Israel represented dissatisfaction with the political compromises that are a part of nationhood.
   3. Henotheistic belief in the Lord as the only God for Israel was expressed in terms of the Lord's incomparability and strength, leading to a nascent monotheism.
   4. The prophets tended to be theological idealists, claiming in any and all circumstances that the best policy was adherence to the word of the Lord.
   5. Prophecy did not inevitably lead to conflict, because some prophets focused attention on the sins of foreign nations that oppressed God's people.

II. Both Amos of Tekoa in Israel and Isaiah of Jerusalem in Judah provide examples of the conflict between the prophet and the governing authorities.

A. Amos is the earliest of the prophets whose oracles are preserved in a book.

    1. Amos was from Judah, but his prophetic ministry in Israel reflects the religious perspective of Israel.

    2. Amos probably prophesied beginning around 750 B.C.E., during the reign of Jeroboam II, whose loyalty to Assyria ensured him a long and prosperous reign.

    3. Jeroboam's reign also saw a widening gap between the rich and the poor in Israel as a result of social injustice.

B. Amos appears to have received his prophetic calling through a series of visions.

    1. Amos distances himself from both official and guild prophecy.

    2. Amos's only recorded appearance is at the shrine at Bethel, where he prophesied against Jeroboam and predicted exile for the people of Israel.

    3. Some of Amos's visions are recorded in Amos 7–8, when he sees everyday objects that convey a symbolic meaning of judgment from the Lord.

C. Amos's first oracle is a series of attacks on Israel's traditional enemies.

    1. Each of these attacks follows the same formula.

    2. In each case, Amos lists the sins of the nation and the punishment that will result.

    3. Amos initially presents himself as a nationalist prophet but then pronounces judgment against Israel in the same terms.

    4. Israel is condemned for sins against the poor, but the punishment will lead to forgiveness.

    5. Amos's message is moderated by the enduring relationship between the Lord and Israel.

D. Isaiah was the first of the three great classical prophets, with Jeremiah and Ezekiel.

    1. Isaiah apparently spent his entire life in Jerusalem and may have been an official court or cult prophet.

    2. Isaiah was married and had at least two sons to whom he gave symbolic names.

    3. Isaiah's career covered about half a century, from about 740 to 676 B.C.E.

    4. During his ministry, Isaiah gathered disciples who preserved his prophecies.

E. One of Isaiah's most well known prophecies was given to Ahaz of Judah around 735–733 B.C.E.

    1. Pekah of Israel and Rezin of Aram-Damascus threatened to attack Judah if Ahaz did not join their anti-Assyrian alliance.

    2. Isaiah's first prophecy (7:1–9) assures Ahaz that the two enemy kingdoms will fall to Assyria.

    3. The second prophecy (7:10–25) provides reassurance with the sign of Immanuel.

    4. In the second prophecy, Isaiah tells Ahaz to take the Lord's covenant with David seriously and to trust in his power.

    5. The prophecy refers to a young woman who is pregnant and will bear the child Immanuel; she may have been one of the king's wives.

    6. The prophecy says that before the child knows right from wrong, Israel and Aram-Damascus will be gone.

    7. The child will eat curds and honey, divine food that will help him grow quickly.

    8. In spite of this prophecy, Ahaz made an alliance with Assyria, bringing Judah under Assyrian control.

    9. The legacy of the prophets is their affirmation of the Lord's faithfulness toward his people, based on his covenantal promises to Israel.

    10. Conviction in the Lord's faithfulness sustained the religious faith of the people after the fall of Israel and Judah.

Essential Reading:

2 Kings 9–25.

Amos.

Joseph Blenkinsopp. *A History of Prophecy in Israel: From the Settlement in the Land to the Hellenistic Period*, pp. 80–118.

Henry Jackson Flanders, Jr., Robert Wilson Crapps, and David Anthony Smith. *People of the Covenant: An Introduction to the Hebrew Bible*, pp. 303–321, 339–347, 355–376.

Siegfried Hermann. *A History of Israel in Old Testament Times*, pp. 187–262.

Isaiah 1–39.

Supplementary Reading:

John H. Hayes and J. Maxwell Miller, eds. *Israelite and Judaean History*, pp. 381–434.

Klaus Koch. *The Prophets*, Vol. 1: *The Assyrian Period*, pp. 36–76, 105–156.

Questions to Consider:

1. What were likely to be the political and religious consequences of an alliance with a military power such as Assyria?

2. Is it possible to combine successfully theological idealism and political realism? Which must accommodate itself to the other? Why?

Lecture Twenty-Six
Israel's Great Crisis

Scope: The last years of the monarchy in Judah were shaped by the imperial ambitions of Assyria, Egypt, and Babylon. Despite a few periods of peace and prosperity, Judah finally fell to the Babylonians, and its aristocracy was sent into exile. During this period, the prophets spoke to the people's hopes and fears, blaming the fall of Judah on the nation's own lack of faithfulness to its covenant with the Lord. Jeremiah and Ezekiel both proclaimed this message, but after the fall of Jerusalem, both adopted a new message of hope and reconciliation. After the Babylonian empire fell to the Persians, the Judahite exiles were allowed to return to their homeland. Second Isaiah preached a message of comfort and restoration based on an overt monotheism. The prophet Haggai encouraged those who returned to Jerusalem to rebuild the Temple and obey the covenant to ensure the Lord's blessing on their community.

Outline

I. The last years of the Judahite monarchy were overshadowed by the imperial powers of Assyria and Babylon.

    A. In Israel, usurpations and shifting alliances led to the nation's conquest by Assyria and the fall of Samaria in 721 B.C.E.

        1. Jehu overthrew Omri's dynasty, made himself king, and submitted Israel to Assyria.

        2. The Assyrian alliance led to peace and prosperity under Jeroboam II, but a series of usurpations and kings with short reigns weakened Israel.

        3. After Tiglath-Pileser III died in 727 B.C.E., Israel rebelled against Assyria.

        4. Assyrian armies laid siege to Samaria, until the capital fell to Sargon II in 721 B.C.E.

        5. About 27,900 Israelites were deported and replaced by foreign nobility, who served as imperial administrators for the Assyrians.

B. Judah had a similar history of obedience and rebellion with Assyria and Babylon throughout the 7th century B.C.E.

    1. Ahaz voluntarily became a vassal to Assyria when he was threatened by Israel and Aram-Damascus.

    2. Hezekiah rebelled against Assyria in 705 B.C.E. by withholding tribute but lost his entire kingdom except Jerusalem.

    3. Hezekiah's son Manasseh restored the alliance with Assyria and enjoyed a long and prosperous reign.

    4. Judah rebelled again under Josiah, who like Hezekiah, reformed religious practice to emphasize national identity.

    5. In the last 20 years of its existence, Judah shifted loyalties between Egypt and Babylon six times, with disastrous results.

    6. In 587 B.C.E., Jerusalem fell to the Babylonian king Nebuchadnezzar, who deported the nobility to Babylon.

C. Jeremiah's prophetic ministry took place in the midst of Judah's national crisis.

    1. Jeremiah's prophetic call was an interior experience reflecting the tension between his message and his sympathy for his people.

    2. Jeremiah endured hardships and condemnation in proclaiming his message.

    3. After Jerusalem fell, Jeremiah began to proclaim a message of hope and reconciliation.

II. The fall of Jerusalem was an unparalleled calamity without apparent remedy and demanded a theological response.

  A. The fall of Jerusalem was a political and military disaster but also a blow to Judah's religious ideas.

    1. The fall of Samaria to the Assyrians left Judah reassured that it was dear to the Lord, while Israel had been punished for its sins.

    2. The fall of Jerusalem, however, removed the benefits the Lord had conferred on Judah: the land, the king, and the Temple.

    3. The means of renewing the covenantal relationship, the sacrificial cult, had been destroyed.

    4. There were two possible theological conclusions: The Lord had been unable to prevent the disaster or had himself brought it about.

5. If the people were to continue to worship the Lord, they had to accept the Babylonians' conquest as a just punishment from the Lord for Judah's sins.

6. It fell to the prophets to make sense of the people's experience of exile as a prologue to reconciliation with their God.

B. Ezekiel's prophetic message among the exiles understood the fall of Jerusalem in terms of Judah's sin and offered hope for reconciliation.

1. Ezekiel was part of the first wave of exiles to Babylon in 597 B.C.E. and acted as their spiritual leader.

2. For the first part of Ezekiel's prophetic career, his primary subject was the fall of Jerusalem; for the second part, it was hope and restoration.

3. Ezekiel's inaugural experience was his vision of "the wheel in a wheel," the throne-chariot of the Lord that allowed him to be wherever his people were, even in exile.

4. Ezekiel proclaims that God's people presumed on their elect status, trusting that the Lord would always protect them.

5. Instead of a punishment, exile had been a blessing, because those in exile escaped the siege and fall of Jerusalem.

6. Ezekiel's vision of the Lord's throne-chariot shows that God is accessible to his people in exile; thus, the possibility of their redemption remains.

III. After Nebuchadrezzar, the fortunes of the Babylonian empire rapidly declined, setting the stage for the exiles' return.

A. After a struggle over the succession, Nebuchadnezzar was eventually succeeded by Nabonidus, who abandoned Babylon to live in an oasis.

1. His son Belshazzar presided in Babylon over a worsening economic and military situation.

2. The Persians under Cyrus invaded Babylon and took power in 539 B.C.E.

B. These events provide the historical context for the prophecies of "Second Isaiah," the author of the oracles in Isaiah 40–55.

1. These chapters stand apart from the oracles of Isaiah of Jerusalem by virtue of their historical setting, their message, and their lyrical beauty.

2. Second Isaiah was apparently a disciple of Isaiah who was also a prophet in his own right and proclaimed the word of the Lord to the exiles.
3. In an atmosphere of despair, Second Isaiah prophesied and revived hope that the Lord would restore the nation's fortunes.

C. Second Isaiah's message is comfort at the end of exile, set in the context of the people's sin.
1. Comfort is possible only because the people have been punished, as the Lord offers renewal of the covenantal relationship.
2. The basis of the comfort is the Lord's sole sovereignty of the earth and his faithfulness.
3. The Lord's glory, power, and incomparability are expressed through images based on his works in creation.

D. In Second Isaiah, a manifest monotheism is proclaimed in rejection of polytheism and idol worship.
1. Second Isaiah satirizes idolatry by equating the idol with the god it represents.
2. This satire is probably consistent with some common polytheistic practices.
3. Second Isaiah's monotheism is illustrated by the ways in which the Lord displays his sovereignty over the cosmos, including fulfilling his word.
4. The idea that the Lord proclaims, then fulfills his word apparently inspired the first written records of prophetic oracles by Isaiah of Jerusalem and Jeremiah.
5. Second Isaiah proclaims the Lord as God of the whole world, including foreign nations and their leaders.

E. Persian policies toward subject peoples were generous in regard to native political and religious traditions.
1. The Persians allowed native aristocracies to reside in their own territories under the authority of Persian political authorities.
2. The Persians also allowed their subjects to worship their own gods, provided they entreated their gods for the king's welfare.

3. In Second Isaiah's oracles, the return to Judah from exile would be the Lord's "day of salvation," when the Lord would reestablish his covenant with the people.
4. But when they returned to Judah, the exiles found a ruined land and people who wanted to join them in a renewed community.
5. Tensions developed and the question arose: What had become of the Lord's promises?

F. Haggai's prophetic ministry addresses this question in the light of God's covenantal relationship with his people.
1. Haggai may have been one of the returnees or he may have lived in Judah all his life.
2. His prophecies reflect traditions that see the Temple as the essential link between the Lord and his people.
3. Haggai was confident that reconciliation with God could be precipitated by reconstruction of the Temple.
4. The people had put off rebuilding the Temple, but Haggai argued that rebuilding the Temple would bring prosperity.
5. Only a renewed Temple cult could ensure the Lord's presence and protect the people.
6. But Haggai also calls the people to forsake sin so that cultic worship can again be effective.
7. In this respect, Haggai is consistent with earlier prophets who said that the cult was effective only if it was supported by the people's obedience.
8. The community of returnees rebuilt the Temple in response to Haggai's prophetic message.

Essential Reading:

Joseph Blenkinsopp. *A History of Prophecy in Israel: From the Settlement in the Land to the Hellenistic Period*, pp. 153–224.

Ezekiel 1–7.

Henry Jackson Flanders, Jr., Robert Wilson Crapps, and David Anthony Smith. *People of the Covenant: An Introduction to the Hebrew Bible*, pp. 380–429.

Siegfried Hermann. *A History of Israel in Old Testament Times*, pp. 263–297.

Isaiah 40–54.

Jeremiah 1:1–4:4, 26, 36.

Supplementary Reading:

Klaus Koch. *The Prophets*, Vol. 2: *The Babylonian and Persian Periods*, pp. 80–151.

Questions to Consider:

1. What are the connections among sin, punishment, repentance, and renewal in religious ideas about the relationship between the human and the divine worlds? To what extent are those same connections in operation in human relationships?

2. Why did the idea of returning to Judah have such a powerful hold over the exiles in Babylon, even though many of them had never been there and their nation was no longer independent?

Lecture Twenty-Seven
Syria-Palestine—The Problem of Evil

Scope: Although polytheistic and henotheistic religions can blame evil on conflicts between gods, monotheistic religions must reconcile belief in an all-powerful and morally perfect God with the existence of evil. In the religious culture of post-exilic Judah, evils that befell the nation were usually understood as punishment for sin. But in other cases, the cause of suffering was more obscure. Apocalypticism maintained that the present world order is under the control of forces hostile to God and looked forward to the Lord's vindication of his people at the end of the age. A belief in an afterlife later arose out of belief in retributive justice for martyrs and their persecutors. Ecclesiastes puts aside retributive justice and presents all human endeavors as "vanity" in the face of death. The book of Job deals extensively with the problem of innocent suffering but ultimately advises acceptance of the Lord's inscrutable will.

Outline

I. The existence of evil is the primary theological problem for a monotheistic religion that posits a single all-powerful and morally perfect deity.

   A. Basic to all religious belief is the conviction that one will receive benefits from the sacred realm in keeping with one's behavior.

   1. Religious activity is a means of maintaining harmony between the human and the divine worlds, including exchange of benefits.

   2. Religious activity reflects the belief that worship and sacrifice will lead the gods to return blessings in equal measure.

   3. If certain forms of behavior are pleasing to the gods, they will accept those who please them and reject others.

   4. In wisdom literature, retributive justice decrees that those who do good will receive good from the gods, and those who do evil, evil.

   B. The existence of evil may be easily explained in polytheistic or henotheistic systems.

1. In polytheistic systems, the gods have competing interests just as humans do, and they often work at cross-purposes with each other.
2. In a henotheistic system, the god worshiped may be hampered by other gods who temporarily afflict his people.

C. A monotheistic religious culture must explain the problem of evil in terms of a single god who is both all-powerful and righteous.
1. The problem is: "If God is God, he is not good; if God is good, he is not God."
2. Either God's power or his righteousness is called into question by the existence of evil.
3. Explanation for the problem of evil is *theodicy*, from the Greek for "God is in the right."

D. As the religious culture of Judah developed an overt monotheism during and after the exile, the need for theodicy arose.
1. Second Isaiah explained the fall of Jerusalem and the exile as punishment for Judah's sins.
2. The same idea was expressed by the historian who wrote Samuel and Kings, who attributes the downfall of Israel and Judah to sin.
3. But after the exile and return to Judah, the fortunes of the community did not improve, despite several religious reforms.
4. Hopes for divine deliverance and independence from foreign dominion were continually frustrated.
5. This, along with the fact that the good were not always rewarded nor the evil punished, raised the problem of evil.
6. This problem led to two related phenomena in response: the hope for an end to history expressed in apocalypticism and the questioning attitude of skeptical wisdom.

II. Apocalypticism is the expectation that, at some point, God will intervene in human history and bring it to a halt to save his people.

A. Apocalypticism considers the current age to be dominated by forces that oppose the Lord and oppress his people.
1. The forces that oppress Israel are identified with cosmic evil that opposes God.
2. Those who obey the Lord suffer at the hands of the wicked but will receive their reward in the new age.

3. The principle of retributive justice remains, but its implementation is postponed until the end of the age.

B. Apocalypticism is, in many ways, a natural outcome of Israelite religious ideas.

    1. The people of Israel understood their history as a history lived out in relationship to the Lord.

    2. The prophets tended to depict historical events as visible manifestations of the Lord's work.

    3. As expectations for the restoration of Israel were continually frustrated, the hope for vindication was recast in supernatural terms.

    4. Israel's tradition about the day of the Lord's vengeance was now understood as the Lord's direct intervention into history to make Israel the center of the world.

    5. Zechariah 14 depicts a final battle when the Lord intervenes and establishes Jerusalem as the place where all the nations will worship the Lord.

C. Apocalypticism is expressed in the presentation of historical events in mythic terms as steps in a progress toward the end.

    1. Apocalyptic literature typically presents a vision experienced by a revered figure of the past.

    2. The vision reviews recent history in symbolic terms as a vision experienced by the person of the past as his or her "future."

    3. Apocalyptic literature is typically concerned primarily with the events leading up to the Lord's victory over the forces of evil.

D. A later form of theodicy related to apocalypticism is belief in a life after death.

    1. This belief arose in response to a king of Syria who outlawed Judaism and killed those who refused to submit.

    2. Martyrdom raised the problem of how God would reward those who suffered and died for their faithfulness.

    3. Belief in retributive justice led some to postulate that divine recompense could come after death for the very good and the very evil.

    4. Life after death necessitated resurrection, because the Jews believed that the self did not exist apart from the body.

    5. The idea of resurrection and life after death received only limited acceptance in later Judaism.

III. The problem of evil was also addressed by the literature typical of *skeptical wisdom.*

    A. In the Hebrew Bible, traditional wisdom is represented primarily by the Book of Proverbs.
        1. Traditional wisdom is comparable to most of the wisdom works from Egypt.
        2. Traditional wisdom reflects practical common sense and belief in the principle of retributive justice.

    B. Skeptical wisdom, by contrast, questions the entire human enterprise of attempting to discern the Lord's intentions.
        1. Skeptical wisdom shares the prophetic perspective that the Lord is beyond human knowledge and known only by what he chooses to reveal.
        2. In Ecclesiastes, the questioning of retributive justice is part of a pessimistic view of human existence in the face of inevitable death.
        3. The refrain "All is vanity!" reflects the conviction that death makes human striving meaningless.
        4. Ecclesiastes argues that the best thing one can do is enjoy what life offers while it lasts.

    C. The problem of evil receives its most thorough examination in the Book of Job, where it appears in the form of innocent suffering.
        1. The problem of evil was usually posed in terms of the prosperity of the wicked.
        2. In Job, a rich and thoroughly righteous man is subjected to a series of misfortunes.
        3. Three friends argue with Job that his sufferings prove he must be guilty of some sin.
        4. Job asserts his innocence in reply and demands to know why he suffers.

    D. The audience knows from the outset why Job suffers: The Lord has made a wager with Satan.
        1. The wager is an attempt to test Job's fidelity to the Lord when he is not rewarded for it.
        2. The prologue to Job provides the audience with a heavenly view of Job's situation.

3. The audience possesses knowledge unavailable to Job and his friends, emphasizing human ignorance of divine actions.

E. Job's protestations of innocence alternate with his wish to confront God and his friends' arguments that he must be guilty of sin.
1. Job argues that he is innocent and, thus, should not suffer, while his friends argue that he is suffering and, thus, must be guilty of sin.
2. Both parties subscribe to the simple equation that good behavior produces blessing while wickedness produces punishment.
3. Both parties also believe that the reasons for God's actions are transparent to human observers.

F. God's reply makes Job aware that he is in no position to understand or judge God's actions.
1. Instead of answering Job, God points to all the marvels of creation whose full purpose only God understands.
2. God asks Job a series of rhetorical questions that demonstrate that God—not Job—is the source of all knowledge and power.
3. In response, Job keeps silence and "repents" for presuming to judge his creator.
4. God commends Job and rebukes his friends, who did not speak justly of God as Job did.

G. The epilogue of the book returns to the storytelling atmosphere of the prologue.
1. God fully restores Job's health and fortunes, thereby "making good" his suffering.
2. This conclusion satisfies the ancient idea that one's last state in life determined one's happiness.
3. The restoration of Job's fortunes does not violate the point of the book, because God's motivations remain mysterious.
4. The answer to the problem of evil is left to God and remains utterly unfathomable to human reasoning.

Essential Reading:

Ecclesiastes.

Henry Jackson Flanders, Jr., Robert Wilson Crapps, and David Anthony Smith. *People of the Covenant: An Introduction to the Hebrew Bible*, pp. 479–492, 499–505.

Job 1–7, 32–42.

Supplementary Reading:

Glenn Holland. *Divine Irony*, pp. 59–81.

Sarah Iles Johnston, ed. *Religions of the Ancient World: A Guide*, pp. 59–70.

James C. Livingston. *Anatomy of the Sacred*, pp. 247–272.

Questions to Consider:

1. Is religion inevitably based on the belief that worshipers will receive a divine reward in some form for their beliefs and actions?

2. Apocalypticism presents the state of the world as hostile to God and his people; how may this view be reconciled with the fundamental conviction that God created the world, declared it good, and continues to rule over it?

Lecture Twenty-Eight
Early Aegean Civilizations

Scope: Settlement in the Greek islands began in the Neolithic era, with Minoan civilization on Crete reaching its height in the early 15th century B.C.E. Despite extensive ruins and intriguing artifacts, its religious culture is almost impossible to reconstruct. Mycenaean civilization arose during the Bronze Age on the Greek mainland, as incursions of Indo-Aryans settled in geographically distinct areas of the Achaean peninsula. Mycenaean civilization is the historical setting for the events of the *Iliad* and *Odyssey*. It is characterized by shaft tombs, fortified building complexes, and a wealth of goods reflecting vigorous trade with the Near East. The civilization declined rapidly around 1200 B.C.E., as much of the eastern Mediterranean sank into a dark age. The religious culture of the Mycenaean era can be generally described but should be distinguished from the culture reflected in later epic poetry.

Outline

I. The earliest civilization around the Aegean Sea appeared in Crete during the Bronze Age.

   A. The Aegean Sea was easily accessible by ship from the major centers of civilization in the ancient Near East.
      1. The earliest archaeological findings in the Aegean date from the late Neolithic era and include female figurines like those found in the Near East or northern Europe.
      2. Among these female figurines are flat, abstract representations from the Cycladic islands.
      3. The many female figurines suggest some form of goddess worship in connection with the fertility of the earth.

   B. During the Bronze Age, Crete was home to the Minoan civilization centered in Knossos.
      1. The Minoans came to Crete about 7000 B.C.E., living in small farming settlements.
      2. From about 3500 B.C.E., there was a rapid increase in population, leading to larger settlements and new forms of craftsmanship and maritime trading.

©2005 The Teaching Company.

3. From about 2000 B.C.E., Minoans began to construct elaborate building complexes, now often called *palaces*.
4. The building complexes are unfortified, indicating that Minoans had little fear of war or invasion.
5. Apart from the public building complexes in the major cities, there were villages and a system of roads protected by guard posts.
6. Minoan civilization reached its height during the first half of the 15th century B.C.E.
7. Many of the island's cities were destroyed by fire around 1470 B.C.E., suggesting an earthquake or the work of invaders.

C. It is very difficult to reconstruct the religious culture of later Minoan civilization with any certainty.
1. The Minoans' written language, Linear A, has not yet been deciphered.
2. A later written language, Linear B, was used primarily for records and inventories.
3. We know almost nothing directly about later Minoan religious belief and practices.

D. A variety of clues point to what might be examples of Minoan religious belief and activity.
1. Building decorations of birds, double-headed axes, and bull horns are often interpreted as religious symbols.
2. A figurine of a bare-breasted woman holding two snakes is usually interpreted as a priestess or fertility goddess.
3. A mural depicting a figure somersaulting over the back of a bull is often said to represent a religious ritual.
4. The bull-leaping scene, bull horns, and the mythological figure of the Minotaur are taken as evidence for a sacred bull in Minoan religion.
5. Minoan religious culture appears to have been concerned primarily with fertility.
6. Most of what is taken as evidence for religious activity, however, is also open to secular interpretation.

II. Mycenaean civilization on the Greek mainland during the Bronze Age combined Indo-Aryan groups into a single culture.

A. The name of the civilization comes from Mycenae, a site excavated by Heinrich Schliemann in the 1870s.

1. Schliemann devoted his life to uncovering the archaeological sites he believed lay behind the stories of the Trojan War.
2. Schliemann unfortunately tended to inflate the significance of his discoveries.
3. Our knowledge of Mycenaean civilization depends on his discoveries, but we must separate archaeological evidence from legendary accounts.

B. Indo-Aryan invaders settled on the Achaean peninsula before the second millennium B.C.E.
1. The mountains, valleys, and plains of Achaea tended to divide its inhabitants into distinctive autonomous communities.
2. The new settlers tended to establish fortified palaces on hilltops overlooking valleys near the coastlines.
3. Most scholars assume that the Indo-Aryans intermingled with or dominated and eliminated earlier inhabitants.
4. Stories about relationships among the gods may symbolically represent relationships among each god's worshipers.
5. Mycenaean writings in Linear B include some mention of divine names from later Greek mythology.

C. Many of the most important early discoveries from early Greek culture were tombs.
1. *Shaft tombs* cut into the rock seem to be characteristic of the Mycenaean era.
2. One such tomb dating from about 1700 B.C.E. contained 19 bodies and a wealth of precious artifacts.
3. The artifacts were made of precious materials that indicate an active trade with the Near East.
4. The tombs show that Mycenaean culture was highly stratified, with a wealthy and powerful elite.
5. From 1500 B.C.E., burials are found in *beehive tombs*: round, domed, underground burial chambers.
6. The burial chambers were reached through a long tunnel with a massive lintel and doorway at the entrance.

D. Mycenaean cities from 1400–1200 B.C.E. were dominated by fortified public *palaces*.
1. These building complexes served as refuge in war and for a variety of public functions during times of peace.

2. The building complex included storehouses, pantries, workshops, living quarters, and public rooms.
3. Fortifications made of boulders or blocks of stone are called *Cyclopean.*
4. These fortifications and other evidence testify to a warrior culture resembling medieval Europe.

E. The Mycenaean era ended in a dark age that affected all the civilizations of the eastern Mediterranean about 1200 B.C.E.
   1. What led to widespread destruction of cities and the collapse of empires is unknown.
   2. The marauding Sea Peoples harried the Mediterranean basin in search of land and plunder.
   3. Economic collapse and the fragmentation of established power added to the upheaval.
   4. Even nations that remained stable experienced upheavals that affected their subsequent history for centuries.

III. Mycenaean religious culture poses the same problems as Minoan religious culture on Crete.

A. Divine names familiar from later Greek religion appear in Linear B inscriptions, implying some continuity.
   1. As disparate regions came to form a single Greek culture, their gods, too, became associated in a process of syncretism.
   2. The gods of the different Greek peoples were identified with each other or associated by family or marriage.
   3. Syncretism brought new influences to bear on the entire religious culture.

B. Zeus was originally an Indo-Aryan god of the invading northerners, Dyaus Pitar.
   1. Zeus was a god of the sky and weather associated with different mountains.
   2. Zeus's primary identification was as sky-father, but he served a range of functions indicated by his many surnames.
   3. Zeus had many divine and human female lovers, but his consort and queen was Hera.
   4. Hera may have been a goddess of earlier Achaeans, because her relationship with Zeus was often difficult.

C. At this point, we may make a few statements about the religious culture of the Mycenaean era.

1. Careful and elaborate burial of the dead posits a belief in an afterlife similar to the present life.
2. Gods of the Mycenaean era are generally the gods of later Greece, although their attributes and place in the divine hierarchy may have differed.
3. Worship of the gods involved ritual sacrifice, either in the cities or the countryside, preferably on mountains or in grottoes.
4. The gods, as well as human beings, were already the subjects of a lively mythology.

Essential Reading:

Robin W. Winks and Susan P. Mattern-Parkes. *The Ancient Mediterranean World: From the Stone Age to A.D. 600*, pp. 36–44.

Supplementary Reading:

Walter Burkert. *Greek Religion*, pp. 10–46.

Sarah Iles Johnston, ed. *Religions of the Ancient World: A Guide*, pp. 206–209.

Questions to Consider:

1. Minoan and Mycenaean religious culture, like prehistoric religious culture, must be reconstructed on the basis of artifacts without the assistance of written texts. Which problems in reconstructing these religious cultures are similar? Which are different? Why?
2. What problems are presented when reconstructing a religious culture, as Schliemann did, in light of legendary accounts of its history? Should the primary business of archaeology be the accumulation or the interpretation of data? Why?

Lecture Twenty-Nine
Religious Culture in the *Iliad* and the *Odyssey*

Scope: The Dark Age (c. 1200–800 B.C.E.) saw a drastic decrease in the scale and quality of life in Greece. Writing disappeared, and memories of the Mycenaean era were preserved in oral stories of gods and heroes. Poets told stories afresh with each performance, using stereotyped phrases and images. Homer's *Iliad* and *Odyssey* reflect the religious culture of both the Mycenaean era and the Dark Age. The *Iliad* tells the story of Achilles's refusal to fight during the last year of the Trojan War because of a dispute with Agamemnon. The poem depicts both gods and human beings at war, under the shadow of Troy's fated destruction. The *Odyssey* tells the story of Odysseus's long journey homeward from Troy and his adventures with goddesses, men, and monsters. Both poems depict the gods as humanity's divine overlords, but they betray a preference for human beings, their bravery, and the comforts of home.

Outline

I. The epic poems of the *Iliad* and *Odyssey* were apparently first composed during the Dark Age.

   A. The Dark Age in Greece (c. 1200–800 B.C.E.) saw a drastic decrease in population and settlements.

   1. Archaeological sites for the Dark Age are scattered and few in number.

   2. Settlements appear to have been isolated from each other and from the rest of the world.

   3. Burials indicate that settlements were small, with structures built of timber and mud brick.

   4. The exception is a burial site at Lefkandi on Euboea, where the remains of a couple were buried with horses and luxury goods.

   5. The general impression of this period is of a very small population scraping out an existence.

      6. Little is known of religious practice at this time, but presumably, many practices of the Mycenaean age continued on a reduced scale.

  B. Written language apparently disappeared, and stories of gods and heroes were passed on by oral storytelling.

      1. The Greeks of the Dark Age considered the Mycenaeans god-like heroes of a better time.

      2. Poets would compose a story afresh each time it was told; thus, each performance of the story was unique.

      3. The most notable products of the poets of the Dark Age are the *Iliad* and *Odyssey*, traditionally attributed to the blind poet Homer.

  C. Homer's *Iliad* and *Odyssey* reflect the religious culture of both the Mycenaean era and the Dark Age.

      1. We cannot simply equate the religious beliefs reflected in the epics with those of the Mycenaean era.

      2. At the same time, scholars assert that parts of the epics reflect early religious beliefs not typical of the time the epics were composed.

      3. We will put this problem aside in favor of considering the nature of the religious culture reflected by the poems as they stand.

II. The *Iliad* depicts a divine world very much like the world of its heroes.

  A. The *Iliad* is set in the 10th year of the war of the Achaeans against Troy.

      1. The *Iliad* is about the anger of Achilles, who withdraws from combat over a dispute with Agamemnon.

      2. Without Achilles, the Achaeans find the war turning against them.

      3. The Trojan prince Hector kills Achilles's comrade Patroclus, prompting Achilles to take revenge against Hector.

      4. The poem ends when Prium, king of Troy, asks Achilles for his son's body, and Achilles returns it.

  B. In the *Iliad*, gods and heroes interact as equal members of a society where a few stand out as leaders.

      1. The gods pursue their own interests in helping one side or the other and often rebel against or try to evade the power of Zeus.

     2. At the same time, the gods recognize that they are under the authority not only of Zeus but also of fate.

     3. The heroes also have their arguments and often must be appeased by offerings, just like the gods.

     4. The heroes seem to regard the gods as supernatural chieftains who are to be served faithfully and obeyed.

C. The goal of the hero's life in the *Iliad* is to gain eternal renown by his feats of valor.

     1. We have already encountered the idea that the best thing for humanity is to enjoy life while it lasts.

     2. But the heroes of the *Iliad* seek to make the most of life by gaining the glory due a mighty warrior.

     3. Homer lists the names and genealogies of the warriors who fall in battle, providing the glory they desire but also reminding his audience of the human cost of war.

     4. Eternal renown is the only reward these warriors seek from the gods; when they die, their souls go "wailing down to Hades."

D. The *Iliad* often shows the gods wielding a direct supernatural influence over human beings.

     1. The Greeks attributed any sort of uncharacteristic behavior to madness, the influence of a god that prevents clear thinking.

     2. The Greeks thought of a person's character as the product of rational thought, because a person always acted according to what he or she believed to be good.

     3. This meant that irrational behavior had to originate outside of a person's character, in other words, with the influence of the gods.

     4. We still talk about love in much the same way, as something that overcomes us from outside.

     5. The *Iliad* portrays a humanity that is under the gods' control yet presents its heroes as fully in charge of their own lives.

III. The *Odyssey* shows different aspects of religious culture in the Mycenaean era and Dark Age than does the *Iliad*.

A. The *Odyssey* is the story of Odysseus and his long journey homeward after the Trojan War.

     1. Odysseus sets out with a fleet of ships, but through a series of adventures, he ends up alone.

2. Odysseus incurs the wrath of Poseidon after blinding the Cyclops, but through constant vigilance, Odysseus eventually escapes all dangers.

3. Odysseus is seduced by a sorceress and a nymph, in turn, but ultimately chooses to return to Ithaca and his wife, Penelope.

4. Once in Ithaca, he finds his home filled with Penelope's suitors and must use his wits and strength to regain his place at home.

B. As in the *Iliad*, the *Odyssey* presents the gods as humanity's divine overlords.

1. Poseidon takes revenge against Odysseus, although he knows that Odysseus is destined to return home.

2. Apollo destroys Odysseus's crew after they slaughter the cattle of the Sun.

3. Athena admires Odysseus's craftiness and assists him, sometimes in opposition to Poseidon.

4. When the nymph Calypso keeps Odysseus on her island for seven years, Zeus orders her to let him go.

5. Despite help or hindrance from the gods, it is Odysseus's resourcefulness and guile that finally bring him home.

C. At one point, Odysseus travels into the underworld to consult with the shade of the prophet Tiresias.

1. The portrait of Hades in the *Odyssey* has influenced subsequent portrayals of the underworld.

2. The poet presents Hades as a dark, joyless place full of mourning, insubstantial spirits.

3. Odysseus sacrifices a goat, and spirits who drink its blood revive sufficiently to speak to him.

4. The shade of Tiresias provides a prophecy, but Odysseus allows other shades to drink and tell their fate.

5. The shade of Achilles notably gains no satisfaction in Hades from the renown he earned in life.

D. Odysseus journeys through a world of wonders in frequent contact with the sacred.

1. All the supernatural beings he encounters prove a hindrance to Odysseus and delay him on his journey.

2. By contrast, human beings are mostly helpful to him, although at home, he faces human foes.

3. Calypso offers Odysseus immortality and everlasting youth, but he chooses to return home instead.
4. Odysseus rejects both the fate of the gods and the fate of the hero, preferring his home and his family.
5. The *Odyssey* finds the value of human life in peace and the pleasures of marriage and raising children.

E. Homer's work played a central role in the religious and literary culture of later Greek civilization.
1. Homer's poems became the primary literature of all educated Greeks.
2. The *Iliad* and *Odyssey* shaped vocabulary and style of Greek rhetoric.
3. Homer's poems also conveyed theological ideas central to later Greek religious culture.
4. Through Homer's poetry, Mycenaean heroes continued to stimulate the imagination of Greek culture.

Essential Reading:

Homer. *The Iliad*, books 1–6, 22–24.

———. *The Odyssey*.

Supplementary Reading:

Walter Burkert. *Greek Religion*, pp. 47–53.

Questions to Consider:

1. What are some consequences of the *Iliad*'s concentration on particular human actors at one point in the Trojan War, in contrast to a story about the entire conflict?

2. Odysseus's courage, guile, and physical appearance make him attractive to both human and divine women, and he has prolonged sexual affairs with two of them. How does this play into the main thrust of the epic, which is about the longing for home and marital fidelity?

Lecture Thirty
Religious Culture in Archaic Greece

Scope: The Archaic Age in Greece (800–480 B.C.E.) saw an increase in population, the renewal of international trade, and the development of the city-state as the primary political entity in the Greek territories. The city-state was governed by a council of its citizens who also served it as soldiers. Although each city-state had its distinctive religious character, certain beliefs and practices united them in a common religious culture. The Greeks shared a pantheon of gods and interacted with them through prayer, dance, music, processions, festivals, and sacrifice. Gods were worshiped in their own sanctuaries, but some sanctuaries attracted worshipers from all over Greece. Similarly, all the Greek territories participated in the athletic contests of the Pan-Hellenic Games every four years. Two poetic works, *The Homeric Hymns* and Hesiod's *Theogony*, grant us insight into some of the prevailing beliefs and attitudes toward the gods in the Archaic Age.

Outline

I. Greece began to emerge from the Dark Age in the 8th century B.C.E., when its population increased and a new culture developed.

    A. The Archaic Age, the period from about 800 to 480 B.C.E., saw the renewal of international trade.

        1. Archaeological remains from about 900 B.C.E. include artifacts apparently obtained in trade with other nations, notably Phoenicia.

        2. Foreign influences include Egyptian elements in temple design and adoption of the Phoenician alphabet.

        3. Population growth led to Greek colonies around the Mediterranean basin.

        4. Growth and international contact led to a greater awareness of Greek identity.

    B. A fundamental component of Greek society from the Archaic Age was the regional city-state (*polis*) ruled by a council of citizens.

1. Citizenship was based on military service as a *hoplite*, an armored infantry soldier armed with a spear, a short sword, and a round shield (*hoplon*).
2. Landowning farmers who could afford to serve as *hoplites* shared the right to govern the *polis* in council.
3. The *polis* represents an essential equality among citizens, in contrast to those denied citizenship.
4. The *polis* included buildings set aside for governance, public facilities, a marketplace, temples, and the surrounding farmlands.
5. The population of a *polis* ranged from several hundred to a few thousand.
6. There was substantial regional variation among the city-states in governance, public and private activities, and attitudes about life.
7. Each *polis* worshiped particular gods and had its own religious celebrations and festival calendar.

II. Despite this variety, certain religious presuppositions, beliefs, and actions united Archaic Greece in a common polytheistic religious culture.

   A. Greek religious culture of the Archaic Age reflected the sense that the sacred and the secular were intertwined.
      1. Because the natural world was alive with the presence of the sacred, every aspect of life had its religious component.
      2. Religious activities were undertaken to maintain social harmony and equilibrium between the human and divine worlds.
      3. All religious activity was public and communal and carried out according to inherited traditions.

   B. The Greeks of the Archaic Age interacted with the divine world through specific ritual actions.
      1. Prayers spoken aloud consisted of calling on the god, asserting a claim on the god's good will, and making a request.
      2. Both music and dance were a means of honoring the god and accompanied other forms of interaction with the divine.
      3. Processions were a proclamation of divine and human honor with ramifications for the community.

      4. The most important ritual action was animal sacrifice, either to accompany a request or as thanks for a benefit received.

C. The focus of ritual worship was the god's sanctuary, the sacred space devoted to worship of the god.
      1. The altar was a necessary part of the sanctuary, the site where animal sacrifices could be offered.
      2. The altar was separate from the temple, the dwelling for the god's statue and storage space to display votive offerings.
      3. The god's sanctuary might also include a sacred grove, dormitories for pilgrims, and dining rooms for private clubs.
      4. The location of a sanctuary varied according to the god's realm of concern.

D. Although most sanctuaries were located in the *polis*, some sanctuaries were located in places sacred to the god.
      1. The sanctuary of the goddess Demeter at Eleusis attracted worshipers from all over the Greek world.
      2. Oracles were usually associated with a specific location, such as the oracle of Apollo at Delphi.
      3. The Pan-Hellenic Games united all Greeks in a common religious observance every four years in Olympia beginning in 776 B.C.E.
      4. Time was calculated by *Olympiads* of four-year periods, instead of by the reigns of rulers.

E. Because Greece had no religious establishment, religious traditions were communicated by action and by word.
      1. Children learned how to perform rituals by watching them performed by others.
      2. Traditions about the gods were passed on through oral storytelling, either among individuals or by a poet to a group.
      3. Mythic stories taught moral lessons, explained how the world worked, provided a common identity, and revealed the character of the gods.

F. Many mythic stories reflect a growing unease about the gods during the Archaic Age and a deepened sense of human insecurity.
      1. The famous pronouncement of the Delphic oracle, "Know yourself," was a reminder to know where you fit in to the cosmic order.

2. The gods were believed to be jealous of their divine prerogatives, and they would lash out at human beings who presumed to rise above their station.
3. Divine jealousy, or *nemesis*, was provoked by human success that led to complacency, then to *hubris*, impudent pride.
4. Every human triumph potentially aroused a sense of guilt and raised the possibility of divine punishment.

III. Two works of the Archaic Age give a sense of the religious sentiments of the era and the attempt to create a consistent mythology.

   A. The two works are a series of songs known collectively as *The Homeric Hymns* and Hesiod's *Theogony*.
      1. Both works share the poetic meter employed in Homer's epics, the hexameter, with six metrical units to a line.
      2. Each metrical unit consists of a long syllable and two short ones (a *dactyl*) or two long syllables (a *spondee*).
      3. This meter, *dactylic hexameter*, was used in most long poetic works by the Greeks and Romans.

   B. *The Homeric Hymns*, from the 7th and 6th centuries B.C.E., provide a sense of the gods and the sentiments toward them.
      1. Some hymns are poetic renditions of well-known myths.
      2. Other hymns list titles and attributes of the gods and the rites and locations sacred to them.
      3. Other hymns are primarily songs of praise, similar to the biblical psalms.
      4. The hymns vary widely in length and are generally agreed to be the work of many poets.
      5. *The Homeric Hymns* represent the poets' attempts to offer new renditions of familiar stories, to honor the gods, and to gain renown.

   C. Hesiod's *Theogony* is a poem about the gods' origins that also attempts to systematize the relationships among them.
      1. The *Theogony*, from about 740 B.C.E., is the work of a poet from Boetia usually identified as Hesiod.
      2. Hesiod's poem bears a resemblance to Mesopotamian and Egyptian theogonies.
      3. Hesiod's account tells how Zeus came to be king of the gods and guardian of the cosmic order.

4. His story is full of violence, with acts of incest, castration, patricide, and usurpation.
5. Each generation rebels against the one before it, only to have the next generation rebel against it in turn.
6. Ultimately, Zeus kills his father, Kronos, and marries Hera, who rules with Zeus as his queen.
7. Hesiod then catalogues the gods and demigods, providing a pocket portrait of each.

D. *The Homeric Hymns* and the *Theogony* reflect the elaborate mythology and imagery associated with the Greek pantheon in the Archaic Age.
1. Both works bears witness to the multitude of gods and divine beings representing the realm of the sacred.
2. *The Homeric Hymns* give a sense of pious regard for the gods and the voice of those who worshiped them.
3. Hesiod's *Theogony* represents an attempt to bring order to the mythic tradition to create a unified and systematic account of the gods' genealogy.

Essential Reading:

Jules Cashford, trans. *The Homeric Hymns.*

Hesiod and Theognis. *Hesiod: Theogony, Works and Days*; *Theognis: Elegies*, pp. 11–57.

Robin W. Winks and Susan P. Mattern-Parkes. *The Ancient Mediterranean World: From the Stone Age to A.D. 600*, pp. 58–74.

Supplementary Reading:

E. R. Dodds. *The Greeks and the Irrational*, pp. 1–63.

Sarah Iles Johnston, ed. *Religions of the Ancient World: A Guide*, pp. 210–219.

H. D. F. Kitto. *The Greeks*, pp. 64–79.

Questions to Consider:

1. Why was the institution of the city-state central to Greek identity and the later development of ancient Greek culture?

2. What are some of the consequences of the belief that human achievements are likely to lead to divine jealousy? In what ways are similar ideas expressed in our own time?

Lecture Thirty-One
Greece—How Things Came to Be

Scope: The Greek story of creation as it is presented in Hesiod's *Theogony* resembles creation stories from Egypt and Mesopotamia. Creation begins when Chaos spontaneously gives rise to divine beings that, in turn, create new beings through sexual generation. Earth and Heaven give birth to the Titans, the Cyclopes, and a race of monsters. One Titan, Kronos, castrates Heaven and becomes king, only to be deposed in turn by his son Zeus. Zeus establishes the cosmic order but has an ambivalent attitude toward humanity, punishing men by creating the race of women. The Greek story of the flood as it appears in a Roman version in Ovid's *Metamorphoses* has many points of contact with the Mesopotamian stories of Atrahasis and Ut-napishtim, as well as the biblical story of Noah. Points of similarity and difference in the Greek creation and flood stories provide insight into Greek religious culture.

Outline

I. The story of creation as it appears in Hesiod's *Theogony* resembles creation stories from Egypt and Mesopotamia.

   A. The poem begins with an invocation of the Muses, giving Hesiod's account a flavor of divine revelation.

   1. The story begins with Chaos, not associated here with the waters of the sea, as it was in Egypt and Mesopotamia.

   2. Gaea, Earth, appears, then Tartaros, the Depths, appears *in* the earth, the foundation for all creation.

   3. The third created being is Eros, Love, whose existence is essential to creation by sexual generation.

   4. The last cosmic elements to appear are Nyx, Night, and Erebus, Darkness, who give birth to Day and Space.

   B. Gaea gives birth to offspring that constitute the natural and divine context for human existence.

   1. Gaea bears Ouranos, Heaven; Earth and Heaven are the boundaries of the divine realm.

2. Gaea produces mountains and seas, the first pleasant, the other "barren."
3. Finally, Gaea mates with her son Ouranos and gives birth to 12 children, the Titans.
4. Gaea and Ouranos next engender the race of Cyclopes, then three monstrous sons whom Ouranos imprisons in the earth's depths.
5. Gaea incites her Titan son Kronos to punish Ouranos for this wicked deed.
6. Kronos castrates Ouranos and throws his genitals across the earth, engendering the Furies, the Giants, and Aphrodite.
7. Night produces offspring, states of mind that oppress human beings or cosmic forces that work against them.

C. The story continues with Kronos, now king of creation, and his sister Rhea, who bears him 12 children.
1. Kronos eats each child at its birth because of a prophecy that one of his children would usurp his throne.
2. Rhea hides her 12th child, Zeus, and instead, gives Kronos a stone that he devours.
3. Grown to adulthood, Zeus overcomes Kronos, releases his siblings, and becomes ruler over the gods.

D. The rest of the poem lists divinities, their partners, and offspring, with some attention to "how things got to be how they are now."
1. The Titan Prometheus brings fire to humanity and tricks Zeus into choosing the worse portion of the sacrifice for the gods.
2. Zeus punishes Prometheus by chaining him to a rock until the Titan is freed by Heracles.
3. To punish human men, Zeus sends them Pandora, the first woman, who brings a box full of ills for humanity.

E. The question arises: What religious ideas are at work in this explanation of "how things came to be the way they are now"?
1. The gods who are involved in the lives of human beings are several generations removed from creation.
2. The gods that now rule are a part of the cosmic order and, thus, subject to forces they cannot control.
3. Since creation, parents are not necessarily the same sort of beings as their offspring.

4. The gods can be ambivalent or even hostile to their own offspring or the offspring of other gods.

5. There is a pattern of hostility between generations, with each new generation rebelling against the previous one.

II. The gods' hostility toward humanity reaches a climax with the Greek version of the story of the flood.

A. Book I of Ovid's *Metamorphoses*, a 1st-century C.E. Latin retelling of Roman mythology, provides the Greek story, using the gods' Latin names.

1. Ovid places the story in the context of the succession of world ages that steadily decline from the Golden Age to the Iron Age.

2. Iron Age humanity is characterized by brutishness; thus, the gods decide to destroy humanity.

B. The gods gather in council to decide how to cleanse the earth of the crimes of human beings.

1. Jupiter (or Jove, the Roman equivalent of Zeus) has traveled the earth in disguise and been an eyewitness to the depravity of humanity.

2. Jupiter argues that the crimes of humanity deserve punishment and threaten the stability of the cosmos.

3. The gods wonder what will happen without human beings to bring them offerings, but Jupiter assures them that he will provide a new race of humanity.

4. Jupiter decides to send a flood to inundate the world and drown all human beings.

C. There are points of contact with the flood stories of Atrahasis and Ut-napishtim in Mesopotamia and Noah in Israel.

1. Like the story of Atrahasis, the story of the flood in *Metamorphoses* is part of the longer story of the creation of humanity.

2. As with the Mesopotamian stories, the gods gather in council and give assent to the chief god's plan.

3. As in the story of Noah, humanity is destined for destruction because of depravity, but a renewed human race is planned.

4. Ovid's version is notable for the gods' reluctance to destroy humanity and the careful deliberations among them.

D. The flood is sent without any regard for the preservation of humanity beforehand.

    1. No human being is singled out before the flood to prepare a means of survival or to save other life.

    2. There is no preparation of a boat, no gathering of animals in couples, no saving of possessions or lies to the neighbors.

    3. Jupiter sends rain, while Neptune (Poseidon) creates an earthquake to send a torrent to sweep humanity away.

    4. Ovid dwells on the effects of the flood and the resulting famine on humanity and animals.

    5. One human couple, Deucalion and Pyrrha, survive by chance when their boat runs aground on Mt. Parnassus.

    6. Like Noah, the couple is unmatched in righteousness.

    7. Deucalion and Pyrrha make landfall in the midst of the flood, which only later subsides at Jupiter's command.

    8. As in the other flood stories, the survivors' first impulse after making landfall is to offer a sacrifice to the gods.

E. As in the other stories, after the survivors sacrifice, they gain the attention of the god.

    1. In the other flood stories, the gods are pleased by the sacrifice.

    2. Here, Jupiter discovers that Deucalion and Pyrrha have survived and knows they are righteous.

    3. When Jupiter commands the flood waters to recede, they reveal a desolated earth.

F. Ovid's story ends in the establishment of a new relationship between the gods and humanity and repopulation of the earth.

    1. Deucalion and Pyrrha consult the oracle of Delphi, who cryptically tells them to throw "the bones of your great mother" (that is, stones) behind them.

    2. When they do so, the stones slowly turn into human beings.

    3. As a result, the human race is now hearty and makes its living from working the soil.

    4. The animals are brought back into existence by spontaneous generation.

    5. Deucalion and Pyrrha are not the parents of the renewed humanity, as Noah and his wife are.

    6. As in the other stories, the flood institutes a new situation for humanity.

7. No mention is made of the fate of Deucalion and Pyrrha, who appear to return to their previous lives but in a new creation.

8. The various flood stories are clearly all related, but what is most significant are the differences between the stories and what they reveal about their different religious cultures.

Supplementary Reading:

W. K. C. Guthrie. *The Greeks and Their Gods*, pp. 27–112.

Hesiod and Theognis. *Hesiod: Theogony, Works and Days*; *Theognis: Elegies*, pp. 11–57.

Ovid. *Metamorphoses*, book I.

Questions to Consider:

1. The story of creation in Hesiod's *Theogony* is in part a story about incest and intergenerational violence. What ideas about the nature of creation and human existence do these stories seem to reflect?

2. What are the consequences of thinking about successive ages of human existence as representing a steady trend downward, rather than a trend upward?

Lecture Thirty-Two
Greece—The Goddess

Scope: Although goddesses in polytheistic religious cultures often have associations with fertility, most of them develop beyond this primary identity. This is the case in Greece, where goddesses represent a wide range of female activity. Athena, goddess of practical wisdom, is a patron of the arts of civilized society in manufacturing and household crafts. She is also the voice of wisdom in the war council. Demeter is the goddess of the cultivated earth and its crops. She appears primarily in the role of grieving mother in the myth of Persephone and Hades, a story that explains the cycle of the seasons. Aphrodite is the goddess of erotic love and the most beautiful of the goddesses. She is portrayed as an active and generous lover, although she may express her anger by inducing *lover's madness*. These three goddesses indicate the many different ways the Greeks thought about the feminine aspect of the divine.

Outline

I. Goddesses in polytheistic religious cultures often originate as fertility deities, but their significance extends beyond fertility.

    A. Isis is associated with the fertility of the Nile Valley in connection with Osiris, his death, and return to life.

        1. Isis is a loving wife to Osiris, a grieving widow at this death, and protectress of Horus, the divine Pharaoh.

        2. Isis gradually acquired other associations and power until she was a dominant goddess in her own right.

    B. We see a similar process at work in Mesopotamia with the goddess Inanna/Ishtar.

        1. Inanna's erotic connection with Dumuzi leads, in time, to her dominion over heaven and earth.

        2. Her sexuality leads to her association with natural disasters, the frenzy of battle, and divine retribution.

    C. In Greece, the character of the gods and goddesses developed over time, as one religious culture collided with another.

1. Some Greek goddesses have little connection with fertility, or those connections are muted.
2. Even goddesses with clear connections to fertility manifest those connections in diverging ways.

II. Athena, goddess of the virtues associated with Greek civilization, shows a markedly Aegean character.

   A. Athena seems to have originated in Minoan and Mycenaean culture as a goddess of fortresses.
      1. The goddess was earth-based and associated with fertility but also with birds and snakes.
      2. The goddess was associated with bluffs and the location of fortresses and, thus, also with fortresses and cities.
      3. The association with fortresses may explain Athena's identity as a warrior, or she may be related to an Indo-European warrior goddess.

   B. Athena was patron goddess of Athens and was associated with cities in general and with the civilized arts.
      1. Her role as protective deity of Athens probably stems from an association with the Acropolis.
      2. In mythology, Athena's patronage of the city was the result of a contest between her and Poseidon to give the most useful gift.
      3. Poseidon created a saltwater spring, while Athena created an olive tree.
      4. Athena's gift was deemed more useful, and olive oil became the economic staple for Athens.
      5. Athena was patroness of civilization and culture, administrative government, and the family.

   C. Athena is also the goddess of the practical wisdom that enables a person to get things done.
      1. She sprang from Zeus's head when Hephaestus struck it with a hammer to relieve the god's headache.
      2. Athena fosters the knowledge that makes civilized life possible, as both domestic and manufacturing arts.

   D. Athena is also a warrior goddess, depicted dressed in battle-gear with a spear and shield.
      1. Athena's interest is not in battle itself but in military skill, strategy, and tactics.

  2. She was associated with several Greek heroes whom she admired for their strength, skill, and cunning.

 E. Athena was a virgin goddess, one of only three immune to the power of Aphrodite.

  1. Athena's virginity allows her to maintain independence and an equal footing with men.

  2. Athena is proud of her beauty and vies with Aphrodite and Hera to be declared the most beautiful by Paris.

  3. Even so, Athena does not use her beauty to influence either gods or men.

III. Demeter was the goddess of the plowed earth, the goddess of grain, and the patroness of agriculture.

 A. Demeter was prominent as a mother but gained that status only reluctantly.

  1. She spurned Poseidon's advances and disguised herself as a mare.

  2. Poseidon then raped her in the form of a stallion, and she gave birth to twins.

  3. Demeter also spurned Zeus, who then had intercourse with her in the form of a bull.

  4. Their daughter Kore was Demeter's dearest child.

 B. Demeter's cultic importance arose from the myth about Hades's abduction of Kore.

  1. When Kore disappeared, a distraught Demeter sought her all over the earth.

  2. During her wanderings, the earth became barren and yielded no produce.

  3. For a time, Demeter served as a nurse in the household of King Celeus in Eleusis.

  4. Zeus sent Hermes to Hades to demand he return Kore, but Hades gave Kore pomegranate seeds to eat before restoring her to Demeter.

  5. As a result, Kore could return to her mother for only a part of each year.

 C. This story has affinities with other fertility myths in which a goddess mourns the loss of a loved one to the underworld.

1. Eleusis became the primary cultic site for the worship of Demeter and later became a center of a mystery religion devoted to her.
2. Most of the mystery religions had their origins in fertility rituals.

IV. The Greek goddess of erotic love was "Golden Aphrodite."

   A. Aphrodite was one of the most popular and widely worshiped Greek deities.
      1. Aphrodite was related to Near Eastern goddesses whose association with fertility has strong sexual overtones.
      2. Aphrodite also shares many attributes with the Indo-European goddess Dawn.
      3. Even with these similarities to other goddesses, Aphrodite remains unique in many respects.

   B. Aphrodite's association with fertility makes her the source of abundant life, inspiring growth of plants and animals.
      1. Aphrodite's connection with the cycle of the seasons appears in stories about the deaths of her lovers Anchises and Adonis.
      2. Aphrodite has an affinity for birds and for sweet flavors and fragrances that stimulate sexual desire.
      3. Aphrodite is associated with the rhythms that govern organic life and, thus, with cosmic cycles.
      4. Despite her chronic infidelity, Aphrodite was also a patroness of the welfare of the family.

   C. Chief among Aphrodite's divine attributes was her unparalleled beauty.
      1. Her beauty was part of her essence, and because it was divine beauty, it was literally stunning to behold.
      2. Aphrodite's essential beauty was unmistakable even when she was in disguise.
      3. In art, Aphrodite is typically depicted adorning herself, bathing, or dressing.
      4. After the 5th century B.C.E., Aphrodite was usually depicted nude in statuary.
      5. The goddess is called "Golden Aphrodite," perhaps because gold is bright, is beautiful, and retains its beauty forever.

   D. Aphrodite's beauty is the physical manifestation of her powerful sexuality.

1. Aphrodite's nature derives from her origins: She was born from the foam created when Kronos tossed his father's severed genitalia into the sea.
2. Aphrodite is "never-virgin," because she always appears as an enthusiastic participant in sexual acts.
3. Aphrodite actively seeks out and seduces her lovers and is generally benevolent toward them afterwards.
4. Sacred prostitution was practiced at some of her temples, where the women were courtesans skilled in the arts of seduction.
5. As a seductress, Aphrodite is also associated with rhetoric, the art of persuasion.
6. Aphrodite is responsible for the lover's madness that makes a person pursue the object of his or her desire at all costs.
7. Aphrodite uses lover's madness as punishment against those who have dishonored her by shunning love.

E. Aphrodite represents one aspect of what the Greeks considered to be the feminine aspects of the divine realm.
1. As Athena apparently represents woman as the mistress of practical wisdom and Demeter seems to represent woman as mother, so Aphrodite represents woman as lover.
2. These roles may represent more extensive theoretical possibilities for female activity than the Greeks are often given credit for imagining.

Essential Reading:

Jules Cashford, trans. *The Homeric Hymns*, pp. 5–26, 85–99, 108–113, 133–141.

Ovid. *Metamorphoses*, books V–VI, X.

Supplementary Reading:

Walter Burkert. *Greek Religion*, pp. 139–143, 152–156, 159–161.

The New Larousse Encyclopedia of Mythology, pp. 107–108, 130–132, 150–155.

Questions to Consider:

1. What do these different goddesses say, if anything, about the roles of women in ancient Greek society? How do we reconcile powerful goddesses with relatively powerless women in Greek society?

2. In many ways, Athena and Aphrodite seem to represent feminine opposites. Is this, in fact, the case, and if so, what does the contrast between them tell us about Greek ideas about women?

Lecture Thirty-Three
The Classical Era in Greece

Scope: The Classical era in ancient Greece (481-322 B.C.E.) fell between the Persian wars and the death of Alexander the Great, when the Greek city-states, especially Athens, achieved a political and cultural synthesis unparalleled in the ancient world. The radical democracy of Athens was based on the active participation of all its citizens. The Classical era brought a new spirit, often characterized as *humanism*, to architecture, statuary, tragedy, and philosophy. But the primary intention of these endeavors was to glorify the Athenian state and honor the gods who preserved its peace and prosperity. Individuals were important primarily as contributors to the common welfare of the *polis*. Art and architecture exhibited idealized proportions as a reflection of divine order, and tragedy depicted how violations of divine propriety were punished. Philosophy saw human reason as a part of divine nature and pursued the virtuous life based on knowledge of the good.

Outline

I. The Classical era is the period between the end of the Persian wars (481 B.C.E.) and the death of Alexander the Great (322 B.C.E.).

   A. The Persian Empire extended to western Asia Minor in the 540s B.C.E., including the Greek cities of Ionia.
      1. In 499 B.C.E., the Ionians revolted against Persia with some support from Athens, but they were defeated.
      2. In 490 B.C.E., an army of 22,000 Persians advanced toward Athens but was routed by an Athenian hoplite army of 11,000 at Marathon.
      3. Athens devoted a good amount of its revenues to building a naval fleet of oared triremes.
      4. In 480 B.C.E., Xerxes moved into Greece with a large army and naval fleet.
      5. A Greek army assembled to meet the Persians but was defeated at Thermopylae, where 300 Spartans remained to delay the Persians' pursuit of the Greek army.

6. With central Greece open to the Persians, the Athenians abandoned their city.
7. The Greek navy attacked the Persians at Salamis, a narrow strait near Athens, and defeated them.

B. After the Persian Wars, Athens became the dominant city-state in Greece and developed a unique political culture.
1. Around 400 B.C.E., Athens developed a radical democracy with full participation in government and debate for all citizens.
2. Most political offices were filled by lot, and a stipend was provided, allowing poorer citizens to hold office.
3. Most decisions were made by majority vote of the assembly of all citizens that met 40 times a year.
4. The body of citizens was now restricted to those free men whose parents were both Athenians.

II. Classical culture in Athens brought a particular approach to art and architecture, as well as theatre and philosophy.

A. This approach is often called *humanism*, because it is said to reflect the importance and integrity of the individual.
1. The importance of the human form in classical sculpture emphasizes the individual person.
2. The evolution of tragedy that focuses on the travails of the tragic hero brings a new importance to the individual.
3. Greek philosophy deals with the duties of human beings and the meaning of the ideals they profess: justice, piety, love.
4. These ideas are said to exemplify the new humanism of the Classical era.

B. In fact, the Athens of the Classical era focused not on the individual but on the *polis*, the city-state.
1. The political impulse behind the development of radical Athenian democracy was a sense of Athenian superiority.
2. Athenians believed that they had proven themselves superior to other Greeks and to non-Greeks by their strategy and bravery against the Persians.
3. The focus of virtue was the Athenian state, and an individual's worth was his worth as a servant of the state.
4. The individual who was most venerated was the one who had contributed the most to the common good of the *polis*.

C. Architecture was intended to present the glory of the Athenian *polis* through a building's beauty and proportion.

    1. The work of the gods was to impose order on the chaos that threatened to overwhelm creation.

    2. In Greece, the divine order of the cosmos was increasingly understood as a function of reason.

    3. Order was represented by the beauty of proportion, a function of mathematical reasoning, a form of divine science.

    4. The most common examples of classical architecture are the temples of the Acropolis, dedicated to glorifying the gods.

    5. As the cosmos was thought of as a well-ordered, rational design, the gods increasingly were thought of in terms of idealized rationality.

D. Statuary idealized the human form as a divine creation of beauty and proportion.

    1. Greek statuary had long taken stylized forms, such as the *kouros*, a young man, and the *kore*, a young woman.

    2. Stylized forms were retained even as sculptors created more naturalistic images of human beings in standardized poses.

    3. The emphasis on the individual human form was secondary to the idealization of the human form.

    4. The same idealized human forms were used to represent the gods as literal embodiments of divine order and design.

    5. There is less emphasis on the human form *per se* than on using the human form to say something about the gods.

III. Theatre in Greece had its origins and its contextual setting in the festival worship of Dionysus.

    A. Every spring saw the Dionysia, four days of performances of poetry, music, and dance in the god's honor.

        1. Choruses of 50 members, who both sang and danced, performed dithyrambs, lyric hymns in praise of Dionysus.

        2. Tragedies retained a smaller chorus augmented with individual actors who portrayed characters taken from mythology.

        3. Comedies presented actors and chorus in lighthearted and usually obscene stories that ended happily.

        4. The plays involved the interaction of human beings with one another and with the gods.

B. The tragedies of Aeschylus, Sophocles, and Euripides reflect on individual actions in the context of the *polis.*

    1. The leading characters are often members of ruling families whose actions have consequences for their cities.

    2. Aeschylus's *Oresteia* trilogy centers on murder, retribution, and purification to restore divine order to Argos.

    3. Sophocles's *Oedipus the King* tells how Oedipus discovers the truth about himself while trying to lift at plague from his city of Thebes.

    4. Euripides's *The Bacchae* tells the story of Pentheus, who rejects worship of Dionysus and is punished, while his family is exiled from Thebes.

    5. In most of these plays, the chorus represents a voice of traditional wisdom and piety.

    6. The resolution of many tragedies is less about the fate of the characters than the restoration of well-being to the *polis.*

    7. The well-being of the *polis* depends on divine favor, and the gods must be appeased at all costs.

IV. Classical Athens saw the emergence of a new religious idea, that human beings were a part of the world of the gods.

    A. Philosophers believed that a person's essence was reason and that each person's reason was a splinter of divine reason.

        1. Human reason was a splinter of divine reason and, thus, the common element uniting human and divine existence.

        2. The use of reason in philosophical contemplation could discern the intentions of the gods.

        3. The Greeks believed that right behavior was an inevitable result of right knowledge; thus, the philosopher was the most virtuous man.

        4. This meant that a person's way of life was the clearest indication of his or her knowledge of the good, the source of all virtue.

        5. Trust in the virtuous person was specifically trust in that person's knowledge of right and wrong.

        6. For most of the philosophers, the truest form of piety was the performance of right actions.

B. The height of classical culture in Athens was not based on human beings as individuals or as the proper focus of art, theatre, and philosophy.

    1. Instead, the emphasis was on the glory of the Athenian *polis*, the common welfare, and the glory of the gods.

    2. Divine glory and the glory of the *polis* were reflected in the beauty of buildings, crafts, and statuary and dramatic stories of violation and restoration.

    3. Philosophy was intended to discern the divine will through the use of the divine element in humanity, the reason.

Essential Reading:

Simon Price. *Religions of the Ancient Greeks*, pp. 1–88.

Robin W. Winks and Susan P. Mattern-Parkes. *The Ancient Mediterranean World: From the Stone Age to A.D. 600*, pp. 74–101.

Supplementary Reading:

E. R. Dodds. *The Greeks and the Irrational*, pp. 179–206.

H. D. F. Kitto. *The Greeks*, pp. 79–135.

Sophocles. *The Three Theban Plays: Oedipus the King*.

Questions to Consider:

1. We often look to classical Athens as the model for our own ideals of government. How did Athenian democracy in the Classical era resemble and differ from our own?

2. Given the emphasis on rationality during the Classical era, why was theatre dedicated, on the one hand, to farcical comedy and, on the other, to tragedies based on traditional mythology? What purpose did such performances serve in Athenian society?

Lecture Thirty-Four
Greece—Philosophy as Religion

Scope: During the Classical era, many of the elite rejected mythology as unworthy portrayals of the gods and turned to philosophy as an alternative. Philosophers revered "the good" as the highest god. Pythagoras taught that the soul was a divine spark trapped in a mortal body, to be released through purification over many lifetimes. The most influential philosopher was Socrates, whose confession that he knew nothing of value led him to question others in pursuit of knowledge. His student Plato developed a philosophical system based on the premise that all knowledge is knowledge of the divine realm, of which this world is only a shadow. The Epicureans found reassurance in believing that the gods didn't care about humanity. The Stoics believed virtue consisted in keeping one's resolve aligned with the dictates of the divine will, while the Cynics were itinerant philosophers who challenged common assumptions and lived a life "according to nature."

Outline

I. The idea of knowledge as the root of virtue led to contemplation as a form of religious activity in the Classical era.

    A. Greece had a deeply engrained mythology that was at odds with emerging principles of rational thought.

        1. The "Greek enlightenment" included attempts at rationalistic explanation of traditional mythology.

        2. Traditional mythological stories were considered unworthy of the true nature of the gods, who would never commit immoral acts.

        3. Myths were dismissed as explanations of the world, as legends about historical people and events, or as a way of "naming" the forces of nature.

        4. Philosophers derided some aspects of religious culture as mere superstition.

    B. Generally, philosophers acknowledged the gods but rationalized them as abstract principles under the power of Zeus.

1. Zeus, or "the god," was understood in terms of "the good," source and summation of all good.
2. "The good" was the god of the philosophers who was best worshiped by living a rational life, pursuing knowledge and virtue.
3. Philosophical investigation was based on reason and observation to the exclusion of emotion.
4. Emotion was generally regarded among the Greeks as the ruling force in human actions.

C. One school that incorporated both philosophical and religious principles was based on the teachings of Pythagoras.
1. Pythagoras is known only through the writings of his followers and other commentators.
2. Pythagoras believed that numbers were the means of understanding the nature and rhythms of the cosmos.
3. Pythagoras believed that the *psyche*, the soul or human essence, was a spark of divine reason trapped in the body.
4. The duty of the rational person is to purify the soul from the corrupting influence of the body by self-denial.
5. Purification can take several lifetimes, because the soul leaves one body at death and enters another in a process called *metempsychosis*.
6. Purification of the soul was a process of acquiring the knowledge that enables one to lead a virtuous life.
7. Ascetic practices notably included abstention from the use of animal products.

II. The most influential figure in Greek philosophy was Socrates, who was claimed as an inspiration by later philosophical schools.

A. We know Socrates primarily through the writings of his student Plato, a philosopher in his own right.
1. Plato presents Socrates as an ironist who is also acknowledged to be the wisest of all human beings.
2. In Plato's dialogues, Socrates constantly pretends to be less wise than he really is, claiming to know nothing of value.
3. It is this claim of ignorance that makes Socrates the wisest person, because his ignorance drives him to seek wisdom.

B. Socrates in the *Apology* traces his philosophical mission to a pronouncement of the Delphic oracle.

1. An *oracle* was a person empowered by a god to speak a revelation, or it can mean the revelation itself.
2. The Delphic oracle was a person empowered by the god Apollo to give yes or no responses to specific questions.
3. A friend of Socrates asked the oracle whether anyone was wiser than Socrates, and the oracle replied, "No."
4. Because a question to the oracle would be answered yes or no, the question had to be phrased carefully.
5. The oracle's reply puzzled Socrates, because he knew that oracles must speak the truth but also that he himself knew nothing of value.
6. Socrates set out to question people reputed to be wise, hoping to find the meaning of the oracle's reply.
7. In each case, Socrates discovered that those reputed to be wise knew nothing of value and were not aware of their ignorance.
8. Socrates decided he was wiser than they, because he knew that he knew nothing of value.
9. Socrates ultimately concluded that the oracle meant that the wisest are those who, like Socrates, know they know nothing of value.

C. The philosophical mission of Socrates was to engage in dialogue and ask searching questions in hope of discerning truth.
   1. Socrates's profession of ignorance and his desire to learn was invariably dismissed as irony by his opponents.
   2. Socrates collected followers, especially among the aristocratic young men of Athens.
   3. Socrates was put on trial for impiety and undermining the welfare of the state by corrupting the morals of his young male followers.
   4. Socrates was found guilty and condemned to death, a death he accepted with calm rationality.

D. Plato (427–347 B.C.E.) wrote dialogues featuring Socrates, but most of them expound Plato's own philosophy.
   1. Plato argued that our world is in a constant state of change and, thus, cannot be a source of knowledge.
   2. Knowledge derives from our inborn awareness of the "real," unchanging divine world.
   3. This world "participates" in the reality of the divine world and recalls to our minds what we know of the other reality.

4. Plato explained this concept in the allegory of the cave, where prisoners see only shadows, and the philosopher is one who escapes the cave to see things as they really are.
5. Plato emphasized the benefits of questioning and contemplation as a means of understanding the cosmos.
6. Philosophical introspection leads to virtuous behavior based on knowledge of the good.
7. Platonism formed the basic presuppositions for philosophical thought for several centuries.

III. Other philosophical schools emphasized instruction in virtue and peace of mind in the face of fate.

    A. Socrates was often at odds with the Sophists, itinerant teachers of the skills that led to a successful life.
        1. Sophists were teachers of rhetoric who could argue any side of an issue and endorsed accepted ideas of virtue.
        2. Sophists charged fees for their teaching, and some of them became famous.
        3. Sophists were not philosophers but similar to Near Eastern teachers of wisdom.

    B. Epicureanism found happiness in the peace of mind that comes from freedom of anxiety about the power of fate.
        1. Epicurus (341–270 B.C.E.) believed that anxiety arose from fear of offending the gods and fear of what happens after death.
        2. Epicurus offered two affirmations to banish these fears: The gods do not care about human behavior, and existence ends with death.
        3. Epicurus intended his philosophy to be a substitute for the "superstitions" of traditional Greek religion.
        4. Happiness lies in the moderate pursuit of pleasure among good friends in a philosophical community.

    C. Zeno, who taught in the *Stoa Poikile* (the colonnade) in 4th-century Athens, founded the school of Stoicism.
        1. Stoicism asserted that the divine exists in and through everything that exists, a position called *pantheism*.
        2. Stoics believed that a human being could control only the inner resolve that determined how he or she behaved.

3. Stoics maintained that virtue was the result of keeping one's inner resolve in agreement with the divine reason.
4. One must remain "detached" from external circumstances to keep one's inner resolve fixed on the divine reason.
5. Stoic cosmology concluded that history is cyclical, repeating itself exactly as determined by the reduplication of astral phenomena.
6. Stoics understood fate as the perfect legislation of the divine reason, the *logos*.

D. The Cynics were wandering ascetic philosophers who stood apart from society as its critics.
1. Cynicism was founded by Diogenes of Sinope, who as a treasury official, felt a call to "change the currency."
2. Diogenes understood this as a call to reject popular cultural values and social conventions.
3. Diogenes believed a person should live according to nature by satisfying natural needs.
4. This meant stripping life down to its barest essentials and being ashamed of nothing "natural."
5. Diogenes's "shamelessness" earned him and his followers the nickname *kunikos*, "dog-like."
6. Cynics were wanderers well known for their scruffy appearance and caustic polemics against society.
7. The Cynics had no systematic doctrine but were deeply influenced by Stoic philosophy.
8. Some of the milder Cynics filled an important function as personal counselors.

E. The philosophical schools widened the breach between the intellectual elite and the rest of Greek society.
1. The persecution of "rationalists" reflected concern for maintaining religious values and instilling them in the young.
2. The common charge against philosophers was that they were "atheists" whose unbelief endangered the state.

Essential Reading:

Plato. *Five Dialogues*, *Apology*.

Simon Price. *Religions of the Ancient Greeks*, pp. 126–142.

Supplementary Reading:

A. H. Armstrong. *An Introduction to Ancient Philosophy*, pp. 21–32, 114–140.

Walter Burkert. *Greek Religion*, pp. 305–337.

Questions to Consider:

1. Which of the philosophies discussed in this session seem most similar to a religious system? Why? Which philosophies seem more of an alternative to religion? Why?

2. The life and philosophical career of Socrates raise questions about the proper role of the philosopher in society. In what ways might the philosopher benefit society at large? In what ways might the philosopher undermine the common good?

Lecture Thirty-Five
Religious Culture in the Hellenistic World

Scope: After the Peloponnesian War, Greece entered a political and economic decline that led to submission to Philip of Macedon. His son Alexander campaigned against the Persian Empire, conquering its territories until his dominion extended from Greece to the Indus River. Macedonian rule was accompanied by the growth of Hellenistic culture, as key elements of classical Greek culture were imposed on the subject nations. Religious syncretism arose when gods, rituals, and mythology of one religious culture were combined with those of another. In the political and social upheaval of the early Hellenistic era, the primary concern was fate's control over human life. Anxiety over the power of fate led to new forms of religious community, as well as the impulse to resort to magical means of seeing into the future and asserting control over one's life. Theophrastus's sketch of the superstitious man portrays the religious anxiety that marked the early Hellenistic age.

Outline

I. The Peloponnesian War between Athens and Sparta (431–404 B.C.E.) weakened both cities, leading to conquest by the Macedonians.

   A. The Peloponnesian War revealed some weaknesses in the Greek city-states and exacerbated others.
      1. Athenian imperial ambitions led the *polis* to overreach militarily, losing a large part of its navy in an attempt to conquer Sicily in 415 B.C.E.
      2. Political strife weakened the Greek economy, already suffering from a trade deficit and a lack of natural resources.
      3. Greek armies became increasingly dependent on mercenaries as the ideal of the citizen-soldier declined.

   B. At the same time, Macedonia was consolidating its power under Philip II.
      1. Macedon had a self-sufficient economy, a citizen army, and a strong monarchy under Philip II (r. 359–336 B.C.E.).

2. Macedon had participated in Greek culture since at least the 5th century B.C.E.
3. Philip conquered Greek cities, made alliances, and quashed rebellions, becoming leader of a Pan-Hellenic alliance in 338 B.C.E.
4. With Greece united behind him, Philip planned a campaign against Persia, but he was assassinated in 336 B.C.E.

C. Philip was succeeded by Alexander III, who invaded Persia and became master of most of the known world.
   1. As Alexander's armies moved east, the Persian Empire fell into his hands piece by piece.
   2. Alexander's conquest of the Persian Empire with a small army was a tribute to his military genius but also to the reforms his father had brought to war.
   3. Alexander crossed the Indus River into India, but his troops refused to fight any longer.
   4. Alexander the Great died of fever in Babylon in 323 B.C.E., at age 33.
   5. His young son soon died, leaving three of Alexander's generals to divide his empire among them.

II. The shape of Hellenistic culture, which prevailed through the early Roman Empire, was largely determined by Alexander himself.

A. Alexander wished not only to conquer but also to create a cosmopolitan culture that would unify his vast domains.
   1. Alexander was a fervent Hellenist who intended to bring the blessings of Greek classical culture to his subjects.
   2. The vast majority of his subjects lived under regional officials who were now subject to Greek-speaking Macedonians.
   3. In Egypt, Alexander presented himself to his new subjects in the trappings of the pharaoh.
   4. Alexander intended to bring the Persian aristocracy into partnership with its Macedonian masters.
   5. His soldiers and officers rejected mixing conquerors and conquered, maintaining Greek superiority over the "barbarians."

B. In time, Alexander's conquests did result in a single cosmopolitan culture, at least among the upper classes.

1. *Hellenistic culture* was primarily Greek but included elements of the native cultures Alexander conquered.
2. The Macedonian kings of Egypt and Syria adopted traditional royal trappings of the native cultures.
3. They also established the institutions of Hellenic culture in their domains to assimilate native aristocracies.
4. A simplified version of classical Greek became the language of government administration and the *lingua franca.*
5. The Greek educational system indoctrinated native aristocrats, while constitutions established or remodeled conquered cities as Greek *poleis.*
6. Hellenistic culture spread Greek athletics, Greek ideals of intellectual culture, and Greek religious culture.

C. The new Hellenistic cosmopolitanism led to widely spread syncretism.
1. *Syncretism* is the synthesis of elements taken from distinct religious cultures into new forms and combinations.
2. This process might include reinterpretation of rituals and mythology to give them more universal significance.
3. Syncretism was often actively encouraged by Hellenistic rulers to legitimate their power and unite their subjects.

D. Syncretism resulted in the creation of new gods, as well as the reinvention of traditional gods as savior figures.
1. Apollo seems to become identified with the sun god only as a result of his identification with Amun-Rē.
2. The Hellenistic god Serapis is a synthesis of the Egyptian god Osiris and the Apis bull of Memphis.
3. Foreign gods tended to become "Hellenized" by being presented and worshiped according to Greek models.
4. The Hellenistic era also saw widespread worship of some traditional Greek gods, notably Demeter and Dionysus.

III. In the aftermath of Alexander's conquests, the irrational again became a major element in religious culture.

A. Greek rationalism reached a high point with Aristotle's founding of the Lyceum in 335 B.C.E.
1. Aristotle (384–322 B.C.E.), a student of Plato, was interested in observation, classification, and theory.

2. The Lyceum was more of a research center than a philosophical school.
3. Aristotle has left works in natural science, logic, mathematics, physics, ethics, rhetoric, and drama.
4. Aristotle's work demonstrates an attempt to submit natural and social phenomena to rational analysis.

B. Greek rationalism contributed to some extent to its own downfall, because it undermined faith in traditional religious culture.
1. The condemnation of Socrates reflected concern with traditional religious culture in a time of political uncertainty.
2. There was a growing breach between the intellectual elite and the rest of society, with popular opinion against the philosophers.
3. Public forms of religion declined, to be replaced by belief in fate as the determining factor in life.
4. This idea was always inherent in Greek religious culture, but events leading to Macedonian hegemony reinforced it.

C. Belief in the power of fate inspired philosophical and religious remedies but also practices pushing the bounds of religion.
1. The Epicureans, Stoics, and Cynics taught how a person might find peace of mind despite the power of fate.
2. Religious interest shifted to gods who were believed to have the power to save their devotees from the power of fate.
3. The gods who received the most attention were those closest to the concerns of the people.
4. The sanctuaries of Asclepius, the god of healing, combined therapeutic and religious methods for treating the ill.

D. Some people during the Hellenistic era turned to predicting or influencing the future.
1. There were various means of gaining insight into the future to determine what fate had in store.
2. Magical practices ranged from spells and rituals intended to gain control of cosmic powers to reliance on amulets.
3. Magical practices tended to focus on three goals: inspiring love, cursing, or turning aside curses.

E. Toward the end of the 4th century B.C.E., Theophrastus created a portrait of the superstitious man.

1. The portrait is part of a series of 30 depicting people dominated by various faults.
2. The superstitious man is particularly concerned with religious purity.
3. He is scrupulous about religious ritual, both around the house and elsewhere.
4. He takes countermeasures against bad omens and seeks advice from dream analysts.
5. He favors religious actions over practical ones.
6. He's particularly wary of crossroads, common sites of religious pollution.
7. This portrait gives a sense of the forms religious anxiety might have taken in the Hellenistic era.
8. It also provides a context for investigating the new religious groups and practices that became popular during the Hellenistic age.

Essential Reading:

Luther H. Martin. *Hellenistic Religions: An Introduction*, pp. 3–15, 35–57.

Robin W. Winks and Susan P. Mattern-Parkes. *The Ancient Mediterranean World: From the Stone Age to A.D. 600*, pp. 101–117.

Supplementary Reading:

A. H. Armstrong. *An Introduction to Ancient Philosophy*, pp. 66–86.

Theophrastus. *Characters*.

Questions to Consider:

1. Alexander's conquests united the eastern Mediterranean into a single Hellenistic culture, based on the Greek language and Macedonian rule. What were the advantages and disadvantages of a single dominant general culture for the subjects of his empire?

2. Syncretism involves the combination of the elements of one religious culture with those of another. What might be the advantages and disadvantages of syncretism, specifically in Hellenistic culture?

Lecture Thirty-Six
Mystery Religions in the Hellenistic World

Scope: The Hellenistic era saw a return to the worship of earth-based deities in mystery religions. These were religious groups with secret rituals that included initiation rites. The gods of the mystery religions, whether Greek or foreign, were generally fertility deities whose mythology was reinterpreted as stories of death and rebirth. A person chose to join a mystery religion on the basis of religious experience and, by so doing, became a devotee of the god, who in turn, became the devotee's patron. The "salvation" provided by the mystery religion was specifically salvation from the blind power of fate, because the god would ensure the devotee's welfare in all circumstances. Demeter was worshiped in a mystery cult at Eleusis and elsewhere, based on her daughter Kore's descent to Hades and return. The cult of Dionysus, the god of wine and ecstasy, focused on the god's life-giving power, celebrated in ritual banquets.

Outline

I. Mystery religions were so called because the central rituals were secret, that is, "mysteries."

    A. The Hellenistic era saw a renewed worship of earth-based (*chthonic*) deities, as their fertility rites were reinterpreted as salvation rituals.

        1. The power of these deities was based on their association with the cycle of fertility and all aspects of dynamic life.

        2. Myths originally associated with the fertility cycle were reinterpreted as myths about death and rebirth.

        3. The deity controlled the cycle of fertility and, thus, the cycle of life, death, and rebirth.

    B. Mystery religions included secret initiation rituals as a prerequisite to membership.

        1. These rituals were expensive and time-consuming and represented the devotee's sincerity.

        2. First, there was a ritual of purification and a vigil.

        3. There was usually a sacrifice to the god, most often a pig whose blood ran into the earth.

4. This was followed by a confession of faith, when the devotee expressed the desire to become an initiate into the cult.
5. The initiation apparently culminated in a revelatory vision of the central cultic symbol.

C. Public rituals and ceremonies publicized the mystery religion and attracted new initiates.
1. Public celebrations included processions accompanied by music, singing, and dancing.
2. Celebrations often included a recital or reenactment of the central myth of death and resurrection or rebirth.

D. The mystery religions offered their devotees a personal relationship with the cult's deity.
1. A person became a follower of a mystery religion by choice on the basis of some sort of religious experience.
2. The mysteries emphasized the bond between the deity and the initiate.
3. The "salvation" offered by the mystery religions was salvation from the blind power of fate.
4. Just as the god in the cultic mythology overcame adversity, so he or she would protect the devotee and bring him or her "home."
5. The mysteries forged a patron/client relationship of worship and protection between the initiate and the god.
6. A person might be an initiate into several different mystery religions at once.

E. Although mystery religions achieved new popularity during the Hellenistic era, many of them were ancient in their origins.
1. Most gods of the mysteries were "foreign," and this emphasized the antiquity and universality of their cults.
2. Some goddesses of the mysteries retained a specifically "foreign" identity.
3. Others became thoroughly Hellenized and cosmopolitan, to the extent they became identified with Greek gods.
4. This is the case with Isis, who is identified with several Greek goddesses.
5. Mystery gods were explicitly deities for the entire world, and their devotees were also missionaries.

II. Demeter was a goddess of the Greek pantheon whose worship evolved into a mystery religion.

A. The Eleusinian mysteries were based on the myth of Kore's abduction and rape by Hades.

    1. Demeter was plunged into despair by Kore's disappearance and served the king of Eleusis as a nurse.

    2. The earth lay fallow until Zeus sent Hermes to demand that Hades return Kore to Demeter.

    3. Kore could return to earth for only a part of each year before returning to Hades.

    4. This myth is typical of stories explaining the fertility cycle that easily become stories of death and rebirth.

B. Demeter's primary sanctuary was in Eleusis, where a temple was built at her command when Kore returned to her.

    1. Eleusis was the site of an early festival celebrating the sowing of grain and, later, the *Thesmophoria*, mourning Kore's annual return to Hades.

    2. The Eleusinian mysteries seem to have evolved out of these celebrations, reinterpreted as festivals of rebirth.

    3. At Eleusis, both men and women worshiped, although elsewhere, only women celebrated the Eleusinian mysteries.

    4. The worship space in Eleusis could hold several thousand worshipers.

    5. Priests of Eleusis served as advisors in the institution and reform of other mystery religions.

C. After Eleusis was conquered by Athens, the "greater mysteries" were celebrated with a procession from Athens to Eleusis.

    1. On the first day, sacred objects and chests were carried from Eleusis to Athens.

    2. On following days, a herald excluded criminals and barbarians; initiates sacrificed and bathed in the sea.

    3. Finally, a procession along the Sacred Way from Athens to Eleusis returned the sacred objects to the hall of initiation to cries of "Iacchos!"

D. Some written and graphic evidence survives indicating what the ceremonies of Demeter might have included.

1. There were three sorts of activities in the Eleusinian mysteries: "things recited," "things shown," and "things performed."
2. The public aspect of the ritual is parodied in *The Frogs* by Aristophanes.
3. Initiation reportedly included fasting, drinking a mixture of barley meal and mint, and manipulating sacred objects.
4. The ultimate revelation is believed to have been a head of grain that revealed the essential nature of life.

III. Dionysus, the god of wine and ecstasy, also became the god of a mystery religion.
   A. Worship of Dionysus forms something of a complement to the worship of Demeter.
      1. Demeter's grain must be made into bread to provide food, just as grapes must be made into the wine of Dionysus.
      2. Dionysus was a son of Zeus and the mortal Semele, who was struck dead during her pregnancy.
      3. Zeus took her unborn child and sewed him into his thigh until he was ready to be born.
      4. Dionysus was later entrusted to nymphs of Mount Nysa, who raised him.
      5. Dionysus discovered wine and traveled throughout Greece to share it.
      6. He was ultimately included in the company of the gods after rescuing Semele from Hades.
   B. Various stories tell about those who refuse to recognize the divinity of Dionysus and suffer the consequences.
      1. The most well known story is told in Euripides's *The Bacchae*, when Pentheus, king of Thebes, imprisoned Dionysus.
      2. Dionysus inspired the women of Thebes to join his followers and persuaded Pentheus to spy on them, but the Bacchae discovered Pentheus and tore him to pieces.
      3. Such stories reflect Dionysus's chthonic identity that runs counter to the official religious culture.
   C. Such stories tell us about the god's power and the effects he was believed to have on his worshipers.

1. Dionysus was originally a rustic deity associated with the rural gods Pan, Silenus, and Priapus, as well as with satyrs, fauns, and nymphs.
2. Dionysus sometimes appears as a bull but more usually as an effeminate young man with long curls.
3. Dionysus was believed to cause ecstasy and madness in human beings.
4. In Euripides's play, the Bacchae eat raw flesh as a means of feeding on Dionysian power in the animal.
5. The intention of Dionysian worship was to ingest the intoxicating power of the god and to exhibit divine possession.
6. Rituals of Dionysus involved eating and drinking wine; banquets in his honor appear to have included sexual activity.
7. Sexual activity and secrecy led the Roman Senate to severely restrict the worship of Dionysus in 186 B.C.E.

D. Dionysus was identified with Osiris and associated with death and rebirth.
1. Dionysus's rescue of Semele from Hades, with his identity as the god of the power of life, made him a potent mystery deity.
2. Dionysus appears to have promised his devotees an afterlife of enjoyment of the sensuous appetites his presence inspired on earth.

Essential Reading:

Luther H. Martin. *Hellenistic Religions: An Introduction*, pp. 58–72, 90–98.

Marvin W. Meyer, ed. *The Ancient Mysteries*, pp. 1–45, 61–109.

Supplementary Reading:

Sarah Iles Johnston, ed. *Religions of the Ancient World: A Guide*, pp. 98–111.

Questions to Consider:

1. What seem to be the most valuable characteristics of the mystery religions? How did they contrast in that respect with the traditional religions of the Hellenistic era?

2. What characteristics do the gods and goddesses of the mystery religions seem to have in common? How are these characteristics reflected in the mystery religions themselves?

Lecture Thirty-Seven
Mystery Religions from the East

Scope: Most major mystery religions worshiped a fertility goddess under
the title "Queen of Heaven," although some mysteries were
devoted to male gods. One of these was Mithras, an Indo-Aryan
god worshiped by men in a hierarchical cult. Apuleius's novel *The
Golden Ass* provides information about two mystery religions: the
cult of the Syrian goddess and the mysteries of Isis. The Syrian
goddess resembles the "Great Mother" worshiped in Asia Minor,
whose rites memorialized and imitated the self-castration of the
goddess's consort Attis. Apuleius ridiculed the eunuch priests of
her cult as charlatans and thieves. Isis came the closest of any
ancient god to being the focus of a worldwide religion. She was
worshiped both in public rituals and in mysteries. Apuleius's hero
Lucius is rescued from his troubles by the goddess's intervention
and becomes her devotee. His story provides some insight into the
nature of the mysteries of Isis.

Outline

I. Most major mystery religions were devoted to a fertility goddess as the
"Queen of Heaven," but some worshiped male gods.

   A. We have already considered several goddesses identified as
"Queen of Heaven."

      1. Inanna represented all aspects of natural cycles and was called
"Queen of Heaven and Earth."

      2. Aphrodite was associated with natural and cosmic cycles
because of her association with fertility.

      3. Associations with life and fertility were more important in
mystery religions than the gender of the deity.

   B. The mysteries of the Indo-Aryan god Mithras appear to be a
product of the late Roman Republic.

      1. The mysteries of Mithras celebrated in the Roman Empire
appear to be independent of his worship in the East.

      2. No central cultic myth of Mithras has come down to us,
although scenes in his sanctuaries suggest its outlines.

3. Mithras was born from a rock, witnessed either by shepherds or by two men who serve as his torchbearers.
4. His birth was associated with that of the sun at the winter solstice, December 25.
5. The central image is a bull-slaying scene showing Mithras pinning a bull and slitting its throat.
6. The scene is accompanied with iconic symbols and two men standing at either side holding torches.
7. The scene is usually accompanied by astral signs that may represent a set of constellations.
8. The primary cultic act appears to have been a banquet in communion with the god.

C. Mithras worship was particularly popular with soldiers, sailors, and merchants, who established its shrines everywhere.
1. The military-style organization of the cult included seven levels of initiation.
2. The hierarchical structure of the group mirrors an upward ascent into the divine realm.

II. Apuleius, a Latin author of the 2nd century C.E., provides information about two mystery religions in *The Golden Ass.*

A. Apuleius (born c. 123 C.E.) is best known for *Metamorphoses*, commonly called *The Golden Ass.*
1. The book tells the story of Lucius, a young man who dabbles in magic and is accidentally turned into an ass.
2. In his new form, he has a series of adventures with different owners.
3. For a while, Lucius is owned by priests of the Syrian goddess Atargatis, and he is finally saved by a revelation of Isis.

B. Atargatis, the Syrian goddess, had traits in common with a number of Greek goddesses.
1. Our only other source for details of her worship is an account written by the satirist Lucian of Samosata.
2. Lucian described a visit to her sanctuary, where he tried to figure out what Greek goddesses Atargatis resembles.
3. Lucian decided that the goddess combined aspects of Hera, Athena, Aphrodite, Selene, Rhea, Artemis, Nemesis, and the Fates.

4. Lucian thereby demonstrates the rationale behind syncretism: Gods with similar traits may be identified with one another.

C. Atargatis appears to be a Syrian version of the Great Mother Goddess, known to us also as Cybele.
 1. Cybele, the "Great Mother," was originally a goddess of Asia Minor associated with fertility and untamed nature.
 2. Cybele was a defender of her people, curing illnesses, sending oracles, and protecting her worshipers in war.
 3. Cybele was worshiped in Rome from the late 3rd century B.C.E.
 4. The mysteries of the Magna Mater ("Great Mother") centered on the story of her consort Attis, the goddess's beloved.
 5. When Attis was about to marry another, Cybele sent the wedding party into a frenzy and Attis castrated himself.
 6. Attis died from his wounds, but his dead body became a source of continued life.

D. The story of Attis was understood as a story of fertility and death and rebirth.
 1. We know the details of worship primarily from the Roman festival of Attis in late antiquity.
 2. The festival took place during 12 days in March and included offerings and fasting.
 3. On the seventh day, a freshly cut pine tree, the symbol of Attis, was brought into the temple and decorated.
 4. On the ninth day, the Day of Blood, devotees would flog themselves in a frenzy while others castrated themselves.
 5. These eunuch priests, called *Galli,* would dress as women and perform women's tasks in the temple.
 6. The rest of the festival included feasting and bathing the cult statue of the Great Mother.

E. The other major ritual performed in honor of the Magna Mater was the *taurobolium.*
 1. In this ritual, a devotee of the goddess stood in the bottom of a pit covered with slotted planks.
 2. A bull or ram was sacrificed over the pit, allowing the blood and gore of the animal to drench the worshiper.
 3. This ceremony was a means of imparting the bull's divine life and vitality to the devotee.

    F. The cult of the Magna Mater was considered foreign and exotic by most Greeks and Romans.

        1. Apuleius's *The Golden Ass* portrays the priests of the Syrian goddess as effeminate homosexual transvestites.

        2. They wear their hair long, dress in brightly colored robes, and mutilate themselves to solicit donations.

        3. The priests also act as fortune-tellers in the story and are ultimately caught stealing from a temple.

        4. Lucius's indenture to the priests of Atargatis is part of the evil fate that dogs him until Isis grants him release.

III. The Egyptian goddess Isis came closer to becoming the deity of a worldwide religion than any other ancient god.

    A. The most relevant aspects of her character for her mystery rituals were her association with Osiris's death and resurrection.

        1. In the Hellenistic era, Osiris was identified with Serapis, essentially a new identity as a universal god.

        2. Sanctuaries of Serapis and Isis were established among the major ports and cities.

    B. The public rituals associated with worship of Isis were the daily rituals of prayer and meditation at her sanctuaries and the major festivals recalling parts of her story.

        1. The Festival of Search and Discovery recalled Isis's search for Osiris's body, followed by its discovery and his return to life.

        2. The *Navigium Isidis*, or "Isis's Sea Journey," recalled the voyage of Isis to Byblos, where she found Osiris's body.

        3. Many details of the stories of Isis and Demeter are similar.

        4. The festival of Isis's sea journey was also believed to calm the seas at the beginning of spring.

    C. Apuleius's description of Lucius's revelation of the goddess is filled with the language of devotion.

        1. After a catalogue of troubles, Lucius the ass purifies himself and prays to the Queen of Heaven.

        2. Isis appears in a dream to promise Lucius that he will regain his human form during the *Navigium Isidis.*

        3. Isis tells Lucius to become her devotee, something he is already eager to do.

        4. Isis promises Lucius that he will live blessed and, after death, will still see the goddess shining in the darkness of Hades.

5. Lucius follows the goddess's directions and regains his human form.

6. Isis becomes Lucius's patroness and protector, guiding him safely through life until he comes "home."

D. The rest of the novel tells how Lucius prepared for his initiation into the cult.

1. He describes the initiation ritual in symbolic language.

2. After his initiation, Lucius appears in public wearing the garb of an initiate.

3. Lucius finally returns home, where he is initiated twice more as a priest of Isis.

4. Through the initiation and symbolic death, Lucius is reborn as a devotee of Isis, who becomes his "Good Fortune."

Essential Reading:

Apuleius, *The Golden Ass*.

Mary Beard, John North, and Simon Price. *Religions of Rome*, vol. 2, pp. 297–319.

Luther H. Martin. *Hellenistic Religions*, pp. 16–34, 72–89, 113–118.

Marvin W. Meyer, ed. *The Ancient Mysteries*, pp. 111–221.

Supplementary Reading:

Robert Turcan, *The Cults of the Roman Empire*, pp. 75–247.

Questions to Consider:

1. What seem to be the primary characteristics that set "Eastern" mystery religions apart from those that originated in the West?

2. What characteristics of the mystery religion of Isis most likely contributed to its widespread popularity? How does Isis differ from such mystery gods as Demeter, Mithra, Dionysius, and Cybele?

3. *The Golden Ass* is a combination of fantasy, satire, traditional mythology, and devotional literature. Do you think the other elements would diminish the sincerity of the devotion to Isis expressed at the conclusion of the novel? Why or why not?

Lecture Thirty-Eight
Roman Religious Cultures Before the Empire

Scope: It is difficult to reconstruct the early history of Roman religious culture, because the earliest sources come from the 3rd century B.C.E. The Romans believed that the cosmos was suffused with spiritual power and recognized its presence not only in the gods and human beings but in groups, places, activities, and the objects of everyday life. As a result, religious ritual accompanied all forms of human activity. The Romans interacted with the gods through precisely enacted rituals and prayers, seeking the gods' patronage. State religion was similar to that of the home and worshiped the same major gods. The Etruscans seem to have inspired the Romans to represent the gods in human form, while the Greeks contributed their full pantheon of gods and their mythology. By the late republic, although Roman religion continued to be part and parcel of everyday life, some sought the reassurance of philosophy or the mystery religions.

Outline

I.   The Romans traced their origins to Trojans who escaped the fall of Troy and came to Italy.

   A. The story of Aeneas was the subject of Virgil's *Aeneid*, modeled on Homer's epics.

      1. Like the *Iliad*, the *Aeneid* dealt with the last years of the Trojan War.

      2. Like the *Odyssey*, the *Aeneid* traced its hero's sea journey westward, but in this case, Aeneas is searching for a new home.

      3. The Romans traced their ancestry to Trojan refugees and to the outcasts who had settled in Rome under Romulus.

      4. The Romans believed that their civilization was the vindication of Trojan superiority.

   B. The Roman legend of Aeneas reflects the cultural predilections of Romans in several ways.

      1. The Romans valued persistence in hardship, poverty, and simplicity.

2. The Romans understood their civilization as the product of both human and divine forces.
3. The Romans believed that they were the vehicles for the well-being of the known world.
4. The appropriation of Greek mythology is typical of the Romans' willingness to assimilate foreign religious cultures.

C. The Latin tribes that were the core of the Roman people were not the original inhabitants of the Italian peninsula.
   1. Most historians place the foundation of Rome around 750 B.C.E.
   2. When the city was founded, the Latins were flanked by Etruscans to the north and Greek immigrants to the south.
   3. The Etruscans sometimes ruled over the Romans and had a profound effect on their culture.
   4. In the 7th and 6th centuries B.C.E., Rome developed as an urban culture under Etruscan influence.
   5. Rome was incorporated in the 6th century B.C.E., when a wall was built around the city.
   6. Most of the Italian peninsula came under Roman control by the mid-3rd century B.C.E.
   7. Rome defeated Carthage, its primary trade rival, at the end of the Third Punic War in 146 B.C.E.
   8. After the defeat of Carthage, Rome was unrivaled in Mediterranean trade and became very wealthy.

D. In the late 6th century, the monarchy was overthrown, and the Roman Republic was established.
   1. The Roman Republic resembled a Greek *polis*, but more power was held by the patrician families who formed the senatorial aristocracy.
   2. Other families—the plebeians—worked to win a more equal distribution of power and finally succeeded.
   3. Roman society was dominated by a system of patrons and dependents that united people of disparate status in mutually beneficial relationships.
   4. This system of patronage was also reflected in Roman religious culture.

II. The earliest written sources for Roman religious culture come from the 3rd century B.C.E.

A. Roman histories about religious culture in early Rome reflect the ideas of their authors' own times.

    1. Roman historians during the republic depicted early Roman religious culture in an idealized way, as a foil to their own era.

    2. Portrayals of religious indifference during the republic—written during the early empire—were intended to justify Augustus's religious revival.

    3. We must use the Roman historical sources carefully, with an awareness of their biases.

B. Roman religious culture is characterized by formality, pragmatism, and a vast array of gods.

    1. Romans believed in all-pervading spiritual power—*numen*—possessed by gods, human beings, groups, places, and things.

    2. Each *locus* of spiritual power was identified as a deity and named.

    3. Many minor gods were no more than sources of spiritual power and were so vaguely conceived that their gender was unknown.

    4. Divine powers were invoked to facilitate human actions and make them prosper.

C. Every human activity, location of human activity, and stage of human life had its own deities.

    1. Every part of the home had its own patron deity, notably the threshold, sacred to the god Janus, and the hearth, sacred to the goddess Vespa.

    2. Members of the family also had their own patron deities, the spiritual essence of each male (his *genius*) or female (her *juno*).

    3. The family and the clan had their household deities, the *Penates*, in addition to the ancestral spirits, the *Lares*.

    4. The head of each household, the *pater familias*, was responsible for the daily religious ceremonies of the family.

    5. These rituals were part of the normal routine of life, a natural accompaniment to human action.

D. State religion was similar to the religion of the home, with many of the same gods and rituals.

    1. Most of the early gods whose names we know were associated with the city of Rome and had a role in official religion.

2. State religious rituals were conducted by priests organized into four *colleges*: the pontiffs, the augurs, the "men for sacred actions," and the fetials.
3. Priests had ceremonial duties 104 days of the year and had to maintain a state of purity.
4. Other religious officials included diviners, who interpreted omens, and prodigies.
5. The most prominent women in Roman religious culture were the Vestal Virgins, who guarded the flame in the temple of Vesta.

E. The well-being of the Roman state depended on the proper worship of the gods in words and rituals.
1. It was extremely important in Roman religion to interact with the right god at the right time in the right way.
2. Religious actions had to be performed in exactly the right way with precisely the right words.

F. The Roman emphasis on formal exactitude and pragmatism had several results.
1. Religious actions, such as animal sacrifices, required several participants.
2. Measures were devised to facilitate proper performance of a ritual.
3. Religious actions could be repeated until they were performed correctly.

III. Later changes and developments in Roman religious culture arose from contact with other cultures and Rome's political evolution.

A. The Etruscans' periodic domination over Rome introduced new religious ideas.
1. The Etruscans apparently introduced to the Romans the idea of portraying the gods in human form.
2. The Etruscans may have contributed to the development of Roman temple architecture.
3. The Etruscans also developed the art of *haruspicia*, finding omens in the entrails of animals.
4. The Etruscans introduced new gods to the Romans, apparently including Minerva.

B. Greek influence introduced religious sentiment, its pantheon, and its mythology to Rome.

1. In the 6th century B.C.E., the written oracles of the Sibylline prophet were brought to Rome.
2. When consulted, these oracles often advised recourse to Greek gods or rituals to address a problem or crisis.
3. Over time, many Greek gods received temples and worship in Rome at the order of the Sibyl.
4. The Romans also adopted the Greek practice of giving votive offerings.
5. The Romans took over the stories of Greek mythology, substituting the names of Roman gods.
6. Romans also deified abstract concepts that they particularly prized and even deified the city of Rome itself.

C. By the last century of the republic, Rome's religious practices reached their height as part of Roman culture.
1. Historians began to bemoan republican religious affairs in comparison with their portrayals of the pious life of early Rome.
2. The political troubles of this period led to social uneasiness that prompted a desire for religious security.
3. Mystery religions offered Romans mysticism, enthusiasm, and community.
4. Many of the intellectual elite turned to philosophy as a substitute for religion while maintaining outward observances.
5. A generation of civil war was blamed in part on Roman impiety, and Augustus initiated a religious revival.

Essential Reading:

Mary Beard, John North, and Simon Price. *Religions of Rome*, vol. 1, pp. 1–72; vol. 2, pp. 1–25.

Ovid. *Metamorphoses*, pp. 311–357.

Robert Turcan. *The Gods of Ancient Rome*, pp. 1–99.

Robin W. Winks and Susan P. Mattern-Parkes. *The Ancient Mediterranean World: From the Stone Age to A.D. 600*, pp. 118–145.

Supplementary Reading:

Sarah Iles Johnston, ed. *Religions of the Ancient World: A Guide*, pp. 225–232.

Virgil. *The Aeneid.*

Questions to Consider:

1. What appear to be the most distinctive traits of Roman religion? What do those traits tell us about the primary concerns of Roman culture?

2. Roman writers of the late republic used an idealized picture of earlier religious culture to criticize the religion of their own time. What eras in history tend to be used to criticize the religious, cultural, and social trends of our own time? Why?

Lecture Thirty-Nine
Rome—Saviors and Divine Men

Scope: When Augustus Caesar became emperor, he instituted a revival intended to restore traditional religious institutions in Rome. But Augustus also gathered religious authority into his own hands and became the central religious figure in the empire. The emperor's *genius* was even worshiped in the provinces during his lifetime. This reflects the era's need for "savior" figures, gods or human beings with the spiritual power and authority to save suppliants from the dangers of this world. The gods of the mystery religions and other gods, such as Asclepius, were often called "savior," as were some military and political leaders. Another sort of savior was the *divine man*, endowed with divine power manifested in wisdom and miraculous works. The 1st-century C.E. Pythagorean philosopher Apollonius of Tyana was presented in a 3rd-century "life" as the ideal divine man, a savior who embodied all Roman philosophical and religious virtues.

Outline

I. The Roman Empire under Augustus Caesar marks a new era in the religious culture of Rome.

    A. Augustus (63 B.C.E.–14 C.E.) came to power after a generation of civil war in Rome.

        1. The republic began to collapse amid class warfare and the growing power of a few aristocratic families.

        2. Successful generals became rivals for political power over the decaying state.

        3. Julius Caesar (c. 100–44 B.C.E.) fought and won a long civil war against his rival Pompey (106–48 B.C.E.).

        4. Caesar's adopted son Octavian formed an alliance with Marc Antony, who later laid claim to the eastern empire.

        5. Antony and Cleopatra were defeated by Octavian's general Agrippa and committed suicide in 30 B.C.E.

        6. Octavian was granted the full sovereign power of the Senate as "first citizen" and ruled as Augustus Caesar.

    B. Augustus Caesar revived traditional public religion in Rome.

1. He revived rituals and priesthoods, repaired old temples, and built new ones.
2. Augustus ordered the collection of all the Sibylline oracles and forbade the creation of new oracles.
3. Augustus presented his religious revival as a return to traditional forms of worship, but his reforms inevitably introduced innovations.

C. The major religious innovation Augustus introduced was the central place of the emperor himself.
   1. Augustus became a priest of all the major colleges, as well as several minor ones.
   2. Augustus became *pontifex maximus* and supervisor of all religious activities in Rome.
   3. All temples built during his reign presented the emperor as the gods' benefactor.
   4. Augustus built a temple of Apollo next to his own house and dedicated part of his palace to public religious use.

D. The office of emperor itself gave Augustus religious significance and power.
   1. Successful generals had long been identified with the divine power believed to be at work in them.
   2. Roman religion did not draw a clear line between gods and others who displayed spiritual power.
   3. Roman subjects in the provinces worshiped Augustus's *genius*, the essence of his male vitality.
   4. This practice reflected the tradition of bestowing divine honors on native kings.
   5. Veneration of the emperor and worship of his *genius* became a means of affirming loyalty to Rome.
   6. Soon after his death, Augustus was declared a god by the Roman Senate.

II. The veneration of Augustus was consistent with the search for salvation from divinely gifted individuals.

A. We have already discussed the search for salvation in philosophical and religious communities.
   1. Pythagoras was believed to "save" his followers from the cycle of death and rebirth.

      2. Epicurus "saved" his followers from the anxiety caused by fear of the gods and what comes after death.

      3. Salvation was a central concern of the mystery religions, in which the patron god "saved" the initiate.

B. The god of healing, Asclepius, was revered as a savior in the Hellenistic and imperial eras.

      1. There were more than 300 sanctuaries of Asclepius throughout the Mediterranean basin.

      2. Sanctuaries combined the facilities of a temple, a spa, and a hospital.

      3. Several of the Asclepius sanctuaries included medical schools.

      4. Asclepius sanctuaries displayed written accounts and mementos of miraculous healings.

      5. "Cures" apparently ranged from the medical to the psychosomatic to the "miraculous."

      6. Asclepius was often called *soter*, "savior," for his ability to deliver his devotees from illness.

C. Political leaders were likely to claim the title *savior* of their people.

      1. A military leader might be called savior for defeating external or internal enemies.

      2. The title *savior* was not a religious claim per se, but it certainly had religious overtones.

      3. The assumption was that the gods had chosen the political leader to govern and had given him success.

III. Another savior figure in the Roman world was the *theios aner*, the "divine man" endowed with spiritual power.

A. The divine man's wisdom and miraculous powers were attributed to divine power at work in him.

      1. The supernatural power of the divine man was believed to envelop his body like an aura.

      2. The divine man's supernatural power was at his command, just as his natural abilities were.

      3. The divine man "saved" a person by a miracle, an insight, or his mere presence.

      4. The divine man was necessarily a religious figure, proclaiming what was pleasing to the gods by his words and his life.

B. A good example of the divine man was Apollonius of Tyana, a 1ˢᵗ-century C.E. philosopher.

    1. Apollonius was born around the turn of the age and still alive during Nerva's reign (96–98 C.E.).

    2. He was a Pythagorean philosopher who taught about the duality of soul and body and purification through self-renunciation.

    3. Apollonius enjoyed some renown during his lifetime, although opinion about him was mixed.

C. Apollonius is known today primarily through the 3ʳᵈ-century work of Flavius Philostratus, *Life of Apollonius of Tyana.*

    1. Philostratus was part of the *Second Sophistic* during the reign of Septimus Severus (193–211).

    2. The Second Sophistic was a literary revival focused on the oratorical skills of the Sophists.

    3. Philostratus claimed to have written the life of Apollonius at the request of the empress Julia Domna (d. 217).

    4. Philostratus presents Apollonius as a divine man who represents the height of Roman religious virtue.

    5. Philostratus's portrait reflects Roman religious interests of the early 3ʳᵈ century C.E., when those interests had already been influenced by Christianity.

D. Philostratus portrays Apollonius as a wise man devoted to his friends and the cause of truth.

    1. Born into a wealthy family, Apollonius chose the life of a wandering philosopher.

    2. He showed an affinity for Pythagoras's teachings "by some mysterious intelligence."

    3. Apollonius wore linen clothing and bark sandals, abstained from meat, and lived celibate.

    4. Apollonius applied himself to wisdom, philosophy, and the proper worship of the gods.

E. Apollonius traveled in search of wisdom but also taught and performed miracles.

    1. He traveled to India and Egypt, traditional homes of ancient wisdom and esoteric knowledge.

    2. Because of his ascetic habits, Apollonius was endowed with powers of healing, insight, and foreknowledge.

3. He dispensed miracles, but Philostratus takes a "skeptical" view and suggests naturalistic explanations for some of them.
4. Apollonius met with opposition, most notably from the "bad" emperors Nero and Domitian.
5. The book's climax is the trial of Apollonius before Domitian and his bodily ascension into heaven.

F. It appears that Philostratus deliberated presented Apollonius as a rival to Jesus.
1. The "lives" of the two men are similar, although Apollonius's portrait often seems drawn in contrast to that of Jesus and his disciples.
2. Some later Roman writers compared Jesus unfavorably with Apollonius.
3. Philostratus portrays Apollonius as the embodiment of all the virtues of Roman philosophy and religious culture.
4. Apollonius was one among a range of gods and men who, by virtue of their divine gifts, could act as saviors for those in need.

Essential Reading:

Mary Beard, John North, and Simon Price. *Religions of Rome*, vol. 1, pp. 167–210.

Robert Turcan. *The Gods of Ancient Rome*, pp. 134–145.

Robin W. Winks and Susan P. Mattern-Parkes. *The Ancient Mediterranean World: From the Stone Age to A.D. 600*, pp. 145–165.

Supplementary Reading:

Philostratus. *Life of Apollonius of Tyana.*

Questions to Consider:

1. What might have motivated people in the Hellenistic era and the early empire to look for salvation specifically from individual gods or men and not from other sources, such as religious or political communities?

2. How does the worship of the Roman emperor resemble and differ from the worship of the Egyptian pharaoh as a god?

3. What traits does the Jesus of the Gospels have in common with the Apollonius of Philostratus's *Life*? What traits set them apart? What similarities and differences are there between their respective stories?

Lecture Forty
Rome—Divination, Astrology, and Magic

Scope: Divination was a means of discerning the will of the gods in a given situation and how best to please them. Divination was a regular part of Roman religious rituals, but unofficial forms of divination also provided guidance for individuals. Diviners might draw on spiritual insight, read signs, or consult written oracles. Babylonian astrology was introduced to the rest of the Mediterranean world by Alexander the Great. It provided a means of gaining insight into divine intentions based on scientific observation and mathematical calculation. Magical practices are difficult to distinguish from religious practices, although emphasis appears to be on the magician gaining power over divine forces through use of "hidden" names that must be obeyed. Magic was used primarily for healing, love charms, and cursing and turning aside curses. Apuleius portrays magical practices alongside religious devotions in *The Golden Ass* as different ways of interacting with the gods.

Outline

I. Divination was a primary concern among the Romans to discern the will of the gods and to do what would please them.

  A. Augury was a formal part of virtually all religious rituals, carried out by designated priests.

   1. The members of the college of the *augeres* oversaw the taking of auspices before a sacrifice.

   2. The auger had several distinct techniques for taking the auspices.

   3. Other priests, the *haruspices*, were diviners who were expert in several methods for discerning the will of the gods.

   4. The diviners examined the entrails of sacrificial animals and interpreted prodigies and other "signs."

   5. All these methods were to read divine messages for the present, not to see into the future.

  B. Prophecy was also a matter of gaining insight into the divine will in the present.

        1. In Israel, for example, the role of the prophet was closely related to the seer.

        2. The duties of a court or cult prophet included giving advice on actions to be taken in the present.

        3. When Israelite prophets foretold the future, they did so as a means of casting light on the present.

        4. Prophecy in all its forms was always primarily about the here and now.

  C. There were also unofficial forms of divination available to the individual for a price.

        1. Some seers could provide oracles on the basis of their own spiritual gift of insight.

        2. Others manipulated objects or read "signs" in random phenomena.

        3. The oracle-monger kept collections of oracles and would provide one to suit the occasion.

  D. In each of these cases, there are elements of foresight into the future, because foresight was believed to guarantee the seer's gift.

        1. The element of foretelling the future is primarily legendary, a literary tradition that runs counter to actual historical practice.

        2. The legendary tradition of ambiguous oracles fulfilled in unexpected ways reflects the contrast between the divine and the human way of seeing things.

        3. This tradition affected common expectations; thus, the oracle-monger could provide new interpretations for old oracles based on divine ambiguity.

II. Alexander the Great's conquests brought astrology from Babylon to the rest of the Mediterranean world.

  A. There had previously been a belief in "astral influences" in Greek religion and philosophy.

        1. Plato spoke of the movement of the stars as an indication of the rational design of the cosmos.

        2. The Stoics believed in "sympathy" between the movement of the stars and events on earth.

        3. The careful observation of astronomical phenomena helped prepare the way for astrology.

  B. Through astrology, one could identify the forces in operation in daily life by watching the stars.

1. Events on earth were thought to be a result of divine powers influencing human actions and emotions.
2. Each divine power was identified with an astral sphere whose movements indicated the waxing and waning of its influence.
3. The nature of a power's influence was always the same, but its intensity was always changing with the movement of the spheres.
4. The divine forces were identified with the god who most closely resembled their influence.
5. Because stars had regular patterns of movement, there was a predictable pattern of influence, allowing the astrologer to predict the future.
6. Because the movement of stars was also cyclical, history was believed to be cyclical.
7. In theory, astrologers could calculate both present and future influences on earthly events for individuals and for nations.

C. Astrology became popular in Greek and Roman culture as a "scientific" form of divination.
   1. Astrology was based on careful observation of the stars and mathematical calculation.
   2. Astrology could be mastered by anyone who was willing and able to undertake the study.
   3. Astrology offered a means of avoiding fate, because one could anticipate its actions and take preventive measures.
   4. The primary use of astrology was to make decisions about actions to be taken in the present.

III. Another response to the problem of anxiety over the blind power of fate was to resort to magic.

A. The distinction between magical and religious actions was not clear in the ancient Mediterranean world.
   1. In Egypt, Isis was venerated in part because of her knowledge of magic and spells.
   2. The gods' role in warding off evil may be regarded as magical when represented by amulets or protective rituals.
   3. The line between observant religious practice and superstitious magical practice was—and remains—hard to draw.

B. One way of differentiating religious from magical practice lies in the intention of the actions involved.
1. Religious rituals try to persuade divine forces, establishing a balance between the benefits given and received.
2. Magical practices try to compel divine forces to act as the magician wishes in an assertion of his or her power over them.
3. This distinction was not necessarily recognized by people in the ancient world.
4. This distinction becomes problematic in religious rituals in which divine reaction follows automatically on correct performance of a ritual.

C. We should also distinguish between magic ritual and the performance of miracles.
1. The magician performs a ritual to call upon outside powers to perform an action.
2. The power to perform the miracle is understood to be available to the miracle-worker much as natural abilities are.
3. The powers are given by the gods but reside in the miracle-worker and are always available for use.
4. Generally, use of the term *miracle* indicates approval, while *magic* usually indicates disapproval.

D. Why would magic be considered an appropriate response to anxiety over the capriciousness of fate?
1. Anxiety over fate was concern over a lack of control, and magic is a means of taking control.
2. Magic could be a response to the loss of faith in traditional religious practices during the Hellenistic era.
3. Magical practices did not address primary "religious" concerns, such as salvation.
4. But such concerns were not necessarily a part of Hellenistic or Roman religious culture either.

E. Magical practices are a product of syncretism.
1. Magic assigns equal importance to almost all aspects of the divine, to all gods and goddesses.
2. The key to magical practice is knowing the "hidden" name to which a divine power must respond.
3. Isis gained magical power through her knowledge of the hidden name of Amun-Rē.

4. Extant magical spells include long recitations of divine names recited in the hope that one would "hook" a god or demon.
5. This practice survives in popular culture in magic words, such as *Alakazam* (from *Allah*).
6. Nonsense syllables imitating foreign languages or arcane rituals were also a common feature, as in *Abracadabra*.
7. Scraps of religious rituals appeared in spells because they were believed to possess inherent power, as in *hocus pocus*, apparently from *hoc est corpus meum* ("this is my body").

F. Magic and magical ritual were used for practical and fairly mundane purposes.
1. Magic was used primarily for love charms, healings, curses, and protection from curses.
2. The concerns of those who turned to magic were much more "practical" than "theological," but this is true of most religious practices of the time.

G. Apuleius combined stories of magical practices with serious religious devotion in *The Golden Ass*.
1. In the novel, Lucius learns that a woman is a sorceress who is able to change herself into a bird.
2. The maid who is his lover brings him the wrong ointment, and he is turned into an ass.
3. The ultimate outcome of this magical predicament is religious, Lucius's induction into the mystery religion of Isis.
4. This casual intermingling of magic and devout religiosity shows that there was no clear line dividing the two in the imperial era.

Essential Reading:

Mary Beard, John North, and Simon Price. *Religions of Rome*, vol. 1, pp. 211–244.

Luther H. Martin. *Hellenistic Religions: An Introduction*, pp. 16–34.

Robert Turcan. *The Gods of Ancient Rome*, pp. 145–154.

Supplementary Reading:

David E. Aune. *Prophecy in Early Christianity and the Ancient Mediterranean World*, pp. 23–79.

Fritz Graf. *Magic in the Ancient World.*

Sarah Iles Johnston, ed. *Religions of the Ancient World: A Guide*, pp. 139–152.

Robert Turcan, *The Cults of the Roman Empire*, pp. 266–290.

Questions to Consider:

1. Why has astrology continued to attract attention and a place in many newspapers, while other ancient forms of divination have largely disappeared?

2. What common religious practices might be considered "magical"? What is the rationale behind them that defines them as "religious" instead?

3. The oracle-monger chose an existing oracle and reinterpreted it to address a new situation. What might be the rationale for this practice, given beliefs about prophetic oracles in the ancient world?

Lecture Forty-One
Rome—Critics and Charlatans

Scope: From the 4th century B.C.E., philosophers subjected the Greek religious tradition to rationalistic criticism. The philosophical critique of religious traditions fell into four categories: explanations of the origins of religious beliefs, apologies for the philosophical pursuit of truth as a form of religious piety, attacks on religious beliefs as either unworthy of the true nature of the gods or inconsistent with worldly reality, and criticism of religious people, either as hypocritical con artists or as gullible fools. Lucian of Samosata, a satirist of the 2nd century C.E., created a devastating portrait of one religious charlatan in a literary parody of an admiring philosophical "life." In another work, he also wrote about the gullibility of Christians that led them to become easy prey to hucksters claiming to be one of them. His "common sense" critiques represent a rationalist's skepticism toward any and all religious claims.

Outline

I. From the early 4th century B.C.E., there was philosophical critique of traditional Greek religious culture.

    A. Philosophy provided not only a critique but also a rival to religion during the Hellenistic era.

        1. Many philosophies offered their own metaphysics, moral standards, cosmology, and means of "salvation."

        2. Philosophical and religious forms of knowledge differed in presuppositions, methodologies, and goals.

        3. Philosophical critique also arose from a sense that traditional religion was inadequate to the needs of a new age.

    B. The philosophical critique of religion may be said to fall into four categories.

        1. Explanations of the origins of religious beliefs, including the origins of the gods and specific mythological stories.

        2. Apologies for philosophical approaches to religion in contrast to traditional ways of worship.

3. Attacks on religious beliefs as unworthy of the gods or as inconsistent with the realities of the world.
4. Critiques of religious people either as gullible believers or as hypocritical charlatans.

C. Explanations for the origins of religious belief ranged from the general to the particular.
1. Aristotle explained that religious beliefs were based on both experiences during sleep and observations about the order of the cosmos.
2. Euhemerus of Messene argued that mythology arose from legendary stories about great human kings.
3. Pausanius explained the origins of some myths based on his observations at the locations involved.
4. Cornutus explained Greek myths through complicated etymological analysis of the names of gods.

D. Arguments that philosophical investigation is the highest form of piety go back at least to Socrates.
1. Socrates argued that his life of philosophical questioning was a pious response to the pronouncement of the Delphic oracle.
2. Given that Socrates was accused of undermining traditional religion, this defense was strategically wise, although it failed.

E. Plutarch wrote an explanation of the myth of Osiris and Isis that defends philosophical piety.
1. Plutarch wrote on a wide variety of topics with moral instruction in mind.
2. Plutarch's *Concerning Isis and Osiris* provides the most complete version we have of the events surrounding the death of Osiris.
3. Plutarch identifies Isis with wisdom and the search for truth with her desire to find Osiris.
4. Plutarch argues that philosophy and religion are merely different ways of reaching the same truth
5. Plutarch also suggests that the Egyptian gods were *daimons*, superhuman creatures that combine the spiritual and physical.
6. Plutarch explicitly rejects the idea that the story of Isis and Osiris is based in the fertility cycle.

F. Another philosophical critique of religion is the claim that the traditional myths do not do justice to reality.

1. Mythology depicts the gods as similar to human beings, but these portrayals wrong the gods.
2. Another viewpoint, espoused, for example, by the Cynic philosopher Cercidas, argued that the gods didn't seem to care about humanity at all.
3. Traditional religious mythology failed to satisfy and was rejected by rationalists, both atheists and the pious.

G. Some criticized traditional religious culture on the basis of the behavior of its adherents.
   1. Theophrastus's portrait of the superstitious man also makes fun of the neurotic anxiety that motivates his behavior.
   2. Religious culture in the Hellenistic and early imperial eras had its share of charlatans.
   3. Such people provoked pointed criticism and degraded the whole religious enterprise.
   4. The fact that gullible people were preyed upon by hucksters deepened the contempt many felt toward religious groups.

II. The satirist Lucian of Samosata provides portraits of religious and philosophical hucksters.

   A. Lucian (c. 115–after 180 C.E.) was first a legal advocate, then a traveling lecturer and satirist.
      1. Lucian's satires reflected common sense and a perspective tempered by an awareness of life's brevity.
      2. Lucian wrote more than 80 humorous pieces that survive.
      3. Lucian's perennial subject was the popular culture of his day.

   B. Lucian wrote an account of a self-styled "divine man," Alexander of Abunoteichos, whom Lucian styles a "quack oracle" and a charlatan.
      1. Lucian makes fun of Alexander but also parodies the admiring "lives" written about notable philosophers.
      2. Lucian covers all the usual details of such a "life" but does so with ironic content.
      3. He describes Alexander's "education" in the streets and under the tutelage of charlatan "masters."
      4. He describes Alexander's appearance, carefully calculated to mimic the stereotype of an inspired prophet.
      5. Alexander even claimed to have a golden thigh like that attributed to Pythagoras.

C. Lucian describes Alexander's inaugural appearance as a prophet but also reveals the trickery behind it.

  1. Alexander planted a blown goose egg containing a small snake and later "found" it in a simulated frenzy.

  2. Soon, he appeared with a full-grown snake tricked out with a false head so that he could make it seem to talk.

  3. Alexander would answer sealed queries with appropriate oracles, either by secretly opening them or by providing vague replies.

  4. Lucian describes the prophet's "mighty deeds," but they are "mighty" only as brazen frauds.

  5. Lucian finally describes Alexander's death and the succession of "worthy" disciples at his shrine.

  6. Lucian also depicts the gullibility of those foolish enough to take all this seriously.

D. Alexander established a mystery religion, and Lucian describes what was expected of its rituals.

  1. An initial "purging ceremony" was intended to roust unbelievers from the crowd.

  2. A proclamation was read to exclude Christians and Epicureans, both considered atheists.

  3. A reenactment of the birth of Asclepius was followed the next day by the "birth" and presentation of "the new Asclepius," the snake Glycon.

  4. The third day reenacted Alexander's own birth and Alexander's romance with the moon goddess Selene.

  5. In fact, a mystery religion associated with Alexander and Glycon lasted for more than a century.

  6. Whether Alexander was a fraud or a sincere prophet is now impossible to judge.

E. Lucian also wrote a treatise about a philosophical con man named Peregrinus.

  1. At one point, Peregrinus traveled to Palestine, where he became a Christian.

  2. He soon became a leader among the Christians and was arrested for his adherence to the faith.

  3. The Christians devoted themselves to making his time in prison as comfortable as possible.

4. The community provided elaborate meals for him, read him their Scriptures, and encouraged him.
5. Apparently, Christians were famous for such behavior, and Peregrinus profited handsomely at their expense.
6. For Lucian, Christians represent the worst sort of religious fools.
7. Peregrinus eventually alienated the Christians and became a wandering Cynic philosopher.

F. Lucian offers a rationalist's skeptical evaluation of the claims of religious leaders and their followers.
1. Lucian has no time for most philosophy or religion because of the foolishness and hypocrisy of the devotees.
2. Although somewhat sympathetic to the Cynics and the Epicureans, Lucian appears to accept no creed.
3. He echoes the evaluation of human life in wisdom literature: Enjoy life's pleasures while they last.

Supplementary Reading:

Lucian of Samosata. *Lucian*, vol. 4, *Alexander the False Prophet*, and vol. 5, *The Passing of Peregrinus*.

Luther H. Martin. *Hellenistic Religions: An Introduction*, pp. 111–113.

Marvin W. Meyer, ed. *The Ancient Mysteries*, pp. 160–172.

Questions to Consider:

1. What characteristics of religious culture seem most likely to come under rationalist critique? What do such critiques tend to overlook, and what characteristics do they tend to misjudge? Why?

2. Which sort(s) of philosophical critique of traditional Greek religious culture seem most cogent or legitimate? Why?

3. When we have only one extensive witness to the life of an ancient person, such as Alexander or Peregrinus, how might we best evaluate the truth or falsehood of that account?

Lecture Forty-Two
Jesus of Nazareth as a Figure in History

Scope: There are many problems in creating a historical portrait of Jesus of Nazareth. Most of the historical information about him is embedded in mythic accounts of his words and deeds, written to induce belief in Jesus as the Son of God. It is difficult not only to isolate historically verifiable data but also to evaluate the data to produce a historical account of Jesus's life and ministry that accords with his cultural milieu. We begin with the hypothesis that Jesus believed he was called to reform the Judaism of his time in light of a radically new understanding of both Israel's covenantal obedience and the Lord's merciful love for his people. This hypothesis is tested and supplemented with widely accepted historical data about Jesus. The result is a theory of Jesus's intentions consistent with his standing as a unique religious thinker whose character and actions substantiated the content of his message.

Outline

I. There are particular problems that face us in creating a historical portrait of Jesus of Nazareth.

   A. The first problem is the sort of evidence historical investigation includes and excludes.
      1. The historical Jesus must be investigated through accumulation, analysis, and comparison of historical sources.
      2. *History* here means "what can be surmised to have happened in the past on the basis of historically acceptable data and analysis."
      3. History explicitly excludes "myth," any idea of the supernatural or what lies behind or above history.

   B. The second problem is that Jesus is important to history specifically because of his mythic significance.
      1. For Christians, what Jesus did and said makes sense only in the light of his mythic identity.
      2. Jesus is a historic figure because of the belief that he revealed God's intentions for humanity.

3. History can neither confirm nor reject mythic identity, because such judgments lie beyond history's competence.
4. At best, we can say that his followers *believed* Jesus to be the Son of God or the Messiah.

C. Most sources of information about Jesus are mythic in nature, concerned with his identity.
1. The Gospels' authors were not interested in Jesus's biography but in proclamation of the good news.
2. The members of the Jesus movement thought about Jesus as the present Lord and future Messiah, always accessible to them.
3. The Jesus movement's earliest proclamations appear to have focused on Jesus's suffering, death, and resurrection.
4. The Gospel accounts dealt only with particular events that illuminated Jesus's mythic identity.
5. The problem is succinctly summarized in John 20:30–31: The Gospels include only what leads their audiences to faith.

D. Each of the canonical and apocryphal Gospels presents a distinctive portrait of Jesus.
1. Each Gospel writer chose and crafted the material available to produce the chosen portrait.
2. None of the Gospels claims to tell the "whole story" about Jesus, nor do all four together.
3. From the beginning, there was a collection of stories about Jesus, coinciding on some points and diverging on others.

E. Even events in Jesus's life that appear in the Gospels cannot simply be accepted as historically accurate.
1. The earliest New Testament writings, Paul's genuine letters, were written at least 10 to 12 years after the end of Jesus's ministry.
2. The earliest written Gospels are no closer than 40 years or so to the end of Jesus's ministry.
3. For decades, stories about Jesus were communicated primarily by word of mouth.
4. Even after the composition of the earliest Gospels, oral transmission of stories about Jesus continued.

F. There are also problems with the proper compilation and analysis of the historical data.

1. Few investigators of the historical Jesus are without a personal agenda that inevitably affects their work.
2. It is difficult to recreate the cultural context of 1st-century rural Palestine to understand Jesus better.
3. Scholars and others often make the mistake of understanding Jesus's culture in terms of our own.

II. To develop a historical portrait of Jesus, we must decide what we wish to know and evaluate the data that are available.

A. Scholars are generally agreed about what they wish to know about the historical Jesus.
    1. They seek historically reliable information about the cultural and social context of Jesus's ministry.
    2. They want accurate versions of Jesus's sayings, distinguished from those attributed to him.
    3. They seek a reliable account of Jesus's deeds and the chronology of his ministry.
    4. They want an idea of Jesus's self-understanding of who he was and what he was doing.
    5. These goals are difficult to achieve with even the most heavily documented figures of the past.

B. The primary sources for the investigation of the historical Jesus are the writings of the New Testament.
    1. Paul preserves historical traditions about Jesus and considers them important.
    2. All four canonical Gospels have a valid claim to contain reliable historical traditions.
    3. The sources are not the New Testament books themselves but the stories they contain.

C. Other sources include apocryphal writings, Roman and Jewish sources, and stray sayings of Jesus.
    1. Apocryphal writings were not accepted as reliable by enough Jesus communities to be included in the canon.
    2. Many of these works provide interesting insights into the early Jesus communities, as well as clearly legendary material.
    3. There is very limited information about Jesus in Roman and Jewish sources, and even that is hard to separate from the beliefs of Jesus's followers.

4. Stray sayings of Jesus include sayings in Paul's letters, Acts of the Apostles, other early Christian writers, and unique Gospel manuscripts.

5. These other writings are sources of isolated stories about Jesus that may have historical worth.

D. How do we determine which stories about Jesus have historical value?

1. Several scholars have developed criteria to determine which of Jesus's sayings are most likely to be authentic.

2. The best known use of such criteria was by the Jesus Seminar.

3. However, a collection of sayings and deeds is not the best way to reconstruct the life of a historical figure.

4. A sounder approach establishes a theoretical structure for the facts of Jesus's life and ministry.

5. We will begin with a concept of who Jesus thought he was and what he was doing.

E. A reasonable theory is that Jesus believed he was called to reform Judaism in light of a radically new understanding of Israel's covenantal obedience and the Lord's merciful love.

1. This theory is based in part on the disciples' title *messiah*, or "anointed one," for Jesus.

2. The messiah was associated with the Lord's impending sovereign rule over the earth.

F. This hypothesis may be tested in light of widely accepted historical information about Jesus's words and deeds.

1. Jesus was baptized by John the Baptist, himself a Jewish reformer, and appealed to his authority.

2. Jesus directed his message to Jews and showed no particular concern for Gentiles.

3. Jesus welcomed "outsiders," people excluded from official Jewish religious concern.

4. Jesus had disciples who accompanied him in his travels throughout Palestine.

5. Jesus made statements emphasizing the paramount importance of responding to the Lord's call.

6. Jesus emphasized the commandment to love the Lord, one's neighbor, and even one's enemies.

7. Jesus prohibited divorce as part of the return to God's original intentions for humanity.
8. Jesus was believed to be capable of performing miracles.
9. Jesus expected a major future event that would initiate the establishment of God's sovereignty over the earth, "the kingdom of God."
10. Jesus made a threat against the Jerusalem Temple, saying that he would destroy and rebuild it again in three days, a threat interpreted in various ways.
11. Jesus used bread and wine at his last supper as symbols of the meaning of his death.
12. Jesus was tried on a political charge by the Romans and executed by crucifixion.
13. After his death, Jesus's followers became convinced that he was alive again.
14. His followers proclaimed this message and became the nucleus of an identifiable Jesus movement.

G. Although these data are consistent with our theory of Jesus's self-concept, the facts alone do not confirm the theory's validity or viability.
1. This historical outline is also consistent with the general outlines of Jesus's career as it is depicted in the New Testament.
2. It also confirms what subsequent history has told us: Jesus was a unique and highly influential thinker whose personality and actions substantiated his message.

Supplementary Reading:

Bart D. Ehrman. *A Brief Introduction to the New Testament*, pp. 158–184.

The Gospel According to St. Mark.

Mark Allan Powell. *Jesus as a Figure in History*.

Questions to Consider:

1. What motivates scholars and others to search for the "historical Jesus"? How might the results affect faith statements made about Jesus by his followers?

2. What factors lead to disagreements about major historical figures? What are some conflicting views of Christopher Columbus, Thomas Jefferson, and Abraham Lincoln, for example?

3. In your opinion, which historical facts about Jesus seem to be most open to question? Which seem to be most reliable? Why?

Lecture Forty-Three
Creating Jesus Communities

Scope: The Jesus movement began as a sectarian group within Judaism, with its own rituals and prayers. It spread extensively among Greek-speaking Jews, who became the leaders of the movement's missionary outreach. Among those converted were "God-fearers," Gentiles who were sympathetic to Judaism but refused circumcision. Paul of Tarsus, who had once persecuted the followers of Jesus, became the movement's most influential missionary. After an initial proclamation of the good news, Paul would teach potential converts while working, forming a congregation over a period of several years. After appointing leaders for the community, Paul would continue his missionary travels, keeping in touch through return visits and letters. Paul created the situation that led to the Jesus movement's break with Judaism when he argued that circumcision should not be a prerequisite to membership in the Jesus community. The break with Judaism left the Jesus movement open to persecution by the Roman authorities.

Outline

I. The Jesus movement began as a sectarian group within Judaism, based on the conviction that Jesus of Nazareth was Messiah, the Lord's anointed.

   A. The Jesus movement arose directly out of Jesus's ministry and was led by Jesus's disciples.
      1. Central to the Jesus movement was the belief that Jesus was alive again after his crucifixion.
      2. Belief in his resurrection inspired the disciples to preach Jesus's message, that establishment of the Lord's sovereign rule—the kingdom of God—was near.
      3. The kingdom was the fulfillment of the Lord's promises to Israel, now certified by Jesus's death and resurrection.
      4. The Jesus movement's proclamation of the kingdom was the same as that of Jesus but now joined to the message "Jesus is Messiah."

5. Jesus's followers expected the Lord to intervene in history and vindicate his faithful people.

6. Jesus's followers shared sympathy with the poor and outcast, expecting a reversal of the fortunes of the rich and the poor at the end of history.

B. The members of the earliest Jesus movement were Jews who observed Jewish practices but added rites of their own to Jewish worship.

1. Baptism became a ritual of initiation from the beginning, as a sign of new life.

2. Jesus's followers practiced "the breaking of the bread" as a communal meal.

3. Followers also had their own prayers and prayed to Jesus "as to a god."

4. "Spiritual gifts" were sometimes practiced during the course of group meetings.

C. The initial growth of the Jesus movement included Greek-speaking Jews who inspired missionary outreach.

1. These cosmopolitan Jews expressed their new faith in Greek terms familiar to Gentiles.

2. The Aramaic term *messiah*, meaning "anointed one," became the Greek *christos.*

3. Jesus's favored self-designation, "Son of Man," a traditional term in Hebrew and Aramaic meaning "human being," fell into disuse.

4. It was replaced by "Son of God," a title that, in the imperial Roman world, indicated superhuman power and authority.

5. Jesus was also designated "Lord" and "savior," both titles with connotations in Roman religious culture.

6. Greek-speaking Jews gave the Jesus movement a new vocabulary that introduced new ideas about Jesus's identity and significance.

D. The early Jesus movement benefited from some aspects of the prevailing religious culture.

1. In the ancient Mediterranean world, to be a member of a society was to be a part of its religious culture.

2. Weakening of traditional religious communities gave rise to new religious communities that one made a choice to join.

3. For example, one chose to join a mystery religion and to form a bond of service and patronage with the mystery deity.
4. There was no threat to the polytheistic worldview when one joined a mystery religion, and one could join several different mystery religions.

E. But the early Jesus movement was also at odds with aspects of the prevailing religious culture.
1. Monotheistic faith was considered a threat to the common welfare, because it angered the traditional gods who protected the empire.
2. Judaism had gained recognition as a *religio licta*, a legitimate non-conforming religion.
3. Romans were also highly suspicious of any religious group that practiced secret rituals.
4. While the early Jesus movement was identified with Judaism, it shared Judaism's privileged status.
5. But because most Jews rejected the Jesus movement, its leaders turned to Gentiles who were sympathetic to Judaism but rejected circumcision.
6. These "God-fearers" became a primary source of converts to the Jesus movement.

II. The most influential of the Greek-speaking Jewish missionaries for the Jesus movement was Paul of Tarsus.

A. Paul was a typical Jew of the Hellenistic world, educated in his own culture and the standard Greek curriculum.
1. Paul was educated, first, at a primary school and, later, with a grammarian to learn rhetoric.
2. Paul was also well-versed in the rabbinic interpretation of Scripture and "a Pharisee in regards to the law."
3. He was zealous in his fulfillment of the covenant and "righteous" in terms of the Law.
4. Paul persecuted the Jesus movement in some official capacity but had a conversion experience he likened to Jesus's resurrection appearances.

B. After his conversion, Paul became a missionary apostle by commission from the Jesus congregation in Antioch.
1. Antioch focused its mission on Greek-speaking Jews in cities of the eastern Mediterranean.

    2. A missionary from Antioch named Barnabas became Paul's mentor and partner.

    3. Paul found that he had the greatest success with Gentiles associated with urban synagogues.

    4. Paul had success establishing congregations with both Jewish and Gentile members.

C. The popular image of Paul's work of spreading the gospel focuses on public preaching.

    1. In fact, public proclamation was only an initial part of spreading information about a religious movement.

    2. Paul did not have the status or reputation necessary for public speaking, and his intention was not to convert individuals but to create a Jesus community.

    3. Paul taught potential converts in the workshop, where he could both work and teach at the same time.

    4. Paul's work and teaching in a secluded environment benefited both his students and those socially connected to them.

D. The process of conversion meant leaving behind one's way of life and the people associated with it.

    1. Conversion might be a joyful experience, but it also produced anxiety and doubt.

    2. Conversion to the Jesus movement required severing all one's kinship and professional ties in favor of relationships within the Jesus community.

    3. There was also the stress of joining what was a disdained "countercultural" movement.

    4. It was the job of the missionary preacher and the community to ease the convert's transition to the new life.

E. The conversion was confirmed through encouragement, example, and reaffirmation.

    1. Paul said converts "received the word in much affliction, with joy inspired by the Holy Spirit" (1 Thess. 1:6).

    2. The "affliction" came from the world left behind, while the "joy" came from the spirit of God.

    3. Paul and other missionaries used kinship language (*brother, sister*) to reassure their converts that they had been "reborn" into a new "family."

4. The mystery religions used similar language and characterized initiation as a "death" and "rebirth."
5. Paul offered his own example for his converts to emulate, much as philosophers provided an example for their students.
6. Paul understood whatever sufferings his converts might experience in the context of their salvation as proof of their faith.

F. Paul would provide for the continued life of the new congregation before moving on.
1. Paul appointed congregational leaders who acted as patrons and provided the congregation with a meeting place.
2. After leaving, Paul would continue to keep in touch with the congregations through visits.
3. When unable to visit, Paul would send a co-worker on his behalf or an emissary with a letter from Paul for the congregation.
4. Paul's letters in the New Testament have been extremely influential, but they were originally occasional documents written to address specific situations.

G. Paul contributed to the break with Judaism by accepting uncircumcised Gentiles into the Jesus community.
1. Gentiles were reluctant to be circumcised, because Roman society disdained the practice.
2. Paul argued that inclusion into the Jesus movement depended on commitment, because circumcision could not guarantee covenantal obedience.
3. His stance created a major controversy that took many years to resolve, but eventually, Paul's position won out.
4. Once separated from Judaism, the Jesus movement no longer enjoyed official protection, and persecution by the Roman authorities began in earnest.

Essential Reading:

1 Thessalonians.

Henry Chadwick. *The Early Church*, pp. 9–31.

Bart D. Ehrman. *A Brief Introduction to the New Testament*, pp. 185–274.

Leander E. Keck. *Paul and His Letters*.

Romans.

Supplementary Reading:

Sarah Iles Johnston, ed. *Religions of the Ancient World: A Guide*, pp. 233–239.

Questions to Consider:

1. What are some of the major similarities between Judaism and Christianity that reflect the Jesus movement's origins as a sect of Judaism?

2. How did the introduction of Greek terminology affect the way Greek-speaking converts understood who Jesus was? Was this development inevitable or a result of circumstances?

3. Paul once wrote, "I have become all things to all people, that I might by all means save some" (1 Corinthians 9:22b). How is this statement supported by his missionary method and teaching?

Lecture Forty-Four
Living and Dying for the God(s)

Scope: The idea that death is sometimes preferable to life has a strong grounding in the Greek religious and philosophical tradition. Among philosophers, suicide was considered an appropriate response when the alternative was to betray the principles that guided one's life. In such a case, suicide was a "fitting death." In the religious sphere, the "fitting death" was execution under persecution. The earliest Jewish martyrs were executed during persecution under Syrian rule in the 2nd century B.C.E. The Jesus movement associated martyrdom with Jesus's death at the hands of the Roman authorities, as well as loyalty to Jesus as Lord instead of Caesar. The political overtones of the Jesus movement brought its members under suspicion. They could gain release after arrest by sacrificing, and most of those arrested capitulated. But those who remained steadfast to endure martyrdom became heroes and gave Christians a reputation for obstinacy to the point of death.

Outline

I. A recurring idea in Greek culture was the desirability of some escape from the tribulations of life, even if it were found in death.

    A. The phrase that concludes Sophocles's *Oedipus Rex*, "Call no man happy till the day of his death," reflected the uncertainties of life.

        1. The idea is that it is only after a person dies that one can accurately assess his or her life as happy or tragic.

        2. Throughout life, a person is constantly subject to the buffets of fate and unexpected turns of events.

        3. A common idea was that the best time to die was at the peak of one's strength and acclaim.

        4. In the face of life's trouble, the Greeks also theorized that it might be better for one never to have been born.

    B. In the *Phaedo*, a dialogue set after Socrates's condemnation to death, Socrates considers the option of suicide.

        1. He says that a person shouldn't take his own life, because doing so is forbidden by common opinion.

2. Socrates believes that one must wait until the gods make it clear that death is the right choice.
3. Socrates argues that a philosopher will die gladly, because he expects blessings in the other world.
4. Socrates's death—execution through poison—was believed to be consistent with his philosophical calling, a "fitting death."

C. Hellenistic philosophers generally considered suicide an appropriate action in some situations.
1. They generally agreed that the rational response to some circumstances of life is withdrawal.
2. This response arose from the obligations of the philosopher's calling that extend beyond this life.
3. It was more important to live a life guided by philosophical principles than simply to live.
4. Suicide was sometimes in keeping with the philosophical vocation, if that was the only way to remain true to its dictates.
5. A related idea was that suicide was a means of avoiding disgrace or a painful death.

D. Lucian of Samosata provides an example of the "fitting death" of a philosopher gone wrong.
1. Lucian gave an account of Peregrinus's brief career as a member of the Jesus movement.
2. Peregrinus became a Cynic philosopher and later decided to immolate himself at Olympia to show the Greeks how to die.
3. He had a pyre built and delivered a long oration claiming that he wanted to die as he had lived.
4. Some of the crowd prodded him to burn, although Lucian claims Peregrinus had hoped to be "persuaded" to live.
5. Peregrinus had to carry out his plan, and his followers invented stories about his "glorification."
6. Lucian asserts that Peregrinus did it all for public acclaim but notes that his followers declined to follow his example.

E. A "fitting death" for a philosopher might also be execution or death in exile.
1. What was important was remaining faithful, no matter what the opposition or the hardships.

2. Philosophers and member of religious communities were persecuted or exiled under some emperors.
3. Domitian (b. 51, r. 81–96 C.E.) was noted for twice banning philosophers from Italy and may have persecuted the Jesus movement.
4. Philostratus tells how Apollonius was arrested and brought before Domitian but managed to gain acquittal.

II. In the religious sphere, these issues are discussed in terms of persecution and martyrdom.

    A. In religious communities, dying for one's beliefs was a means of "bearing witness."
      1. The word *martyr* is taken from the Greek *marturein*, meaning "to bear witness."
      2. Martyrdom was believed to be the ultimate witness to one's faith, the crown of a faithful life.

    B. The first notable example of Jewish martyrdom is the persecution under Antiochus IV Epiphanes, the Hellenistic king of Syria.
      1. Antiochus IV Epiphanes (r. 175–164? B.C.E.) was a fervent Hellenist and expected all his subjects to adopt Hellenistic culture.
      2. Antiochus had supporters among the Jews in Judea, but a conservative reaction led to an insurrection.
      3. Antiochus put down the revolt and imposed Hellenization on Jews by desecrating the temple and making it illegal to obey Torah.
      4. The persecution and martyrdom of faithful Jews had several notable consequences, including veneration of martyrs, belief in resurrection, apocalyptic expectations, and a guerilla movement.
      5. The persecution under Antiochus became a model for all later persecutions of the Jews.
      6. The experience of persecution contributed to the tradition that all the prophets had died as martyrs, a tradition without biblical support.

    C. For the early Jesus movement, the ideal of martyrdom was buttressed by the death of Jesus.
      1. Jesus's death was understood as a sacrifice for sins and an example of innocent suffering.

2. Paul emphasized the solidarity between Jesus and the believer in both life and death.

3. In Acts, the stoning of Stephen, the first martyr of the Jesus movement, is modeled on Jesus's death by crucifixion.

D. The ideal of martyrdom was strengthened by the idea that God's kingdom was near.

    1. The idea of Jesus as "Lord" displaced loyalty to the emperor and exalted God over the state.

    2. This idea is expressed, for example, in *The Martyrdom of Polycarp*, written c. 120 C.E.

    3. The expectation that God's kingdom would soon come gave reassurance to those who suffered.

    4. An idea in the early Jesus movement was that conflict with worldly powers was inevitable.

E. The political aspects of the Jesus movement were emphasized in Roman proceedings against its members.

    1. The welfare of the Roman state was believed to lie in the spiritual benefits conferred by the gods.

    2. Similarly, worship of the emperor or his *genius* was an expression of loyalty.

    3. Because members of the Jesus movement did not honor the Roman gods, they were labeled "atheists."

    4. They were suspected of subversive tendencies, in part because of their secret meetings.

    5. Proof that one was not a follower of Jesus was to burn incense in front of an image of the emperor.

F. Imperial policy against members of the Jesus movement evolved gradually.

    1. Trajan (r. 98–117 C.E.) was asked by one of his governors, Pliny the Younger, how to proceed against those accused of being Christians.

    2. Trajan's reply allowed Pliny some latitude but also established several points of procedure.

    3. Despite the example of the martyrs, the majority of those who were persecuted for being Christians capitulated under pressure.

4. These people might later return to the Jesus movement after the persecution, seeking forgiveness and readmission to the community.

5. The reaction to such attempts usually depended on how severely a local community had suffered.

G. Whatever the reality, members of the Jesus movement became notorious for their obstinacy.

1. Polycarp saw his death by martyrdom as a sacrifice supplementing the sacrifice of Jesus.

2. The perseverance of the few to the point of death led to their veneration by the community.

3. The earliest heroes of the Jesus movement were the martyrs, and each of their deaths was regarded as the crown of a pious life.

4. Marcus Aurelius (r. 161–180) commended those who remained steadfast in their beliefs under pressure but made an exception for those who were obstinate like the Christians.

Essential Reading:

Acts of the Apostles 6–7.

Henry Chadwick. *The Early Church*, pp. 32–83.

Henry Jackson Flanders, Jr., Robert Wilson Crapps, and David Anthony Smith. *People of the Covenant: An Introduction to the Hebrew Bible*, pp. 465–474.

Supplementary Reading:

1 Maccabees 1–6.

2 Maccabees 6–10.

Michael D. Coogan, ed. *The Oxford History of the Biblical World*, pp. 317–351, 388–419.

Questions to Consider:

1. What considerations seem to lie behind the Greek idea that the best death is death at the height of one's powers and renown? How do our own ideas differ in this respect?

2. What are some of the points of similarity and difference between the idea of the philosopher's "fitting death" and religious martyrdom? What is the significance of the similarities and differences?

3. If the majority of those who were persecuted for being members of the Jesus movement capitulated, why did the official persecutions ultimately fail to suppress Christianity?

Lecture Forty-Five
Women's Religious Roles in the Early Empire

Scope: Our picture of women's participation in early imperial religious culture is hampered by lack of reliable sources. Literary sources tend to overlook or degrade women's religious activities, while artifacts provide only limited information. Roman women had religious duties in the home and the Vestal virgins performed similar duties for the state. Both the Vestals and priestesses of mystery religions were under the supervision of male priests. Women may have found some autonomy in magic, but our knowledge in this regard is scanty. Evidence from later rabbinic tradition tends to restrict Jewish women's religious activities to the home, while archaeological findings suggest that Jewish women served as patrons and leaders of synagogues. In the early Jesus movement, women served both as congregational patrons and as missionaries. Depictions of women in the Gospel traditions tend to grant them equal status with men. Later accommodation of Christianity to Roman social expectations led to suppression of female leadership.

Outline

I.   The primary problems in reconstructing women's religious practices are finding sources and defining parameters.

    A. The first set of problems concerns the sources available to us for reconstructing women's participation in religious activities during the early empire.

        1. Our primary sources are literary and, thus, tend to downplay women's activities.

        2. Literature was the province of educated men who were generally unconcerned with women's activities.

        3. Moreover, classical literature was preserved and copied by monks, who themselves considered women inferior to men.

        4. We have virtually no written record of women's religious activities from women themselves.

    B. Those ancient literary works that do deal with women's religious activities were written with specific objectives.

1. Historians in the late republic presented the Roman past, including women's religious activities, in an idealized form.
2. Greek and Roman authors most often depicted women's religion as illegitimate in some way.
3. A common way to discredit a religious movement was to associate it with unsupervised women.
4. At the least, we must be cautious in using literary sources for reconstructing women's religious activities.

C. There are also non-literary written sources for women's involvement in religious activities.
1. Some of these sources are artifacts, such as funerary and dedicatory inscriptions.
2. Others are non-literary writings, such as letters, prayers, spells, listings of festivals, and regulations.
3. Given that the survival of such sources is accidental, it's difficult to determine how representative they are of women's religious activities.
4. Potential sources can be overlooked if fragmentary names are restored in their male forms.
5. The question is: What sort of information is most likely to provide an accurate picture of women's religion?

D. Another problem is whether gender is a primary line of division in ancient religious practices.
1. Obviously, sexual identity is not the only division in ancient imperial society.
2. Paul wrote in Galatians 3:28 that in Christ, there is no longer Jew or Greek, slave or free, male and female, and to these divisions we may add rank and status.
3. One's place in imperial society was determined by the combination of one's life circumstances.
4. To what extent can we talk about women's religion per se, with other aspects of social identity set aside?

E. Given these caveats, it still appears possible to talk about women's involvement in early imperial religious cultures.
1. We will concentrate on women's presence and leadership in religious activities.
2. Later sources will be supplemented with material from earlier witnesses.

II. Women filled a variety of roles both as leaders and participants in mainstream religious culture.

    A. Roman women had their own realm of religious activity with specific duties in the family home.

        1. Women's household rituals centered on the hearth and its protective goddess, Vesta.

        2. The mistress of the house had cultic responsibilities on the calends, nones, and ides of each month.

        3. Periodic festivals in honor of women were celebrated throughout the year.

    B. The primary female religious officials in Rome were the six Vestal Virgins.

        1. The Vestals were chosen by the *pontifex maximus* from among patrician girls aged 6 to 10.

        2. Those chosen lived in the sanctuary of Vesta for 30 years, first learning, then serving and teaching.

        3. Their primary duty was to tend the flame of Vesta and to prepare the flour for sacrificial victims.

        4. The institution of the Vestals was very old, and archaic elements continued to mark their practices.

        5. Despite their standing in Roman society, they were under the authority of the *pontifex maximus*.

    C. As we have seen, most of the mystery religions were dedicated to patron goddesses.

        1. This was true of Demeter's cult at Eleusis and the mysteries from the East.

        2. Although most worshipers of Demeter were women, the priests of the Eleusian mysteries were men.

        3. The cultic personnel of the mysteries of Cybele and Atargatis were men, many of them eunuchs.

        4. There were notably prominent priestesses of Isis, but the dominant cultic personnel were men.

        5. Mystery religions offered opportunities for women's religious expression but were controlled by men.

    D. The religious situation of women was comparable to their general situation in Roman society.

        1. Women derived their status and social identity from the men in their extended families.

    2. In religious activities, women might act as sacred personnel, but they were under the authority of men.

    3. What power they did have operated in covert and unregulated ways, in spite of dominant structures.

E. This also appears to be the case in women's participation in magical rituals.

    1. Despite the common depiction of women practicing magic, surviving spells assume that the practitioner is male.

    2. Contrary to literary convention, spells invariably depict men binding women with spells, not the reverse.

    3. To the extent that women practiced magic, they most likely acted as independent agents.

III. Women in the early empire found larger scope for religious participation in Judaism and the early Jesus movement.

A. Our sources for women's religious lives in Judaism are the Mishnah and archaeological artifacts.

    1. The Mishnah is a collection of rabbinic commentary on the teachings of Torah, compiled c. 200 C.E.

    2. The Mishnah was the product of one group within Judaism; thus, it may not reflect practice among the majority of Jews.

    3. Within the rabbinic sources, women are responsible for maintaining the purity of the Jewish home.

    4. The rabbis exclude women from the most valued activities, notably from learning Torah.

B. Archaeological sources present a different picture of women's roles in Judaism in the early empire.

    1. Women often acted as financial patrons of synagogues, providing for them in part or whole.

    2. Funerary tributes to Jewish women resemble similar tributes to Gentile women.

    3. These tributes include titles such as "elder," "leader of the synagogue," and "mother of the synagogue."

C. We find a similar situation in the early Jesus movement, especially in Paul's letters.

    1. Paul's letters refer to about 80 persons by name, about a fifth of them women.

    2. Most of these women's names appear without reference to a relationship with a man.

3. These women generally appear to be independent merchants or patrons of congregations, the urban bourgeoisie.
4. Women in this position would have been subject to a conflict between their low status as women and their higher status as successful people of business.
5. This conflict was resolved in Jesus communities, where social status was based on accomplishments, not gender.
6. Paul refers to women who are his "fellow workers" and women who act as patrons to Jesus congregations.
7. Despite some attachment to traditional Jewish views of men and women, Paul endorsed sexual equality.

D. An open attitude toward women in the Jesus communities is also reflected in the Gospel traditions.
1. For Luke, women provide one example of those "outsiders" who gain special attention from Jesus.
2. The attention given women in Gospel stories is limited, but most grant women equal standing with men.
3. In Luke 10:38–42, of two models for women's roles, Jesus commends the woman who acts as a disciple instead of serving food.
4. Luke also gives prominence to Mary, the mother of Jesus, primarily in the story of Jesus's birth.
5. Jesus's mother gained a special status and was later credited with many of the titles attributed to goddesses.
6. Women's equality in the Jesus community was muted as the movement entered mainstream Roman society.

Essential Reading:

Bart D. Ehrman. *A Brief Introduction to the New Testament*, pp. 295–306.

Ross Shepard Kraemer. *Her Share of the Blessings*, pp. 50–70, 80–156.

Supplementary Reading:

Rodney Stark. *The Rise of Christianity*, pp. 95–128.

Questions to Consider:

1. Do religious cultures that include goddess worship necessarily reflect the interests of women? What connections exist between the gender of a deity and the interests of women or men as worshipers?

2. Why was magic traditionally associated with female practitioners in ancient literature even though most practitioners appear, in fact, to have been men?

3. Why did Judaism and the early Jesus movement apparently offer more opportunities for religious leadership to women than traditional Roman religious cultures? Does this have more to do with the beliefs and practices of the religious groups involved or with their institutional structures?

Lecture Forty-Six
The Jesus Movement in the Greco-Roman World

Scope: As the Jesus movement entered the final third of the 1st century, a new generation of leadership had to deal with a series of crises, including official persecution, the death of Jesus's disciples, and the fall of Jerusalem after a revolt against Rome. Responses to these crises shaped the New Testament and other works of the Jesus movement. By the mid-2nd century, there was a list of standard philosophical attacks on the Jesus movement and the continuing threat of persecution. The apologists wrote treatises defending their faith as rationally sound and consistent with the highest standards of morality. Within the Christian movement, Marcion and the Gnostic teachers rejected the authority of Jewish scriptures and the Lord of Israel in favor of forms of redemption based on esoteric knowledge. The rejection of their teachings reaffirmed mainstream Christianity's roots in Judaism and the non-rational revelation that formed the core of its teaching.

Outline

I.   The Jesus movement experienced several crises with the death of its first generation of leaders in the last 40 years of the 1st century C.E.

  A.   These crises arose from historical events, the passage of time, and specific beliefs among Jesus's followers.

  1.   The leaders of the Jesus movement had been Jesus's disciples, and their deaths silenced the living voice of witness to his ministry.

  2.   In 64 C.E., the emperor Nero launched a persecution of Jesus's followers in Rome.

  3.   The first generation of Jesus's followers had expected Jesus to return quickly, but they died before he appeared.

  4.   A Jewish revolt against Rome ended with the fall of Jerusalem and the sacking of the Temple in 70.

  B.   These crises presented several different sorts of questions for the second generation.

  1.   What would be the source of authoritative doctrine and reliable traditions about Jesus?

    2. Who was best qualified to lead the movement, and how should they be selected?

    3. How should the movement's traditions be handed on and protected from misinterpretation?

    4. How should Jesus's followers live in a hostile world until the appointed time of his return?

C. Most of the writings in the New Testament and others known as the *Apostolic Fathers* come from this era and address these issues.

    1. The New Testament writings, apart from the genuine letters of Paul and possibly 1 Peter, date from 70 to 130 C.E.

    2. Gospels provided written versions of still-evolving oral traditions about Jesus's life and ministry.

    3. Letters written in the names of earlier leaders addressed problems of discipline or belief.

    4. Other writings deal with leadership, apostolic teachings, problems, martyrs, or "false" teachings.

D. Persecution by Roman authorities was a constant threat, although it was localized, random, and sporadic.

    1. Members of the Jesus movement continued to be liable to persecution after Nero's attack on them in 64.

    2. Domitian (81–96) is usually included among the emperors who persecuted Jesus's followers, although there is no firm evidence that he did so.

    3. Trajan (98–117) outlined policies for proceedings against those accused of being Christians, but they were not to be sought out.

    4. Persecution was a danger, but the fear or expectation of persecution was a continuing part of Christian life.

    5. Popular opinion in the empire was that Jesus's followers were atheists and a criminal threat.

II. In the latter 2nd century, Christianity was engaged in a dialogue with the prevailing intellectual culture.

A. Celsus's *On the True Doctrine* (c. 178) made a number of by-then standard charges against Christians:

    1. The Christian concept of God is unworthy, because its God is unable to control his creation.

    2. If Jesus had been divine, he would not have been betrayed by his followers or died on a cross.

3. Christians share the superstitions of the Jews without the ethnic justification and, in fact, sunder religious belief from national identity.
4. Christians belittle learning in favor of their own fables and take converts from among women and members of the lower orders.
5. Anything of real value in Christianity is stolen from Greek culture and philosophy.

B. Popular attacks provoked attempts among Christians to produce an intellectually defensible presentation of their faith.
1. This movement is represented by the writings of the Christian apologists, a name taken from the Greek word for a literary defense of a person or movement.
2. The apologists wanted to reconcile basic Christian doctrines with concepts from Greek philosophy.
3. Literary defenses of Christianity first appeared during the reign of Hadrian (117–138).

C. The best-known apologist, Justin Martyr (c. 100–165), argued that philosophy was derived from Scripture.
1. Justin wrote several apologies before being arrested and beheaded c. 165.
2. Justin argued that the divine *logos* identified with Jesus in John 1 was the rational mind that governs the cosmos.
3. Human beings participate in the *logos* by virtue of behaving rationally; thus, all rational people are Christian.
4. Justin presented two pictures of Christianity, as a philosophical system and as a non-rational religious revelation.
5. Justin Martyr laid the foundations for later attempts to synthesize Christian doctrine and philosophy.

D. Another attempt to create a "rational" Christian doctrine was the work of the sectarian leader Marcion.
1. Marcion came to Rome around 140 and was excommunicated in 144 but won many followers.
2. Marcion rejected Jewish Scriptures, claiming that the Jewish god was an inferior divinity who was responsible for material creation.

3. This god was subject to emotion and unjustly chose one nation in the world for his people.
4. The Christian God was the true God, who sent Jesus to reveal him to the world.
5. This God was characterized not by law and punishment but by love and forgiveness.
6. Jesus's mission was to overthrow the power of the lowest divinity, the Jewish god, in favor of the worship of the true God.
7. Marcion rejected the Old Testament and books of the New Testament that he felt were "tainted" by Jewish beliefs.
8. Marcion's scriptures were his own edited versions of Paul's letters and Luke's Gospel.

E. The most extreme example of Hellenized Christian belief was Gnosticism.
1. *Gnosticism* refers to various related interpretations of Christian teaching that first appeared around 80 C.E.
2. A cache of Gnostic works was discovered at Nag Hammadi in Egypt in 1945, providing firsthand knowledge of the movement.
3. Basic to Gnosticism is a dualistic view of the cosmos, dividing creation into equal but opposing forces.
4. Gnostic belief teaches redemption through "saving knowledge" of the true nature of the self.

F. The saving knowledge is best understood in terms of the Gnostic myth of creation.
1. The highest God is the *Monad*, existing in total isolation from other lower orders of being.
2. The Monad emanates divine power that spontaneously creates a series of lower divinities.
3. This process ends with the lowest divinity that is incapable of creation by emanation.
4. This divinity falls in love with its reflection in matter and creates the cosmos by "falling" into matter.
5. Humanity is part of this accidental creation, a spark of divinity trapped in gross matter.

G. Gnostic redemption consists in "recalling" one's true identity as a divine spark entombed in a material body.

1. Although humanity is ignorant of the Monad, the Monad chooses to redeem humanity.
2. The Monad sends a Redeemer who "awakens" the elect to their true status.
3. The Redeemer returns to the Monad, while those he awakened are freed from material existence.
4. After death, the divine spark released from the body will ascend to the Monad.

H. The consequences of these beliefs set Gnosticism apart from mainstream Christianity.
1. The important thing in Gnostic salvation is an esoteric knowledge necessarily reserved for the few.
2. Gnostic teachings provide no impetus toward community, with no command to love others.
3. Dualism encourages a distinction between "good" spirit and "evil" matter that denies creation any value.
4. The result is an elitist, exclusivist form of Christian belief that denies the validity of Jewish Scripture.

I. Both Marcion and the Gnostic teachers helped mainstream Christianity reaffirm its basic principles.
1. Marcion and Gnosticism led mainstream Christianity to reaffirm its foundations in Judaism.
2. Exclusivist tendencies in Marcionite and Gnostic doctrine bolstered mainstream support for hierarchical church government to ensure proper interpretation of Jesus's teachings.
3. Marcion's limited scripture led mainstream Christian leaders to develop their own list of authoritative books for defining Christian belief and practice.
4. Mainstream Christianity tarred other non-conforming groups with the Gnostic brush.
5. Hellenistic philosophy that influenced Gnostic systems continued to influence mainstream Christianity, as well.
6. The basic non-rational revelation at the core of Christian faith remained stoutly non-philosophical.

Essential Reading:

Luther H. Martin. *Hellenistic Religions*, pp. 134–154.

Elaine Pagels. *The Gnostic Gospels*.

Robin W. Winks and Susan P. Mattern-Parkes. *The Ancient Mediterranean World: From the Stone Age to A.D. 600*, pp. 184–195.

Supplementary Reading:

Bart D. Ehrman. *Lost Christianities*.

Questions to Consider:

1. Which of the "crises" facing the second generation of leadership in the Jesus movement do you think would be the most influential on that generation's understanding of their faith?

2. Does any of the catalogue of charges Roman writers made against the Christian movement seem valid in any sense? What replies might a Christian apologist have made?

3. Both Marcion and the Gnostic teachers rejected the Jewish scriptures and the God of Israel. What important elements in the mainstream Christian movement of the time derive directly from a perceived continuity with the faith and history of ancient Israel?

Lecture Forty-Seven
The Death and Rebirth of the Old Gods

Scope: Christianity steadily gained strength in Roman culture from the late 2nd century. After a half-century of relative peace, the Christian movement was subject to a series of persecutions during the reigns of the "Barracks Emperors," who gained power through assassination and usurpation. Persecution of Christians often seemed to be a response to pressure on the empire from the Persians and barbarians, as well as internal political unrest. Increasingly repressive persecutions failed to suppress Christianity, and under Constantine, Christianity became the dominant religion of the empire. The collapse of polytheistic religious culture in the ancient Mediterranean world arose, on one hand, from the growing desire for a personal connection with the divine and, on the other, from the expectation that the divine represents absolute moral authority. Even as Christianity triumphed over the Roman world, polytheism reappeared in devotions to the saints and ancient customs continued to be honored.

Outline

I. The era between the reigns of Marcus Aurelius and Constantine saw a shift in the religious balance toward Christianity.

   A. Attacks against Christianity in the latter 2nd century indicate an awareness of its growing power.
   1. Celsus's *On the True Doctrine* (c. 178) was a traditionalist counterattack against a religious rival.
   2. The philosophical synthesis of the Neoplatonic teacher Plotinus was, in part, an alternative to Christian theology.
   3. During this time, Christian thinkers were developing systematic ways of thinking about doctrine.
   4. Christianity's fortunes now most often depended on the policies of individual emperors.

   B. The 50 years between 185 and 235 brought a relative peace and security to Christians in the empire.

1. This period saw only one organized persecution of Christians, in Egypt in 202–203.
2. This was a time of growth and consolidation for the Christian movement.
3. A consensus developed about what books constituted authoritative Scripture by about 200.
4. Creedal statements began to evolve from both theological affirmations and baptismal confessions of faith.
5. Powerful bishops arose in the major territorial churches, although not yet in Rome.

C. This relatively peaceful period ended with the accession of Maximinus (r. 235–238).
1. He objected to favor shown Christians in the imperial household and purged his court of them.
2. Maximinus was the first of a series of "Barracks Emperors" who ruled from 235–284 and generally came to power by assassination and usurpation.
3. Maximinus initiated a short-lived persecution in Palestine and Cappadocia in Asia Minor.
4. Other emperors could be ambivalent in their opinions about Christians.

D. Successive waves of Gothic invasions may have led to changes in religious policy under Decius.
1. Decius (r. 249–251) wanted to ensure stability by enforcing conformity to traditional religion.
2. Decius required every subject to offer sacrifice to the gods and obtain certification.
3. The problem of how to treat those who sacrificed or bought certificates troubled the church for many years afterwards.

E. Outside pressure on the empire led to persecution again under Valerian (r. 253–260).
1. Valerian ruled with Gallienus (r. 253–268) in an effort to make imperial rule more manageable by dividing power among regional rulers.
2. In 257, Valerian ordered church leaders to sacrifice and prohibited congregational meetings.
3. Later, he moved against aristocratic Christians, threatening them with loss of life and property.

    4. Both the edict and its method of enforcement were archaic, and Gallienus instituted religious freedom after Valerian's death.

F. The era of the Barracks Emperors ended with the reign of Diocletian (r. 284–305).
    1. Diocletian established a tetrarchy to ensure the smooth succession of imperial rulers.
    2. Diocletian issued a series of edicts against Christians beginning in 303.
    3. In 309, another tetrarch, Galerius, reimposed the religious regimen of the Augustan era on all citizens.
    4. The edicts only created more Christian converts, and in 311, Galerius issued an edict of toleration.

G. Constantine presided over the conversion of imperial Roman religious culture to Christianity.
    1. He and eastern emperor Licinius issued the Edict of Milan in 313, guaranteeing religious toleration.
    2. Constantine gained control of the empire after defeating Licinius in 324.
    3. Constantine considered himself a Christian from 313 and appointed bishops as state officials.
    4. Constantine played a major role in the Council of Nicea in 318.
    5. Constantine was finally baptized as a Christian when he was near death in 337.
    6. Late baptism was considered the most effective way of ensuring forgiveness of the sins committed during one's lifetime.
    7. Despite a brief relapse to traditional Roman religion under Julian (r. 361–363), Christianity had triumphed.

II. What accounts for ethical monotheism's triumph over the traditional polytheistic religious cultures of the ancient Mediterranean world?

A. Traditional polytheistic religious cultures envisioned the divine world on a human model.
    1. The multitude of gods reflected the multitude of human beings engaged in their own activities.
    2. Some gods dominated other gods as leaders, just as some human beings ruled over others.

3. The gods, like human beings, were part of the created order and subject to its laws.
4. The best one might hope for was a divine patron, a defender and protector among the gods.

B. Hierarchical arrangement unavoidably directs attention to a relatively few major gods.
1. Initially, these are the gods most involved in daily human life, gods of the political order.
2. Even among the major gods, one or two take on special importance as chief deities.
3. The gods are jealous of their prerogatives, administering justice against those who offend them.
4. The gods become moral arbiters, and human presumption is thought of in moral terms as sin.
5. Once gods become dispensers of divine justice, they can no longer be thought of as themselves immoral.
6. The official rituals of sacrifice and cult idols fail to match the moral imperatives of the gods.

C. There is the allied question of whether the gods care about individual worshipers.
1. Is a faithful individual important to the god as a member of the worshiping community?
2. In state-based religious culture, the king is both political and cultic head of the nation.
3. In a voluntary religious community, worshipers receive unmediated divine benefits.
4. Devotion to one deity in a polytheistic context assumes that the god will protect the worshiper's interests.
5. Singling out a god as a patron in a polytheistic system is very similar to worship of a single god.

D. Mediterranean religious culture ultimately seemed to demand a single god as patron and moral arbiter.
1. Such a deity requires both ritual worship and moral behavior in every aspect of life.
2. This was offered by Christianity, the protection of the one God who governed the cosmos.
3. Christianity was inclusive, offering membership to all who confessed Jesus as Lord and accepted baptism.

  4. Christians were set apart by a distinctive moral code based in mutual love and support.

  5. Christian teaching also provided a rationale for suffering among the faithful, by positing a world hostile to Christians.

  6. Moral behavior was enforced by a hierarchical institutional structure.

  7. Christianity successfully redefined what it meant to be religious in the Roman world.

E. Transition from traditional Roman religious culture to Christianity was not instantaneous.

  1. When Christianity became the religion of the empire, it also became part of Roman identity.

  2. Traditional Roman religious culture continued to find adherents for two centuries.

  3. Government made the church wealthy and opened church vocations to Roman aristocrats.

  4. The personal connection that was part of the appeal of Christianity began to erode.

  5. As Jesus withdrew into heaven, worshipers often looked for reassurance and comfort elsewhere.

F. From this search for new patrons in the divine realm arose veneration of the saints.

  1. The saints could be invoked to intercede with the Lord Jesus on behalf of their devotees.

  2. Saints were associated with different concerns, and their prayers sought through acts of devotion.

  3. Devotion to the saints found its fullest expression in the veneration of the Virgin Mary.

  4. Mary soon was glorified in terms that recalled the praises of Isis and other goddesses.

  5. The old gods assumed new faces and continued to be honored in both old and new ways.

Essential Reading:

Mary Beard, John North, and Simon Price. *Religions of Rome*, vol. 1, pp. 364–388.

Henry Chadwick. *The Early Church*, pp. 116–136.

Robert Turcan. *The Gods of Ancient Rome*, pp. 155–165.

Robin W. Winks and Susan P. Mattern-Parkes. *The Ancient Mediterranean World: From the Stone Age to A.D. 600*, pp. 195–205.

Supplementary Reading:

Rodney Stark. *The Rise of Christianity*, pp. 129–215.

Questions to Consider:

1. Once the Jesus movement had gained a place in Roman society, was there any real possibility of eliminating it? What social and political factors worked against successful persecution?

2. What were some of the consequences, for good or ill, of Christianity gaining dominance over traditional Roman religious culture?

3. The only major religion to arise in the Mediterranean world after Christianity is another form of ethical monotheism, Islam. Why have no new polytheistic religious cultures arisen in the last 2,000 years?

Lecture Forty-Eight
Conclusion—Persisting Ideas and Yearnings

Scope: The beliefs and practices that seem most typical of ancient Mediterranean religious cultures involve very literal ideas of the human nature, concerns, and needs of the gods. From such ideas arise mythology about the gods' romances, battles, and interactions with humanity, as well as ritual practices that focus on the care of a god's cult statue and the nearly universal practice of animal sacrifice. The ancient religious beliefs and practices that seem best to reflect humanity's enduring religious aspirations focus on the essential nature of the human and the cohesiveness of humanity as a whole. The transcendence of the divine world over the human world leads to the desire for some ultimate reconciliation of the two worlds, either in the present life or the afterlife. The final establishment of harmony between the human and the divine represents the consummation of the religious yearnings humanity has felt since its beginning.

Outline

I. The practices that seem most typical of ancient Mediterranean religious cultures involve literal ideas of the human nature of the gods.

    A. It seems reasonable to think of the divine realm in terms of the human world, because the human world is our mode of reference.

        1. From the earliest human cultures, there is a sense that the relationship between the human and divine is dependent on human efforts to maintain harmony.

        2. The relationship to the divine is assumed to be a relationship between similar sorts of worlds and similar sorts of beings that share common values.

        3. There is a sense that the divine world is one that human beings can understand, to some extent, because our own world resembles it.

    B. A literal understanding of anthropomorphic conceptions of the gods is a defining characteristic of ancient religious cultures.

1. The divine world was essentially a mirror image of the human world, with similar sorts of beings engaged in similar sorts of activities.
2. These were gods with human bodies but with supernatural abilities and life spans extended by eons beyond human lives.
3. In Egypt and Mesopotamia, daily rituals were dedicated to feeding and caring for cult statues, and annual festivals were held, when the statues were transported to other temples.
4. The almost universal practice of animal sacrifice provided sustenance or a "sweet savor" for the gods.
5. Animal sacrifices were considered compensation for human offenses against the gods, because the gods "needed" the sacrifice.
6. In short, what is most typical of ancient religious culture is belief in gods who are like human beings and the forms of worship arising from that belief.

II. More enduring aspirations of ancient Mediterranean religious cultures have to do with the essential nature of humanity and its relationship to the divine.

A. Ideas about the essential nature of humanity are tied up with the concept of the *soul*.
1. This essential personal identity was apparently believed to survive the death of the body even in the earliest religious cultures.
2. There was apparently no sense that the person had ceased to be, but only that he or she had passed from one mode of existence to another.
3. What was believed to survive can be loosely termed a *soul*, but we have no idea what prehistoric peoples believed it to be.

B. The Egyptians had the most complex notion of the person, comprised of the body, the name, the shadow, the *ba*, and the *ka*.
1. The name was the essential expression of the person in both life and afterlife, while the shadow was the person's "presence."
2. The *ka* relates to the interaction of mind and body that comes into being at birth.
3. The *ba* was the person's spiritual presence in what he or she did in life and the mode of existence for the dead.

©2005 The Teaching Company.

C. Mesopotamian religious culture shared the idea that a person's essence survives death but relegated it to a gloomy underworld.

    1. This reflects the belief that the body was a necessary part of human life that had to be activated by divine breath to live.

    2. Bereft of the body, the personal essence was without sensory pleasure or freedom of movement.

    3. This belief is similar to the Israelite concept of Sheol or the Greek idea of Hades as the realm of shadows.

D. During the Classical era in Greece, a new concept arose that the human soul was a spark of divine life.

    1. Pythagoras believed that the *psyche*, the soul or human essence, was a spark of the divine trapped in the physical body.

    2. Philosophers tended to think of this divine spark as the reason, a splinter of the divine reason that governed the cosmos.

    3. The soul was seen as the locus of the divine within human beings; thus, the essential human identity was divine.

    4. Death provided the opportunity for the *psyche* to escape the bonds of the mortal body and return to the divine realm.

E. The inherent divinity of the soul was not an idea at home in Israelite religious culture, where all life was a gift of the Lord.

    1. The Jews' experience of persecution and martyrdom led to the conviction that those who resisted until death deserved some reward for their faith.

    2. As a result, some Jews concluded that the very good and the very wicked would return to life to receive reward or punishment.

    3. Because the personal essence could not have true life without the body, this belief in new life took the form of belief in resurrection.

    4. Although belief in resurrection was not shared by all Jews, it was characteristic of the Pharisees and of Jesus's followers.

III. Another aspect of the essential nature of humanity has to do with the cohesiveness of humanity and the transcendence of the divine.

A. Ancient religious cultures share a sense of the basic equality of all human beings, who all share a common situation in life.

    1. This basic equality was rarely expressed in political terms but often appears in religious cultures.

2. We find this idea in stories about how the human situation came to be the way it is now and about heroes striving against human limitations.

3. Even where a single figure stood out as a favorite of the gods, his or her ability to benefit others depended on his or her solidarity with the rest of humanity.

B. The cohesiveness of humanity is the basic assumption of wisdom literature and philosophical ethics.

1. Wisdom literature is pragmatic advice based on common experience in a life that follows predictable patterns.

2. Even skeptical wisdom offers advice that is presented as appropriate for every human being, including the command to "seize the day."

3. Similarly, ethical systems devised by the Greek philosophers were meant to be applicable to all people in all times.

C. The cohesiveness of humanity is the basis of religious community, as human beings in a group intercede with the divine world.

1. Religious beliefs arise in and create communities that devise common practices to ensure harmony with the divine world.

2. What is done in ritual worship is done in and for the sake of the religious community.

D. The counterpart to the cohesiveness of human beings is the corresponding sense of divine transcendence.

1. Different Mediterranean religious cultures conceived of divine transcendence in different ways but always with a sense of its "otherness."

2. With literal ideas of the gods' human nature went the acknowledgement that the gods were also very different from human beings.

3. Sometimes the difference was thought of in terms of location or in terms of the gods' greater power.

4. But there is a more basic difference: that the gods represent a sacred mystery that cannot be fully understood by human beings.

5. The sense that human beings live in relationship to a sacred realm is coupled with a conviction that humanity must ensure harmony with that realm.

6. Despite the transcendence of the divine, ancient Mediterranean peoples sought a way to achieve equilibrium between the human and the divine worlds.

E. But given the finitude of human existence, there was also a yearning for some final resolution between human and divine.
   1. In Egypt, harmony was achieved in life through the actions of the pharaoh, who established *ma'at*, but in death, harmony came through judgment.
   2. Mesopotamian, Greek, and Israelite religious cultures looked for some sort of final resolution in the earthly sphere.
   3. Beginning in the Hellenistic era with the rise of mystery religions, we find a growing hope of salvation from the human condition.
   4. Whatever the case, the prevailing assumption was that human beings needed to do what was necessary to bring about the desired reconciliation.

F. But in some cases, awareness of the finitude of human existence led to the desire for resolution as a result of divine action.
   1. Among some Jews and among followers of Jesus, this hope took the form of apocalypticism, the expectation that the Lord would intervene in human history.
   2. God would vindicate his people, and all people and nations would acknowledge the Lord's sovereignty over the earth.
   3. Zechariah provides this image of all nations coming to Jerusalem to worship the Lord together, with the Jews acting as their intercessors (Zechariah 8:22–23).
   4. Here is a vision of both human cohesiveness and ultimate reconciliation with the divine, with the final achievement of harmony.
   5. But here, the harmony between the human and the divine world that is the ultimate goal of all religious action finally arises from the action of divine love.
   6. The final establishment of harmony between the human and the divine represents the consummation of the religious yearnings humanity has felt since the beginning.

Supplementary Reading:
1 and 2 Thessalonians.

Daniel 11–12.

Revelation 20–22.

Zechariah 8, 14.

Questions to Consider:

1. Why is the essential nature of a human person so often thought of as something separable from the body and its needs and sensations? What are the consequences of this belief for the religious cultures we have discussed?

2. What are some of the qualities of human life that lead us to think of humanity as a cohesive unity, in some sense? What factors in human life might argue against such a conception?

3. In what other aspects of human life beside the religious do we find the desire for a final resolution of a continuing attempt to achieve harmony and balance? Is this desire a natural result of our awareness of human finitude or, instead, an attempt to rise above it?

Map

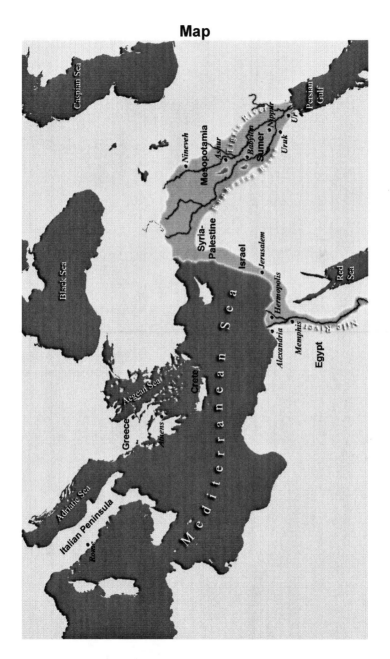

255

Timeline

2,000,000 years ago– c. 17,000 B.C.E.	Paleolithic era (Old Stone Age)
130,000–30,000 years ago	Neanderthals appear, flourish, and decline
70,000–30,000 years ago	Middle Paleolithic era, Mousterian material culture
30,000 years ago– c. 17,000 B.C.E.	Paleolithic era

B.C.E.

c. 17,000–c. 8300	Mesolithic era (Middle Stone Age), Natufian material culture in Syria-Palestine
c. 8300–c. 4000	Neolithic era (New Stone Age)
c. 3500–1450	The Aegean: Minoan civilization in Crete
c. 3000–2670	Egypt: Archaic era—Dynasties 1 and 2
c. 2900	Mesopotamia: Amorites settle to the north of Sumer
c. 2670–2198	Egypt: Old Kingdom—Dynasties 3–6
2654–2635	Egypt: Djoser; career of Imhotep, later deified as god of medicine
2571–2548	Egypt: Khufu (Cheops)
2334–2279	Mesopotamia: Sargon the Great of Akkad
c. 2200–1200	Middle and Late Bronze Ages
c. 2198–1938	Egypt: First Intermediate Period— Dynasties 7–11

Glossary

Achaeans: The people of mainland Greece who made war against Troy.

agora: Greek, public space, open marketplace.

Akkadian: Semitic language, dominant in Mesopotamia from the 19th century B.C.E.

Amorites: Semitic peoples from the west who settled to the north of Sumer c. 2900 B.C.E.

ankh: Egyptian symbol of eternal life.

anthropomorphic: In human form.

Anunnaki: Sumerian, the gods of earth and the underworld.

apocalyptic reversal: The vindication of the poor and the outcast over the rich and powerful at the end of the age.

apocalypticism: The expectation that God will directly intervene into human history to save and vindicate his people.

Aramaeans: Ethnic group of nomads appearing in Genesis.

Aramaic: Alphabetic Semitic language, dominant in Mesopotamian from the 12th century B.C.E.

Archaic Age in Greece: 800–480 B.C.E.

Archaic era: Era in Egyptian history, Dynasties 1 and 2, c. 3000–2670 B.C.E.

aretology: A list of titles and attributes of a god and often rites and locations sacred to him or her.

asheroth: Hebrew, poles or trees sacred to the Canaanite goddess Asherah.

atê: Greek, madness or self-delusion.

audition: An ecstatic experience that is primarily aural.

augurs: Roman priests who oversaw auspices to determine whether a sacrifice was accepted.

auspices: A form of divination involving birds.

ba: Egyptian, a person's activity or spiritual presence perceivable in what he or she does.

Bacchae: Ecstatic female worshipers of Dionysus (sing. Bacchante).

Bacchanalia: Festival in honor of Dionysus.

bamoth: Hebrew, "altars," "high places," national shrines.

barbarians: Greek, "babblers," those who don't speak Greek, non-Greeks.

B.C.E.: Before the Common Era.

Bel Matati: Akkadian, "Lord of the World."

benben: Egyptian, a primeval hill shaped like a pyramid.

calends (new moon): A Roman division of the month.

canopic jars: Containers for a mummy's internal organs.

Capitoline temple of Jupiter: The primary temple of Jupiter, on the Capitoline hill in Rome

C.E.: Common Era, the current era, theoretically reckoned from the birth of Jesus.

cenotaph: A memorial stone.

Chaldeans: A Semitic people who established the Neo-Babylonian empire.

charismata: Greek, "spiritual gifts."

chresmologos: An oracle-monger with large collections of oracles to provide clients.

chthonic deities: Earth-based gods and goddesses.

Classical era: In ancient Greece, 481–322 B.C.E.

Coffin Texts: Instructions for the dead painted inside Middle Kingdom coffins in Egypt.

consul: One of the two chief magistrates of the Roman Republic.

"Cyclopean" walls: Fortifications made of unworked boulders or blocks of stone.

dactyl: Metrical unit consisting of a long syllable and two short ones.

daimons: Supernatural creatures that combine characteristics of the spiritual and physical.

Dark Age: In Greece, c. 1200–800 B.C.E.

Day of the Lord: The day when the Lord acts decisively to deliver and vindicate his faithful people.

deiknymena: Greek, "things shown."

deities: Self-conscious controllers of numinous power.

Deshret: Egyptian, "the red land," the Egyptian desert.

dingar: Sumerian, "god," "one of heaven."

dithyrambs: Lyric hymns in praise of Dionysus.

droît du seigneur: From French, "right of the lord," a lord's prerogative to deflower virgin brides before they marry.

dromena: Greek, "things performed."

dromos: Greek, a walkway; long tunnel leading to a Mycenaean burial chamber.

duality: The idea that all that exists is an expression of one or the other of two equal, opposed, and contrasting realities.

ecstatic phenomena: What is experienced in a state of mind when one "stands outside" one's self, and one's normal perception of reality is temporarily interrupted.

effective cursing: Using access to the spiritual world to call wrath down upon one's enemies.

Ennead: Greek, "group of nine," the nine principal gods of Egypt.

epic poem: Story about a historical hero who undertakes a series of adventures lived out in conscious relationship to the divine world.

ethos: Greek, a person's way of life.

Etruscans: Neighboring people to the Romans who sometimes ruled over them.

execration texts: Names of enemies on clay vessels that are then smashed, effectively breaking the enemy's power.

fauns: Young men with the horns and legs of a goat, attendants of Dionysus.

fetials: Roman priests who undertook rituals to initiate a war and ensure that it was "just."

fetish: An object made by human skill, venerated for its spiritual power.

First Intermediate Period: Era in Egyptian history, Dynasties 7–11, c. 2198–1938 B.C.E.

Galli: Self-castrated transvestite priests of Cybele (sing. *gallus*).

genius: Latin, the male spiritual essence of the man.

Gnosticism: A form of Christian teaching that emphasized esoteric knowledge as the means of salvation.

"God-fearers": Gentiles who were sympathetic to Judaism and observed most of its tenets but rejected circumcision and full conversion.

guild prophets: Prophets who lived and prophesied in groups, usually under a leader.

haruspicia: Latin, "looking at entrails," finding omens in the entrails of animals sacrificed to the gods.

Hashem: Hebrew, "the Name."

Hellenic: From Greek, *Hellas* ("Greece"), "Greek."

Hellenistic: From Greek, *hellenistikos*, "Greek-like."

henotheism: A religious culture devoted to worshiping one god out of the many gods that exist.

hieros gamos: Greek, "sacred marriage."

history: A realm of discourse concerning what can reasonably be surmised to have happened in the past on the basis of historically acceptable data and analysis.

hoc est corpus meum: Latin, "this is my body."

Homo sapiens: the species of modern human beings.

hoplite: Greek, an armored soldier armed with a spear and short sword and carrying a large round shield, a *hoplon*.

humanism: A literary and artistic movement reflecting the importance of the individual in the face of the gods and human society.

HWY: Hebrew, "to be."

Hyksos: West Asian rulers of Egypt in Dynasties 15 and 16.

"Iacchos!": Cry of the festival procession to Eleusis, presumed to be the name of a god.

ides (full moon): A Roman division of the month.

Igigi: Akkadian, the (10) great gods.

ilu: Akkadian, "god," "one of heaven."

imperator: Latin, the holder of the *imperium*.

imperium: Latin, the full sovereign power of the Roman Senate.

inaugural experience: A vision or audition (something seen or something heard) that first calls the prophet to prophesy.

independent prophets: Individual prophets who speak on the Lord's behalf without royal authority.

ironist: A "dissembling rascal" who pretends to be less than he really is.

juno: Latin, the female spiritual essence of the woman.

ka: Egyptian, the interaction of the mind and the body as a person.

Kemet: Egyptian, "the black land," the Nile Valley.

koiné: Greek, "common," the Greek of Hellenistic culture.

kunikos: Greek, "dog-like."

kykeon: A watery mixture of barley meal and mint.

Lares: The ancestral spirits of a Roman clan or family.

Latin tribes: The early core of the Roman people.

legomena: Greek, "things recited."

lingua franca (Italian, "Frankish tongue"): the common (second) language of a people.

logos: Greek, "word," "reason"; divine reason.

ma'at: Egyptian, divine harmony or balance.

mana: Spiritual power.

"martyr": From the Greek *marturein*, meaning "to bear witness."

material culture: The physical remains of a human culture, discovered through archaeology.

Matralia: Festival of the goddess Dawn on June 11.

Matronalia: Festival in honor of women, especially mothers, on March 1.

matzeboth: Hebrew, "sacred pillars."

m e: Sumerian, "authority," "supernatural power."

megaron: Greek, a large room; a circular room with an open hearth at the center and four supporting columns.

"men for sacred actions": First 2, later 10, men who kept the Sibylline books in Rome.

Mesolithic era: The Middle Stone Age, c. 17,000–c. 8300 B.C.E.

Mesopotamia: Greek, "between the rivers."

messiah: From Aramaic *mesiach*, "anointed one" (= Greek *christos*), the Lord's designated agent for a particular purpose on earth.

metempsychosis: Greek, the transmigration of the soul from one body to another at death.

Middle and Late Bronze Ages: c. 2200–1200 B.C.E.

Middle Kingdom: Era in Egyptian history, Dynasty 12, c. 1938–1759 B.C.E.

Middle Paleolithic era: 70,000–30,000 years ago.

Middle Platonism: A form of Platonic philosophy current from the 1st century B.C.E. to the early 3rd century C.E.

Minoan civilization: The civilization of Bronze Age Crete, c. 3500–1450 B.C.E.

Mishnah: A collection of rabbinic commentary on the teachings of Torah compiled c. 200 C.E.

Mithraea: Sanctuaries of Mithras (sing. Mithraeum).

Monad: Greek, "unity"; God as an indivisible unity, absolutely simple and perfect.

monism: The assertion that all that exists is based in and an expression of a single reality manifested in myriad forms.

monotheism: A religious culture reflecting devotion to the one and only god believed to exist.

Mousterian culture: The material culture of the Middle Paleolithic era.

Mycenaean civilization: A civilization of Bronze Age Greece, c. 1600–1200 B.C.E.

mystery religions: Religions devoted to "savior gods," with secret initiation rituals.

myth: A realm of discourse involving any idea of what motivates or drives history, the supernatural, or what lies behind or above history.

mythology: Legendary accounts of gods and heroes.

natron: Hydrated sodium carbonate ($Na_2CO_3.10H_2O$), used in mummification.

Natufian culture: The material culture of Syria-Palestine during the Mesolithic era.

"natural" religious communities: Religious communities coextensive with a social community.

Navigium Isidis: Latin, "Isis's Sea Journey," a festival recalling Isis's voyage to Byblos.

Neanderthals: Early human beings, fl. between 130,000–30,000 years ago.

necromancy: The summoning up of the spirits of the dead to gain insight into the present or foresee the future.

Neolithic era: The New Stone Age, c. 8300–c. 4000 B.C.E.

New Kingdom: Era in Egyptian history, Dynasties 18–20, c. 1539–1075 B.C.E.

nome: Small territories under military leaders in early Egypt.

nones (first quarter of the moon): A Roman division of the month.

Nones Caprotinae: A festival celebrated by free and slave women on July 7.

numen: All-pervasive spiritual power.

Nun: Egyptian, the dark waters of the limitless depths.

Ogdoad: Greek, "group of eight," four pairs of primeval Egyptian gods and goddesses.

official prophets: Professional prophets who worked within the context of the royal court or the shrine.

Old Kingdom: Era in Egyptian history, Dynasties 3–6, c. 2670–2198 B.C.E.

omophagia: Greek, the eating of raw flesh.

Paleolithic era: The Old Stone Age, began about 2 million years ago, ended c. 17,000 B.C.E.

panentheism: The idea that deity is not only present in all things but expresses itself and grows in the processes of natural and human history.

pantheism: The idea that deity suffuses the cosmos and that all its creatures are extensions and expressions of the divine.

pater familiaris: Latin, "father of the family," the head of the household.

patricians: Influential families who formed the senatorial aristocracy in the Roman Republic.

Penates: The household deities of a Roman clan or family.

pharaoh: The Egyptian king, from *Per Ao*, "great house."

plebeians: The commoners who sought greater power during the Roman Republic.

polis: Greek, the regional city-state ruled by a council of citizens.

polytheism: A religious culture with many gods.

pontifex maximus: Latin, "highest priest," the chief office of the college of pontiffs.

pontiffs: Roman priests who oversaw sacrifices and served as the guardians of sacred law.

principiate: Latin, "rule of the chief of state [*Princeps*]," the emperor's rule.

prophetes: Greek, "forth-teller," "proclaimer"; a prophet.

prophetic action: A particular behavior enacted by a prophet as part of the prophetic message.

psyche: Greek, the essence of a person, "soul."

Pyramid Texts: Egyptian religious inscriptions in the chambers of Old Kingdom pyramids.

Rabshakeh: Hebrew, "chief officer," an emissary of the Assyrian king to Hezekiah.

religio licta: Latin, a legitimate non-conforming religious culture within the empire.

Sabine women: Women from a territory neighboring Rome taken as wives by early Romans under Romulus.

sacred, the: That which permeates, influences, and relates to material reality, yet is recognized as part of another reality not subject to the limitations of the material.

šā mūti: Akkadian "bread of death."

šāmūti: Akkadian, "bread of heaven."

sanctuary: The sacred space devoted to worship, including temple, altar, and associated buildings and space.

Saturnalia: A festival of misrule celebrated December 17–23.

satyrs: Part-animal attendants of Dionysus.

Second Intermediate Period: Era in Egyptian history, Dynasties 13–17, c. 1759–1539 B.C.E.

shamans: Spiritual adepts who are believed to commune with the spirit world while in a trance.

Sibylline Oracle: An oracle of the gods located at Cumae in Campania.

si deo, si dea: Latin, "whether god or goddess."

sistrum: A type of musical rattle.

soma sema: Greek, "the body is a tomb."

Sophists: In the classical world, itinerant teachers of the skills and knowledge that led to a successful life.

soter: Greek, "savior."

spondee: Metrical unit consisting of two long syllables.

sub-apostolic period: About 70 to 130 C.E.

suzerainty treaty: A treaty in which a subject people accepts a king as its sovereign, with stipulations placed on both sides.

syncretism: The synthesis of elements taken from distinct religious cultures into new forms and combinations.

Tanakh: The Hebrew scriptures, the Christian Old Testament.

taurobolium: The ritual slaying of a bull in the mystery religion of Cybele.

tauroctony: Greek, a bull-slaying scene.

Telesterion: The hall of initiation at Eleusis.

tetrarchy: Greek, "rule of four," form of government with four co-rulers.

theios aner: Greek, "divine man," a man endowed with spiritual power manifested in supernatural wisdom and miracle-working.

theodicy (Greek, "god is in the right"): Showing a god is in the right in taking particular actions despite appearances to the contrary.

theophoric element (Greek, "god-bearing"): A god's name appearing as part of a person's name.

Thesmophoria: Festival of Demeter at Eleusis celebrated three days each October.

Third Intermediate Period: Era in Egyptian history, Dynasties 21–25, c. 1075–664 B.C.E.

tholos: Greek, dome; a "beehive" tomb.

tribune: A plebian magistrate who could cancel the actions of the other magistrates.

trireme: A large battleship powered by oarsmen, with a bronze ram at the prow.

tyché: Greek, "fate."

Tychē Agathē: Greek, "Good Fortune."

Ubaidians: Neolithic settlers in southeastern Mesopotamia.

Upper Paleolithic era: 30,000–17,000 years ago.

Urim and Thummin: An apparatus to discover the Lord's will, part of the high priest's apparel.

ushebtis: Egyptian, "answerers," tomb models of male and female slaves.

Vestal Virgins: Women who guarded the flame of Vesta on the "hearth" of the city.

vision: An ecstatic experience that is primarily visual.

"voluntary" religious communities: Communities one chooses to join as a result of conversion.

Yahweh: Vocalization of YHWH, the name of the Lord of Israel.

YHWH: Hebrew, the name of the Lord of Israel.

ziggurat: Massive pyramidical brick building intended to represent the sacred mountain.

Biographical Notes

Alexander III ("the Great") of Macedon (356–323 B.C.E.). The son of Philip II of Macedon, Alexander succeeded him as king in 336 B.C.E. He crossed the Hellespont in 334 B.C.E. with an army of 40,000 to challenge the Persian Empire. Alexander gradually gained supremacy over Persian holdings in the west, then defeated the Persians to take Babylon and the Persian capitals. Ultimately, his empire stretched from Greece and Macedon in the west to the Indus River in the east and from Bactria in the north to Egypt in the south. Alexander brought his domains not only Greek forms of government and the Greek language but Hellenistic culture. Alexander's domains fostered a cosmopolitan religious culture characterized by syncretism, the synthesis of gods and rituals from different national traditions. Alexander died of a fever in Babylon at age 33, leaving his empire to his young son. It was soon divided among Alexander's commanders into separate kingdoms, but the territories of his empire remained essentially Hellenistic in language and culture until the Muslim conquest.

Amenophis IV/Ankhenaten, king of Egypt (1353–1336 B.C.E.). A pharaoh of Dynasty 18 during the New Kingdom, Amenophis IV sparked a religious and cultural revolution during his reign. Devoted to the solar god Aten, originally a manifestation of Rē-Horakhty, Amenophis built a temple for the Aten at Karnak with decoration that ushered in a new artistic era. The king replaced the traditional representations of the gods with the image of the sun disk radiating beams that terminated in hands bringing blessings to Egypt. Amenophis changed his name to Ankhenaten and built a new capital in Middle Egypt, Akhetaten, now known as Tell el-Amarna. Ankhenaten ordered the systematic obliteration of the names and images of Amun and other gods throughout his kingdom in favor of the sole depiction and glorification of Aten. The reign of Ankhenaten was a blow to the deeply traditional Egyptians, and he imposed his will with shows of force. Despite his efforts, his theological and cultural revolution was gradually reversed during the reign of his eventual successor, Tutankhamun.

Apollonius of Tyana, philosopher (c. 4 B.C.E.–after 96 C.E.). Apollonius was born in Cappadocia in Asia Minor and began to follow the life of a philosopher at an early age. Through his devotion to the ascetic life of a Pythagorean philosopher, he lived a life of simplicity and gentle wisdom, although he could be stern with his opponents or scoffers. He traveled widely, including in India, and was reputed to have the power to work miracles. He was subject to persecution under both Nero and Domitian but, in both cases, escaped condemnation. The most extensive account of his life was written by the Sophist Flavius Philostratus at the behest of the empress Julia Domna at the beginning of the 3rd century C.E. Philostratus is far from reliable, and there are only scattered references to Apollonius elsewhere, although the satirist Lucian of Samosata dismissed him as a libertine and a charlatan.

Augustus Caesar (Gaius Octavius), Roman emperor (63 B.C.E.–14 C.E.). The son of the niece of Julius Caesar, Octavius was Caesar's adopted son and chief heir after his death. He managed to make allies among the leading citizens of Rome and, through military and political skills, gained the status of senator and consul and later became a member of a triumvirate that also included Marc Antony. His growing power in Italy led to a confrontation with Antony and Cleopatra in Egypt. Octavius emerged victorious and unopposed, ultimately acquiring the *imperium*, or power to rule, from the Senate in 27 B.C.E., as well as the title Augustus. As emperor, Augustus placed himself under the patronage of Apollo and the god Julius, his deified adoptive father. He was a traditionalist and undertook a campaign to restore the glory of Rome after a generation of civil war but, in the process, also consolidated and institutionalized his own power. He built new temples in Rome and rebuilt old ones, ordered a definitive collection of the Sibylline oracles, and placed himself and the imperial family in the center of Roman religious culture. Within a month of his death, Augustus was declared a god.

Constantine (Flavius Valerius Constantinus), Roman emperor (c. 285–337 C.E.). Constantine was the son Constantius Chlorus. When Constantius became part of the tetrarchy ruling the empire, young Constantine was sent to the court of Diocletian in Nicomedia. Constantine showed promise as a commander and became a member of the tetrarchy after his father's death in 306. In 313, Constantine and his co-emperor Licinius issued the Edict of Milan, ending persecution of Christians in the empire and granting them certain rights. Through a series of alliances and battles, Constantine gained sole control over the empire in 324. He oversaw an overhaul of the imperial administration, issued new coinage, and established a new capital in Byzantium on the Bosporus, named Constantinople in his honor. Both traditional Roman and Christian rituals solemnized the city's founding. Among Constantine's building projects in the new capital were many churches, including the Church of the Holy Wisdom, but no temples of the traditional gods. Christians regarded Constantinople as the "Christian Rome." Constantine's own religious ideas are far from clear, but he intervened in Christian doctrinal disputes, most notably at the Council of Nicea in 325. The emperor was finally baptized a Christian in 337 on his deathbed.

Cyrus II ("the Great"), king of Persia (559–530 B.C.E.). Cyrus was originally a ruler over part of Iran and a vassal to the Medes, but he slowly consolidated power in the surrounding territories. The Babylonians under Nabonidus (556–539 B.C.E) asked for Cyrus's assistance against the Medes, and by 550 B.C.E., Cyrus was ruler of both Persia and Media. Cyrus compounded one military success with another, conquering Lydia in 546 B.C.E. and Babylonia in 539 B.C.E. Cyrus soon ruled over an empire of unprecedented size. His policy toward his subject people was remarkably enlightened for its time. He allowed those peoples the Babylonians had exiled to return to their native lands and to observe the customs of their own religious cultures, provided they prayed to their gods for the well-being of the Persian king and his empire. It was during his reign that many of the exiles of Judah returned to Jerusalem, taking with them much of the Temple furniture that the Babylonians had seized. Isaiah 45:1–3 portrays Cyrus as a deliverer of God's people and refers to him as God's anointed one, or *messiah.*

David, king of Israel (1000–961 B.C.E.). The son of a Moabite mother and a father from the Jebusite city of Bethlehem, David first became associated with Israel by serving its first king, Saul, as a military commander. David's military successes led to a break with Saul, and David was, for a time, a mercenary commander for the Philistines. He later became king of Judah, with his capital in Hebron. After Saul's death, David fought against Saul's son and successor, Ishbaal. After Ishbaal's death, David became king over Israel by virtue of a covenantal agreement made with its leading citizens. David ruled over the united kingdoms of Israel and Judah and greatly increased their territories, becoming the strongest and most influential of the kings of Judah and Israel. His later years were taken up in part by rebellions arising from dissension among several of his sons over the succession. In spite of a challenge from his son Adonijah, at David's death, his kingdom passed peacefully to Solomon.

Diogenes of Sinope, Greek philosopher (c. 400–328 B.C.E.). Diogenes reportedly came to Athens as an exile after serving as a treasury official and being accused of "changing the currency." This became his philosophical mission, as he flouted conventional ideas of morality and propriety in an attempt to make life as simple and, therefore, as happy as possible. He believed happiness consisted in living "according to nature," in the sense of doing what satisfied basic human needs without regard to public opinion or social conventions. The public shamelessness of Diogenes and his followers led the public to compare them to dogs and brand them *kunikos*, or "dog-like," the origin of the name *Cynic*. Diogenes and other Cynics lampooned popular standards and opinions in public diatribes. The distinguishing characteristics of the Cynics were their simple clothing, their staff and bag, and their brusque and offensive manner.

Epicurus, Greek philosopher (341–270 B.C.E.). Epicurus was born the son of a teaching master in the Greek colony of Samos. He studied philosophy in Athens at the Academy and became familiar with the atomistic theories of Democritus. He established philosophical schools in the eastern Aegean before returning to Athens in 307 or 306 B.C.E., when he bought a house and garden that became the setting for his philosophical community. Epicurus believed that the best thing for a human being to do was to enjoy the pleasures of life in moderation and to live without anxiety. He identified the primary sources of anxiety as fear of offending the gods and fear of what comes after death. He argued that the gods exist but have no interest in human beings and, thus, cannot be offended by them; on the other hand, at death, the atoms that make up the body are dispersed and consciousness ends, so there is nothing to fear after death. Epicurus and his followers lived a quiet life of contemplation. His school was famous—or notorious—for including women among its members, and this, as well as the school's supposed hedonism and atheism, made Epicureans the subject of popular disdain.

Hammurabi, king of Babylon (1792–1750 B.C.E.). Hammurabi inherited from his father, Sin-muballit, a relatively small domain centered in Babylon and surrounded by larger, more powerful kingdoms. Within a few years, he enlarged his territory considerably by military conquest and eventually united most of Mesopotamia under his own royal rule and the authority of Babylon. He reformed the Babylonian administration and created the first major written law code. The *Code of Hammurabi* shows concern both for individual rights and the demands of justice. During his long reign, Hammurabi presided over a flourishing of the arts and literature, established Babylon as the capital and principal city of Mesopotamia, and granted divine preeminence to Babylon's patron god, Marduk.

Jesus of Nazareth, Jewish religious reformer (c. 4 B.C.E. – c. 30 C.E.). Jesus, a native of Nazareth in Galilee, was an associate of John the Baptist who, after John's imprisonment, began his own ministry. His message was the approaching kingdom of God, and the need for repentance to obtain God's forgiveness in anticipation of the new era. Jesus collected a body of followers who shared his travels and proclaimed his message. Jesus had a reputation as a miracle-worker, and aroused opposition among the Jewish authorities in both Galilee and Judaea because of his criticism of their policies and practices. While in Jerusalem to celebrate Passover, Jesus was arrested by the Temple police and handed over to the Roman authorities, who crucified him. His followers claimed Jesus was alive again a few days after his execution, and continued to spread his message, initially as a sect within Judaism, but later as an independent religious movement.

Moses, leader of Israel (early to mid-13th century B.C.E.). A member of the people of Israel born in Egypt, Moses rose to a position of authority in the Egyptian government, most likely in connection with the forced labor provided by his people for building projects in the eastern Nile Delta during the reign of Ramesses II. He left Egypt and lived among the Midianites and, during that time, married. He later returned to Egypt, where he became a leader of his people in their attempts to gain their freedom, both from forced labor and from Egypt. After a successful escape from Egypt, the people of Israel looked to Moses as their chief lawgiver and religious mediator. He oversaw construction of the Tabernacle, the portable sanctuary for sacrificial ritual, and installed his brother Aaron as high priest. According to tradition, Moses led Israel in the wilderness for 40 years and died on Mt. Nebo in Moab shortly before his people entered Canaan.

Nebuchadnezzar II, king of Babylon (604–562 B.C.E.). Nabû-kudurri-usur (Nebuchadrezzar) campaigned against the Egyptians while still crown prince under his father, Nabopolassar, and successfully drove them from Syria-Palestine. At his father's death, he returned to Babylon to be crowned king. He mounted campaigns in Syria-Palestine on a regular basis to keep the Egyptians in check and to ensure loyalty among his vassals. When Jehoiakim of Judah stopped paying tribute, Nebuchadnezzar captured Jerusalem in 597 B.C.E. and exiled the king, his court, and other leading citizens to Babylon. Ten years later, Nebuchadnezzar's chosen client king in Judah, Zedekiah, also rebelled, and once again, Babylonian armies moved against Jerusalem, taking the city in 587 B.C.E. Another exile of leading citizens from Judah to Babylon followed, although some of the people sought refuge in Egypt instead. Nebuchadnezzar established peace throughout his domains by extensive and effective use of force but was unable to eliminate the forces that led to the fall of Babylon less than a quarter-century after his death.

Nero (Nero Claudius Caesar), Roman emperor (37–68 C.E.). Nero was adopted as a son by the emperor Claudius after Claudius married his niece, Nero's mother, Agrippina. Nero displaced Claudius's son Britannicus, who died—and was, perhaps, murdered—soon after Nero became emperor in 54. Agrippina dominated Nero at first, but he soon exerted his own will and, in 59, had his mother murdered. Nero had artistic ambitions, but his pursuit of vanity and his ruthless use of power turned the Roman public against him. After a suspicious fire destroyed half of Rome in 64, Nero placed the blame on the city's Jews, who in turn, shifted the blame to the followers of Jesus. Nero's persecution of the followers of Jesus in Rome included grotesque forms of execution, inspiring fear and disgust toward the emperor and pity for his victims among Roman citizens. Conspiracies against the emperor arose as conditions worsened in the empire. When the Praetorian Guard finally turned against Nero to support Galba as emperor, Nero committed suicide at the age of 30.

Paul of Tarsus, Christian missionary (c. 10–c. 64 C.E.). Paul, a native of Tarsus in Cilicia in southeastern Asia Minor, received a typical education for a Jew of his time, including study with a rabbi and training in rhetoric. Paul made a living as a tentmaker and leatherworker but also worked for the Jewish authorities in Jerusalem in the attempt to suppress the Jesus movement. While engaged in this work, Paul experienced a vision of the risen Jesus. As a result, he became a member of the Jesus movement and, some years afterwards, a missionary. Paul had his greatest success among Gentiles allied with Jewish synagogues who would not undergo circumcision and full conversion. Paul welcomed such people into the Jesus movement, prompting a reaction from those who thought of the movement as a sect within Judaism. In response, Paul developed the idea that salvation was a free gift of God's grace appropriated by those, Jews or Gentiles, who trusted in his promises. Paul founded congregations in several prominent cities and wrote a number of letters expounding his theology and encouraging his congregations to live a moral life. He apparently died in Rome in 64 C.E. during Nero's persecution of Jesus's followers.

Plato, Greek philosopher (427–347 B.C.E.). Plato was an Athenian of good birth who became a follower of Socrates. After Socrates's death, Plato traveled extensively before returning to Athens and there founded a philosophical school, the Academy, around 385 B.C.E. He devoted the rest of his life to philosophical teaching and writing, producing around 25 dialogues. Although his early dialogues are believed to bear the stamp of the historical Socrates to some extent, Plato's interests and willingness to theorize went far beyond what Socrates had taught. His interest in politics and his creation of the "philosopher-king" led to his involvement with political affairs in Syracuse. The Academy survived Plato's death and continued as a center of philosophical inquiry until the school was finally closed by the Byzantine emperor Justinian in 529 C.E.

Ramesses II, king of Egypt (1279–1213 B.C.E.). A pharaoh of Dynasty 19 during the New Kingdom, Ramesses II is often identified as the pharaoh of the Exodus. His 66-year reign was notable for massive building projects, including the city of Pi-Riamsese in the eastern Nile Delta. Initially through combat and later through diplomacy, Ramesses came to an accommodation with the Hittites, Egypt's long-time rival for hegemony in Syria-Palestine. The treaty led to a long period of peace, freeing Ramesses to devote his attention to his building projects, many of which included colossal representations of the king. In addition to his harem, Ramesses had 2 official wives, and produced more than 50 children. Ramesses II was succeeded by his son Merneptah (1213–1203 B.C.E.). A stele commemorating a campaign into Syria-Palestine by Merneptah includes the first mention of Israel as a people.

Sargon II, king of Assyria (721–705 B.C.E.). Sargon was the successor of Shalmeneser V, although it is unclear whether he was a son of the royal house or a usurper. Assyria's enemies Egypt and Elam fostered rebellions among Sargon's vassals, and Sargon devoted much of his attention to maintaining control of his empire. He was able to assert his authority over most of the rebellious territories, including Babylon and the nations of Syria-Palestine. Sargon captured Samaria, the capital of the northern kingdom of Israel, and deported its leading citizens, replacing them with a foreign aristocracy that served as provincial administrators under Sargon's authority. Sargon built a new capital, Dûr-Sharrukîn near Khorsabad, 24 kilometers northeast of the traditional Assyrian capital, Ninevah, but died in battle a year after the city was completed.

Socrates, Greek philosopher (469–399 B.C.E.). Socrates served as a hoplite in the Athenian army but devoted his life to philosophy early on. He was primarily concerned with ethics, the right way to live one's life, and conducted his philosophical investigations through dialogue, cross-examining his interlocutors in pursuit of truth. The Delphic oracle, in reply to a question from Socrates's friend Chaerephon, proclaimed that no one was wiser than Socrates. Socrates was puzzled by this answer and saw his subsequent philosophical career as a way of determining what the oracle meant by her reply. In 399 B.C.E., Socrates was tried before the Athenian council on a charge of introducing strange gods and corrupting Athenian youth. His self-defense before the council is the substance of Plato's early work *Apology*. Socrates was found guilty and sentenced to death by poison, a death he accepted with good grace. After his death, Socrates's example continued to serve as the model of the ideal philosopher appealed to by many different philosophical schools.

Zeno of Citium, Greek philosopher (c. 333–262 B.C.E.). Zeno came to Athens about 313 B.C.E. and studied at the Academy. He sampled several philosophical schools before finally developing his own philosophy, Stoicism, named after the *Stoa Poikile*, or painted colonnade, where he taught. Zeno maintained that the only thing a person can truly control is his or her inward disposition, which should at all times be aligned with the dictates of the *logos*, or divine mind, that governs the cosmos. In order to keep one's inner resolve in agreement with the *logos*, it was necessary for a person to distance the self from the influence of emotions and relationships. Such lack of feeling (*apatheia*) allowed the inner resolve to dictate the Stoic's actions with no other intention than conforming to the will of the *Logos*, leading to a virtuous life. Zeno's system included logics and physics, but the most influential aspect of his philosophy was the proposition that virtue is the only good, and virtue depended only on the Stoic's determination to conform his or her will to the dictates of the *logos*.

Bibliography

Essential Reading:

Egypt

Baines, John, Leonard H. Lesko, and David P. Silverman. *Religion in Ancient Egypt: Gods, Myths, and Personal Practice*. Edited by Byron E. Shafer. Ithaca, NY: Cornell University Press, 1991. An excellent survey of the primary components of Egyptian religious culture, both official and popular.

Foster, John L., ed. and trans. *Ancient Egyptian Literature: An Anthology*. Austin, TX: University of Texas Press, 2001. A collection of texts from ancient Egypt, including hymns, wisdom literature, love poetry, and *The Tale of Sinuhe*, in clear, readable translations.

Gahlin, Lucia. *Egypt: Gods, Myths and Religion*. New York: Barnes and Noble, 2002. A beautifully illustrated, accessible survey of Egyptian religious culture, incorporating color photographs and helpful charts.

Hornung, Erik. *History of Ancient Egypt: An Introduction*. Translated by David Lorton. Ithaca, NY: Cornell University Press, 1999. An authoritative short history of Egypt from the prehistoric era to its incorporation into the Persian Empire in the 4th century B.C.E.

Redford, Donald B., ed. *The Ancient Gods Speak: A Guide to Egyptian Religion*. New York: Oxford University Press, 2002. A reliable resource for information about ancient Egyptian religious culture presented in dictionary form; well suited to the needs of general readers.

Mesopotamia

Black, Jeremy, and Anthony Green. *Gods, Demons and Symbols of Ancient Mesopotamia: An Illustrated Dictionary*. Austin, TX: University of Texas Press, 2003. A guide to Mesopotamian religious culture from its beginnings to the turn of the age, presented in dictionary form, with a variety of helpful illustrations.

Bottéro, Jean. *Religion in Ancient Mesopotamia*. Translated by Teresa Lavender Fagan. Chicago: University of Chicago Press, 2001. A brief, authoritative account of the history of Mesopotamian religious culture that places it in the context of religious study in general and traces its influence on other ancient Mediterranean religious cultures.

Dalley, Stephanie, ed. and trans. *Myths from Mesopotamia: Creation, the Flood, Gilgamesh, and Others.* Oxford World's Classics. Rev. ed.. New York: Oxford University Press, 1989. A collection of the primary religious texts from ancient Mesopotamia, in translations that convey the sense without disguising some of the difficulties the current state of the texts presents; includes useful notes.

Roux, George. *Ancient Iraq.* 3rd ed. New York: Penguin, 1992. A comprehensive history of ancient Mesopotamia from the prehistoric era to the Hellenistic age, intended for general readers.

Wolkstein, Diane, and Samuel Noah Kramer. *Inanna, Queen of Heaven and Earth: Her Stories and Hymns from Sumer.* New York: Harper & Row, 1983. A collection of texts from ancient Sumer intended to portray the "history" of Inanna, with translations that demonstrate an admirable frankness and clarity. Includes helpful commentaries on Sumerian history and the problems presented by the sources.

Syria-Palestine

Blenkinsopp, Joseph. *A History of Prophecy in Israel: From the Settlement in the Land to the Hellenistic Period.* Rev. ed. Philadelphia: Westminster John Knox, 1996. A history of the phenomenon of prophecy in ancient Israel, set in its larger historical and cultural context in the ancient Near East.

Flanders, Henry Jackson, Jr., Robert Wilson Crapps, and David Anthony Smith. *People of the Covenant: An Introduction to the Hebrew Bible.* 4th ed. New York: Oxford University Press, 1996. A textbook intended for use in college courses, including a thorough introduction not only to the Hebrew Bible but also to the history of Israel in the ancient Near East and the critical methods used by modern scholars to make sense of the biblical texts.

Herrmann, Siegfried. *A History of Israel in Old Testament Times.* 2nd ed. Philadelphia: Fortress, 1981. A readable history of Israel from the ancestors to the beginning of Roman rule that offers reasonable interpretations of its subject's many problems.

Greece

Cashford, Jules, trans. *The Homeric Hymns.* Introduction and notes by Nicholas Richardson. New York: Penguin, 2003. A sound introduction to these important religious texts in elegant translations.

Guthrie, W. K. C. *The Greeks and Their Gods*. Boston: Beacon, 1985. First published in 1950 "to serve as a kind of religious companion to the Greek classics" and now a classic itself as an introduction to the primary ideas at work in Greek religious culture.

Hesiod and Theognis. *Hesiod: Theogony, Works and Days*; *Theognis: Elegies*. Translated by Dorothea Wender. Penguin Classics. New York: Penguin, 1973. An intelligent translation of the archaic Greek poems, intended to convey both the style and the content of the originals, with a helpful introduction and notes.

Homer. *The Iliad*. Translated by Robert Fagles. Introduction and notes by Bernard Knox. New York: Penguin, 1990. This and the following entry are Homer's two great epic poems, in what are arguably the best translations for the modern reader.

———. *The Odyssey*. Translated by Robert Fagles. Introduction and notes by Bernard Knox. New York: Penguin, 1996.

Plato. *Five Dialogues: Euthyphro, Apology, Crito, Meno, Phaedo*. Translated by G. M. A. Grube. Indianapolis: Hackett, 1981. A good, readable translation of the Platonic dialogues that focus on the events leading up to the death of Socrates.

Price, Simon. *Religions of the Ancient Greeks: Key Themes in Ancient History*. New York: Cambridge University Press, 1999. A scholarly introduction to Greek religious culture from the 8th century B.C.E. to the 5th century C.E., addressing a number of subjects with data from an array of sources.

The Hellenistic Era

Martin, Luther H. *Hellenistic Religions: An Introduction*. New York: Oxford University Press, 1987. A brief, comprehensive overview of the religious cultures of the Greco-Roman world from the 4th century B.C.E to the 4th century C.E.

Meyer, Marvin W., ed. *The Ancient Mysteries: A Sourcebook: Sacred Texts of the Mystery Religions of the Ancient Mediterranean World*. San Francisco: HarperCollins, 1987. A well-chosen collection of texts relevant to mystery religions of the ancient Mediterranean world, intended to give the modern reader a view of the mysteries through the eyes of those familiar with them.

Rome

Apuleius. *The Golden Ass*. Translated by Robert Graves. New York: Farrar, Straus and Giroux, 1998. A clear and witty translation of Apuleius's novel by the author of *I, Claudius*, with proper appreciation for its notes of humor, pathos, and religious solemnity.

Beard, Mary, John North, and Simon Price. *Religions of Rome*. Volume 1: *A History*. Volume 2: *A Sourcebook*. New York: Cambridge University Press, 1998. A revisionist approach to the religious cultures of the Roman world, the result of carefully chosen texts and other forms of evidence and a convincing analysis. The second volume provides most of the texts and other sources referred to in the first volume.

Kraemer, Ross Shepard. *Her Share of the Blessings: Women's Religions among Pagans, Jews, and Christians in the Greco-Roman World*. New York: Oxford University Press, 1992. A survey of the forms taken by women's religious activity in the Greco-Roman world, including surveys of the mystery religions, the traditional religious culture of Rome, Judaism, and the early Jesus movement.

Lucian of Samosata. *Lucian*. Translated by A. M. Harmon. Loeb Classical Library. Volumes 4 (*Alexander the False Prophet*) and 5 (*The Passing of Peregrinus*). Cambridge, MA: Harvard University Press, 1925, 1936. Scholarly, readable translations of Lucian's work, with introductions and notes; the Greek text and the English translation appear on facing pages.

Ovid. *Metamorphoses*. Translated by Mary M. Innes. Penguin Classics. New York: Penguin, 1955. An excellent translation for the general reader of Ovid's Latin retelling of the myths that formed part of the Greek religious inheritance of early imperial Rome, as well as the founding myths of Rome and the empire itself.

Turcan, Robert. *The Gods of Ancient Rome: Religion in Everyday Life from Archaic to Imperial Times*. Translated by Antonia Nevill. New York: Routledge, 2001. A brief traditional introduction to the religious cultures of the Roman world, covering the religious beliefs and actions associated with the family and the land, the city, and the empire.

Christianity

Chadwick, Henry. *The Early Church*. Penguin History of the Church. Rev. ed. New York: Penguin, 1993. A standard history of the early Christian movement from its beginnings to the end of the ancient period; intended for general readers.

Ehrman, Bart D. *A Brief Introduction to the New Testament*. New York: Oxford University Press, 2004. A short textbook intended for use in college courses, including an introduction to the books of the New Testament, their historical and cultural context, and the methods used to study them, reflecting the most recent scholarship.

Keck, Leander E. *Paul and His Letters: Proclamation Commentaries*. 2nd ed. Philadelphia: Fortress, 1988. An excellent short companion to the genuine letters of Paul, with major sections devoted to the "historical" Paul, the gospel message Paul proclaimed, and the primary concerns that motivated Paul's evangelical mission and the controversies with his opponents.

Pagels, Elaine. *The Gnostic Gospels*. New York: Vintage: 1989. An award-winning study that uses Gnostic texts from the Nag Hammadi library to illuminate the diversity of earliest Christianity.

Powell, Mark Allan. *Jesus as a Figure in History*. Philadelphia: Westminster John Knox, 1998. An excellent review for the general reader of recent scholarly attempts to identify the "historical Jesus," with a clear explanation and careful analysis of each of the "portraits" that results.

General

The Concise Oxford Companion to Classical Literature. Edited by M. C. Howatson and Ian Chilvers. New York: Oxford University Press, 1993. Primarily a companion to Greek and Roman classical literature and its authors, including brief sketches of the gods and other characters appearing in myths, with helpful information about figures from Greek and Roman history, as well.

Winks, Robin W., and Susan P. Mattern-Parkes. *The Ancient Mediterranean World: From the Stone Age to A.D. 600*. New York: Oxford University Press, 2004. A brief history of the ancient Mediterranean world, from the prehistoric era to the end of the ancient period, with helpful maps, charts, and illustrations; intended for the general reader.

Supplementary Reading:

Prehistory

Cunliffe, Barry, ed. *The Oxford Illustrated History of Prehistoric Europe*. Oxford Illustrated Histories. New ed. New York: Oxford University Press, 2001. An illustrated overview of the prehistoric era in Europe by a number of scholars, intended to reconstruct as accurately as possible the full range of the lives of prehistoric people.

Egypt

Assmann, Jan. *The Search for God in Ancient Egypt.* Translated by David Lorton. Ithaca, NY: Cornell University Press, 2001. A specialized investigation and analysis of the full realm of Egyptian religious culture in terms of the categories of religious scholarship.

Hart, George. *Egyptian Myths: The Legendary Past.* Austin, TX: University of Texas Press, 1990. A review of primary themes in Egyptian mythology, with clear retellings and explanations of different myths.

Ray, John. *Reflections of Osiris: Lives from Ancient Egypt.* New York: Oxford University Press, 2002. A selection of biographical sketches of figures from more than 2,000 years of Egyptian history, illustrating both the familiarity and the strangeness of the Egyptian world.

Traunecker, Claude. *The Gods of Egypt.* Translated by David Lorton. Ithaca, NY: Cornell University Press, 2001. A comprehensive introduction to conceptions of the divine in Egyptian religious culture, in a clear and systematic presentation.

Mesopotamia

Bottéro, Jean. *Everyday Life in Ancient Mesopotamia.* Translated by Antonia Nevill. Baltimore: Johns Hopkins University Press, 2001. A collection of essays by Bottéro and others on a variety of subjects, from cuisine to astrology, to love and sex, to the role of women in ancient Mesopotamia, helping to make its peoples and civilizations more real for the modern reader.

Jacobsen, Thorkild. *The Treasures of Darkness: A History of Mesopotamian Religion.* New Haven, CT: Yale University Press, 1976. A history of Mesopotamian religious culture, focusing on literary evidence and the controlling metaphors for each era of Mesopotamian religious history.

Kramer, Samuel Noah. *History Begins at Sumer: Thirty-Nine Firsts in Recorded History.* 3rd ed. Philadelphia: University of Pennsylvania Press, 1981. A popular account of Sumerian civilization, organized by historical "firsts," such as "The First Case of 'Apple-Polishing'" and "The First 'Farmer's Almanac.'"

—. *Sumerian Mythology: A Study of Spiritual and Literary Achievement in the Third Millennium B.C.* Rev. ed. Philadelphia: University of Pennsylvania Press, 1972. A scholarly retelling and assessment of Sumerian mythology, with discussion of the problems surrounding the present state of the texts.

—. *The Sumerians: Their History, Culture, and Character.* Chicago: University of Chicago Press, 1963. A scholarly but accessible history of all aspects of ancient Sumer, by one of the leading authorities on the subject.

Mitchell, Stephen. *Gilgamesh: A New English Version.* New York: Free Press, 2004. A literary translation meant for the general reader, with an introduction and notes.

Nemet-Nejat, Karen Rhea. *Daily Life in Ancient Mesopotamia.* Peabody, MA: Hendrickson, 2002. An account for general readers of the history, society, and culture of ancient Mesopotamia.

Oates, Joan. *Babylon.* Rev. ed. New York: Thames & Hudson, 1986. A history of Babylon and its peoples from its beginnings until the Hellenistic era, including the city's archaeological history and the influence of the Babylonian empires on the surrounding peoples.

Syria-Palestine

Cross, Frank Moore. *Canaanite Myth and Hebrew Epic: Essays in the History of the Religion of Israel.* Cambridge, MA: Harvard University Press, 1973. A collection of scholarly essays on the development of Israelite religion, focusing on its context among the other religious cultures of Syria-Palestine.

Hayes, John H., and J. Maxwell Miller, eds. *Israelite and Judaean History.* Old Testament Library. SCM 1977. A scholarly history of Israel and Judah by primary periods, with a review of the available sources and possible historical reconstructions preceding the history of each period from the ancestors to the Roman era.

Koch, Klaus. *The Prophets.* Volume 1: *The Assyrian Period,* Volume 2: *The Babylonian and Persian Periods.* Philadelphia: Fortress, 1983, 1984. A good introduction to the prophets of the Hebrew Bible, both those of the historical books and those credited with books of prophecy, dealing with each of the major prophets in turn.

Greece

Armstrong, A. H. *An Introduction to Ancient Philosophy*. 3rd ed. Lanham, MD: Littlefield Adams Quality Paperbacks; original edition, 1957. A brief history of Greek, Hellenistic, and Roman philosophy, continuing into Christian thought to the end of the ancient period; intended for general readers.

Bremmer, Jan N. *Greek Religion*. Greece & Rome: New Surveys in the Classics 24. The Classical Association. New York: Oxford University Press, 1994. Intended as a supplement to Walter Burkert's *Greek Religion*, concentrating on developments in the field after the appearance of Burkert's original German edition in 1977.

Burkert, Walter. *Greek Religion*. Translated by John Raffan. Cambridge, MA: Harvard University Press, 1985. A comprehensive and authoritative scholarly introduction to all aspects of Greek religion.

————. *Homo Necans: The Anthropology of Ancient Greek Sacrificial Ritual and Myth*. Berkeley: University of California Press, 1987. An authoritative examination of the practice of animal sacrifice in ancient Greece, with ramifications for the notion of blood atonement in other religious cultures, both ancient and modern.

Dodds, E. R. *The Greeks and the Irrational*. Berkeley: University of California Press, 1951. A classic work on the role of the primitive and the irrational in the history of Greek thought, including the "rationalism" of the classical era in Athens.

Easterling, P. E., and J. V. Muir, eds. *Greek Religion and Society*. New York: Cambridge University Press, 1985. A collection of scholarly essays on specific aspects of Greek religion understood in the context of ancient Greek society, including the influence of religious ideas in Greek poetry, art, and education.

Kitto, H. D. F. *The Greeks*. Rev. ed. New York: Penguin, 1991. A brief overview of the history and culture of ancient Greece to the decline of the city-states; first published in 1950.

Sophocles. *The Three Theban Plays: Antigone, Oedipus the King, Oedipus at Colonus*. Translated by Robert Fagles. Introduction and notes by Bernard Knox. New York: Penguin, 1982. An excellent translation of Sophocles's tragedies, capturing the subtleties of his wordplay and presenting his work as stage plays fully suitable for modern performance.

Hellenistic Era

Graf, Fritz. *Magic in the Ancient World.* Translated by Franklin Philip. Revealing Antiquity 10. Cambridge, MA: Harvard University Press, 1997. A scholarly investigation of magic among the Greeks and Romans, from the 6th century B.C.E. to end of the ancient period, including the presentation of magical practices in literary works.

Konstan, David. *Friendship in the Classical World.* Key Themes in Ancient History. New York: Cambridge University Press, 1997. An examination of the concept of friendship in the Greco-Roman world from Homer to the 4th century C.E., including its role in larger social, political, and religious contexts.

Theophrastus. *Characters.* Herodas. *Mimes. Sophron and Other Mime Fragments.* Edited and translated by Jeffrey Rusten and I. C. Cunningham. Loeb Classical Library. Cambridge, MA: Harvard University Press, 2002. A scholarly translation with introductions and notes; the Greek text and the English translation appear on facing pages.

Rome

Philostratus. *Life of Apollonius of Tyana.* Translated by F. C. Conybeare. Loeb Classical Library. 2 vols. Cambridge, MA: Harvard University Press, 1950. A scholarly translation with introductions and notes, in two volumes; the Greek text and the English translation appear on facing pages.

Turcan, Robert. *The Cults of the Roman Empire.* Translated by Antonia Nevill. The Ancient World. Oxford: Blackwell, 1996. A scholarly account of the multiplicity of religious cultures within the Roman Empire, focusing on the mystery religions.

Virgil. *The Aeneid.* Translated by Robert Fitzgerald. Vintage Classics. New York: Vintage, 1990. A faithful poetic translation for the modern reader of Virgil's incomplete epic of the travels of Aeneus, with a glossary and a thoughtful postscript.

Christianity

Aune, David E. *Prophecy in Early Christianity and the Ancient Mediterranean World.* Wipf & Stock Publishers, 2003. A comprehensive scholarly account of the phenomenon of prophecy in the Greco-Roman world in the early years of the Jesus movement, including a definitive treatment of the nature of prophecy among the earliest followers of Jesus.

Ehrman, Bart D. *Lost Christianities: The Battle for Scripture and the Faiths We Never Knew*. New York: Oxford University Press, 2003. A review and analysis of the variety of competing visions of the Jesus faith that vied for supremacy in the first four centuries of the Christian movement's history.

Hopkins, Keith. *A World Full of Gods: The Strange Triumph of Christianity*. New York: Plume, 2001. A clever, lighthearted attempt to recreate for the modern reader the Greco-Roman world at the turn of the age, the better to understand the triumph of Christianity over traditional Greco-Roman religious cultures.

Stark, Rodney. The Rise of Christianity: A Sociologist Reconsiders History/How the Obscure, Marginal Jesus Movement Became the Dominant Religious Force in the Western World in a Few Centuries. New York; HarperCollins, 1997. A clear, compelling examination of the reasons for Christianity's ultimate triumph over traditional Roman religious culture, based on contemporary studies of the growth of religious movements.

General

Aharoni, Yohanan, and Michael Avi-Yonah. *The Macmillan Bible Atlas*. 3rd rev. ed. New York: Macmillan, 1993. An excellent reference for better understanding events in the history of Israel, later Judaism, and the early Jesus movement.

Coogan, Michael D., ed. *The Oxford History of the Biblical World*. New York: Oxford University Press, 1998. A detailed, accessible history of Syria-Palestine from the prehistoric era through the end of the ancient period, written by leading experts in the subjects covered.

Holland, Glenn. *Divine Irony*. Selinsgrove, PA: Susquehanna University Press, 2000. A discussion of irony as the result of looking at human events from the divine point of view, drawn on examples from the Tanakh and Greek religious culture, with special attention to Socrates and the letters of the apostle Paul.

Johnston, Sarah Iles, ed. *Religions of the Ancient World: A Guide*. Cambridge, MA: Belknap/Harvard University Press, 2004. A comparative overview of the religious cultures of the ancient Mediterranean world produced by a number of distinguished scholars, incorporating introductory materials on each religious culture and a series of comparative surveys on such topics as sacrifice, divination, deities, rites of passage, death and the afterlife, and mythology.

Livingston, James C. *Anatomy of the Sacred: An Introduction to Religion.* 5th ed. Upper Saddle River, NJ: Pearson/Prentice Hall, 2005. An introduction to the various issues involved in the study of religion, focusing primarily on modern and contemporary religious cultures, with helpful case studies illustrating particular phenomena.

The New Larousse Encyclopedia of Mythology. Crescent Books, 1987. A classic presentation of world mythologies, profusely illustrated in a large format, with an introduction by Robert Graves.

Notes

Notes

Notes